SOUTH COTSWOLD PUBS
THROUGH TIME
Geoff Sandles

AMBERLEY PUBLISHING

To Ric – More Beer!

First published 2012

Amberley Publishing
The Hill, Stroud
Gloucestershire, GL5 4EP

www.amberley-books.com

Copyright © Geoff Sandles, 2012

The right of Geoff Sandles to be identified as the Author of this work has been asserted in accordance with the Copyrights, Designs and Patents Act 1988.

ISBN 978 1 4456 1074 0

All rights reserved. No part of this book may be reprinted or reproduced or utilised in any form or by any electronic, mechanical or other means, now known or hereafter invented, including photocopying and recording, or in any information storage or retrieval system, without the permission in writing from the Publishers.

British Library Cataloguing in Publication Data.
A catalogue record for this book is available from the British Library.

Typeset in 9.5pt on 12pt Celeste.
Typesetting by Amberley Publishing.
Printed in the UK.

Introduction

For the fourth book in my series looking at Gloucestershire pubs *Through Time* I have selected pubs that are located in the GL7, GL8, GL9, GL11 and GL12 postal code areas – a considerable geographical spread, which I have conveniently called the South Cotswolds. The area encompasses the towns of Lechlade, Fairford, Cirencester, Tetbury, Dursley and Wotton-under-Edge.

The pages within this book contrast archive photographs of pubs with modern day scenes. Although some pubs have closed and are now in alternative use, there is only one pub in this selection for which the corresponding present day landscape has changed beyond recognition. In the context of the subject matter of this book that may disappoint, but serves as a reminder that pub closures in Gloucestershire are not nearly as prevalent as they are in other parts of Britain. Indeed there are some pubs that have recently closed, boarded up and face an uncertain future, such as the Crown and Royal Oak in Tetbury, but they might be revitalised to positively thrive in the future.

Take for example the Fox and Hounds in Dursley. This was a run-down boozer in the early 1990s with a 'rough' reputation. The beverage of choice was cheap cider and strong lager and the clientele (to put it politely) were from the very lowest social-economic groups of society. In 1992 Ric Sainty saw the potential of the Fox and Hounds and set about converting it to a superb real ale pub which fifteen years later was declared the Campaign for Real Ale (CAMRA) National Pub of the Year (2007). Today the Old Spot continues to thrive and has won numerous awards. Its continued success can be put down to a very simple formula – great beer, great company, good food and efficient and friendly staff.

The inspiration behind the transformation of the failed Fox and Hounds to the prized, and much loved, Old Spot was the bearded Eric 'Ric' Sainty. He had a previous life working for Cambridgeshire County Council as a draughtsman-designer for the planning department. After twenty-five years of service he opted for redundancy in 1978, and left with dreams of opening a pub in Devon. Somehow or other he ended up purchasing a pub tucked away down a warren of countryside lanes in the quirkily named hamlet of Waterley Bottom near North Nibley. (Perhaps it was the absurdness of the address that attracted him.) At his first pub the New Inn, Ric, and his first wife Ruby, started a real ale revolution that was to influence and, indeed, inspire generations of beer drinkers and pub lovers.

Ric loved the South Cotswolds but desperately missed his favourite beers from East Anglia – particularly Greene King Abbot Ale. In true pioneering spirit he arranged for a fortnightly delivery of Abbot and his other favourite beers to the New Inn in a converted trailer pulled by his friends Range Rover and for the return journey the empty casks were filled with beer from the new Smiles Brewery in Bristol. It was an enterprising venture that would benefit beer drinkers both east and west.

Meanwhile Chas Wright was doing much the same thing, but on a larger scale, transporting beer north to south from Carlisle to Wickwar. He was the local rep for Theakstons Yorkshire Brewery who, at the time, were brewing their Best Bitter in Carlisle. Theakstons were still using wooden barrels and an 18 gallon cask weighed over 200 lbs when full. The cellars of the old Arnold Perrett brewery at Wickwar were ideal for storing the beer before being distributed to fifty outlets throughout the west. It was obviously hard work and frustrating too – a significant proportion of the wooden casks were returned contaminated.

In March 1985 Chas recommenced brewing at a long defunct brewery in the village of Uley. He called his new venture the Old Spot Brewery and all the beers had a porcine theme – Hogshead Bitter, Pig's Ear, etc. Twenty-seven years later the Uley Brewery is still producing superb traditional beer and the real ale revolution, which Ric and Chas were part of from the beginning, has spawned many new breweries and dedicated real ale pubs in Gloucestershire.

Given their background and a shared passion for beer, it was inevitable that Chas and Ric would become great friends. Both larger than life characters in every sense of the word, they enjoyed life and beer to the full. Ric changed the name of his Dursley pub to the Old Spot and the 'house beer', brewed by Chas at the Uley Brewery, was called 'Old Ric'.

Both Chas and Ric shared a wicked sense of humour. When an Ipswich based brewery marketed a beer in Gloucestershire called 'Cobbold's Cotswold's IPA' in the 1990s Chas complained to the Trading Standards Authority, stating that the brewery was some 200 miles away from the Cotswolds and also added that he was incensed with the redundant apostrophe. Outraged by the interloping beer he sent a batch of his own beer to East Anglia with pump clips proclaiming 'Suffolk Mountain Ale'. Ric's sense of humour was also legendary. On a hot summers day a customer walked into the Old Spot wearing a colourful Hawaiian shirt and asked for an ice cool pint of lager. Unbeknown to him Ric was sat at the bar. An embarrassing silence filled the pub immediately after Ric bellowed: 'Quiet please, some w—— in a loud shirt wants to drink lager in my pub!'

Ric Sainty passed away on 16 July 2008 whilst holidaying in France with his best friend Chas. He died of a heart attack, whilst doing one of the things he loved most – having a good time. He was seventy-four. Old Ric may have passed away but his memory (and his beer) is still very much alive.

I would like to express my gratitude to those that have helped me in the preparation of this book, whether providing archive images or helping me with the research: Chris Arrowsmith, Andy Barton, Paul Best, Annie Blick, Peter Corfield, Tim Edgell, *Gloucestershire Echo*, Dave Hedges, Darrel Kirby, Terry Luker, Rick Martin, Joe Stephens, Ian Thomas, Wadworth Brewery, Michael Wilkes and, of course, the anonymous gentleman who so kindly donated so many of those wonderful 1930s and 1940s photographs.

Finally, a special thanks to my wife Kathy for being so patient with me during the preparation of this book. She's getting used to my obsessive nature now!

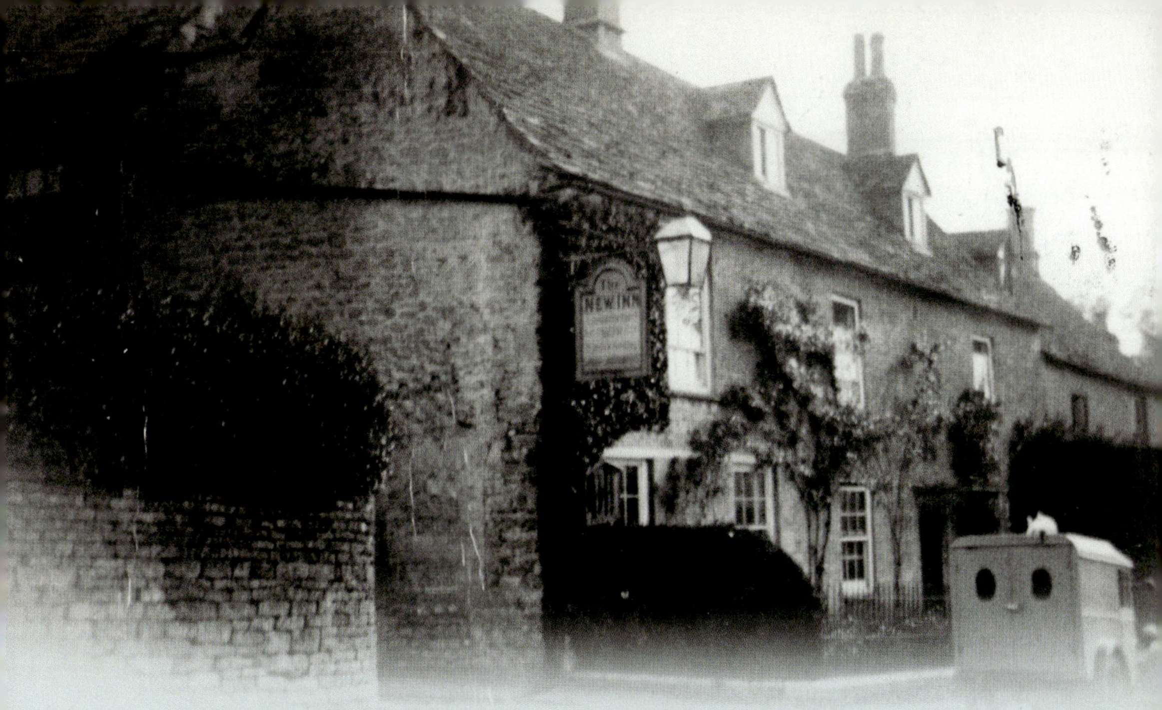

CHAPTER 1

Fairford, Lechlade & the Cerneys

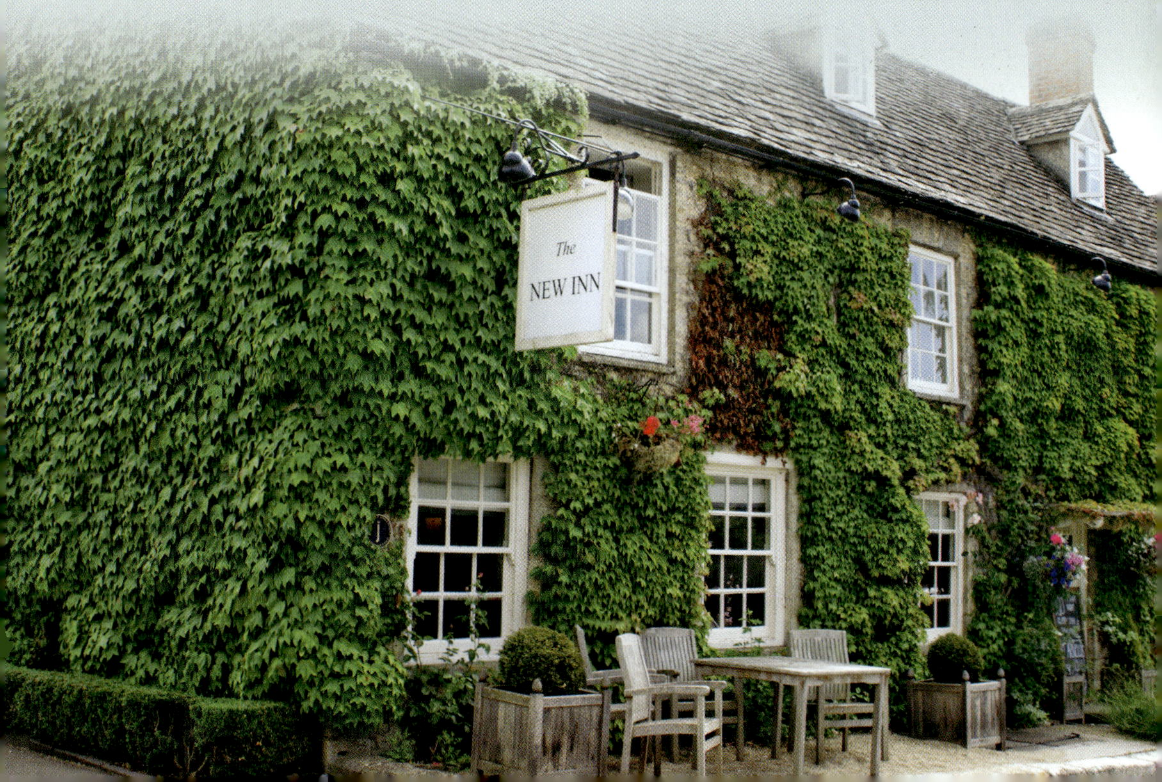

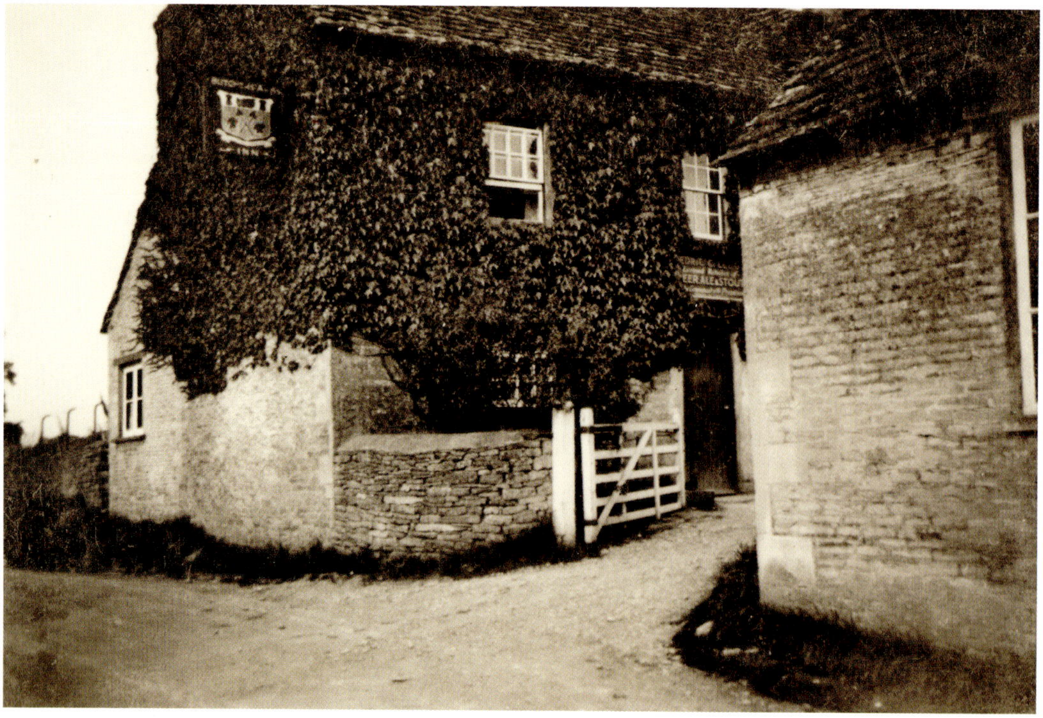

Butchers Arms, Ampney Crucis

The Butchers Arms once brewed its own beer. On 4 September 1899 the Butchers Arms and brewery were sold to the Stroud Brewery Company for £1,875 due to the illness of the owner, Charles B. Radway. The Butchers Arms called 'last orders' for the final time on Friday 21 February 1997. A resident of Ampney Crucis, Tony Truman (sixty-four), said: 'I'm very emotional about it and quite upset. I've been going into the pub since I was six.'

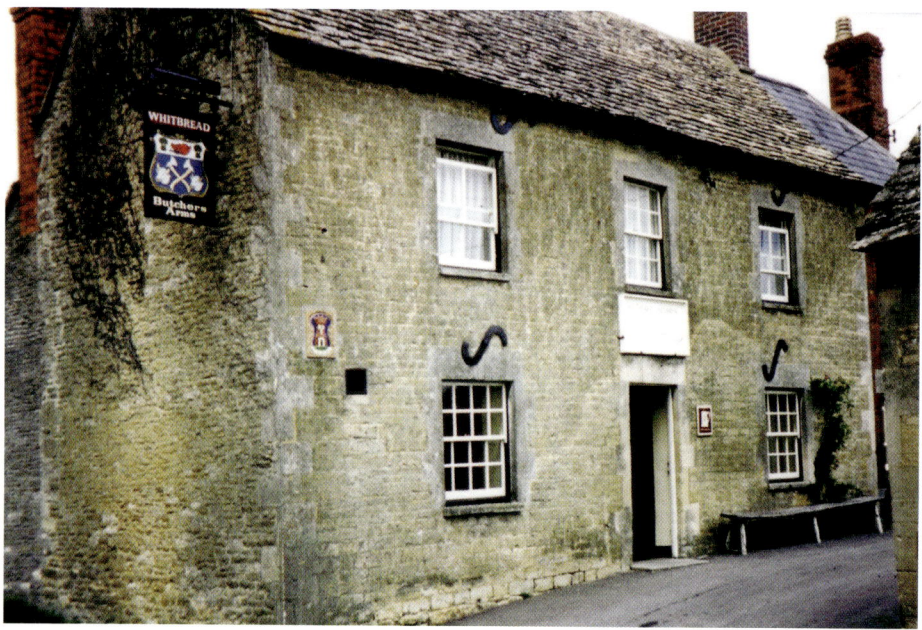

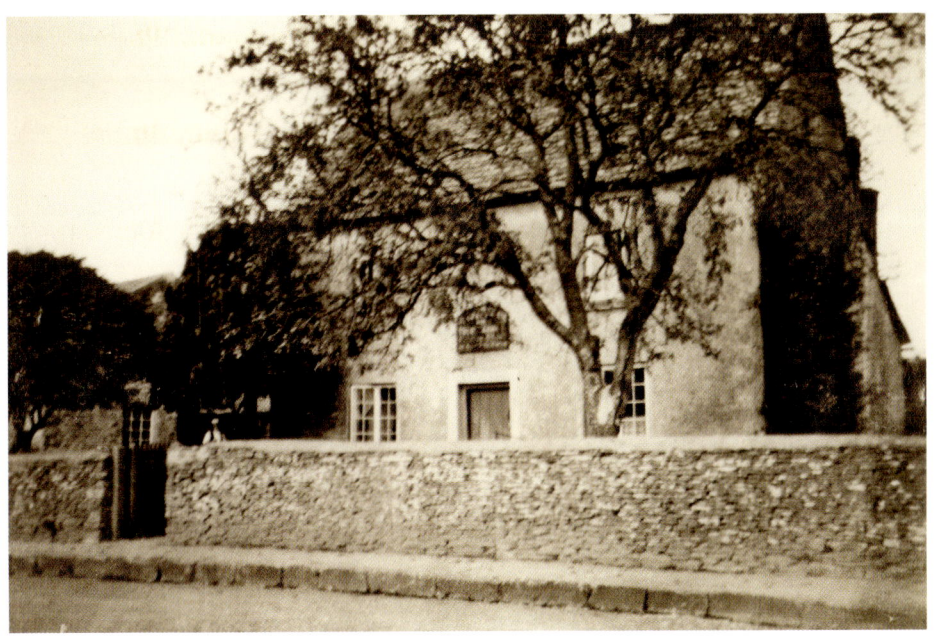

Packhorse Inn, Ampney St Peter

Laura Bechtolsheimer from Ampney St Peter scooped Olympic Gold in the London 2012 Olympics for team dressage on her horse Mistral Hjoris. In celebration a post box in the village was painted gold by Royal Mail. A champagne reception greeted Laura on her return. The names of the closed pubs in the village are perhaps a reminder of her fantastic achievement – the Hope, the Star and the Packhorse ... well maybe not the last one!

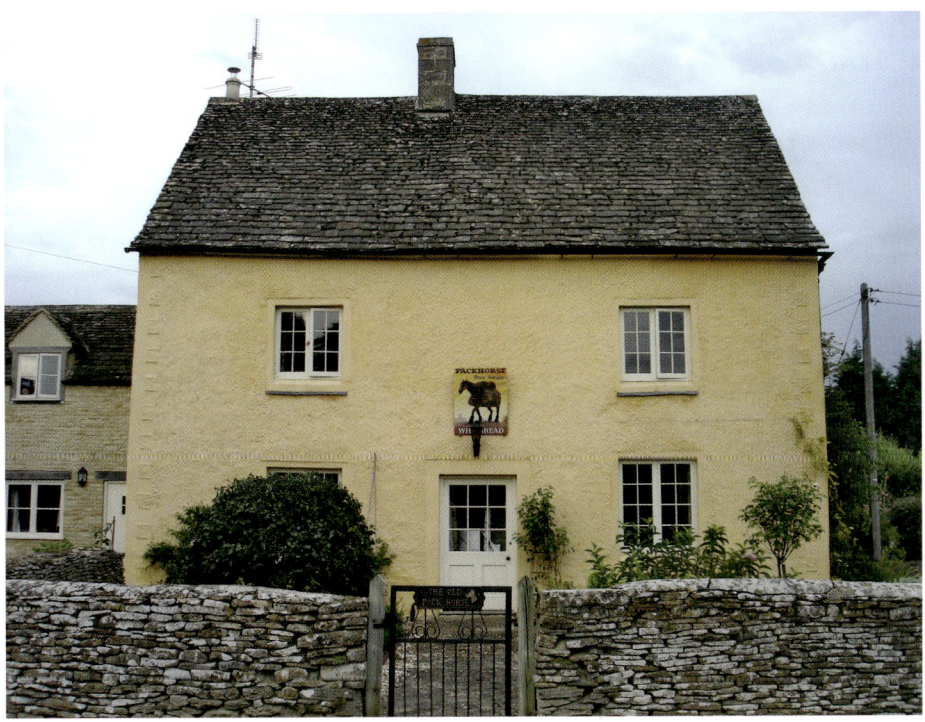

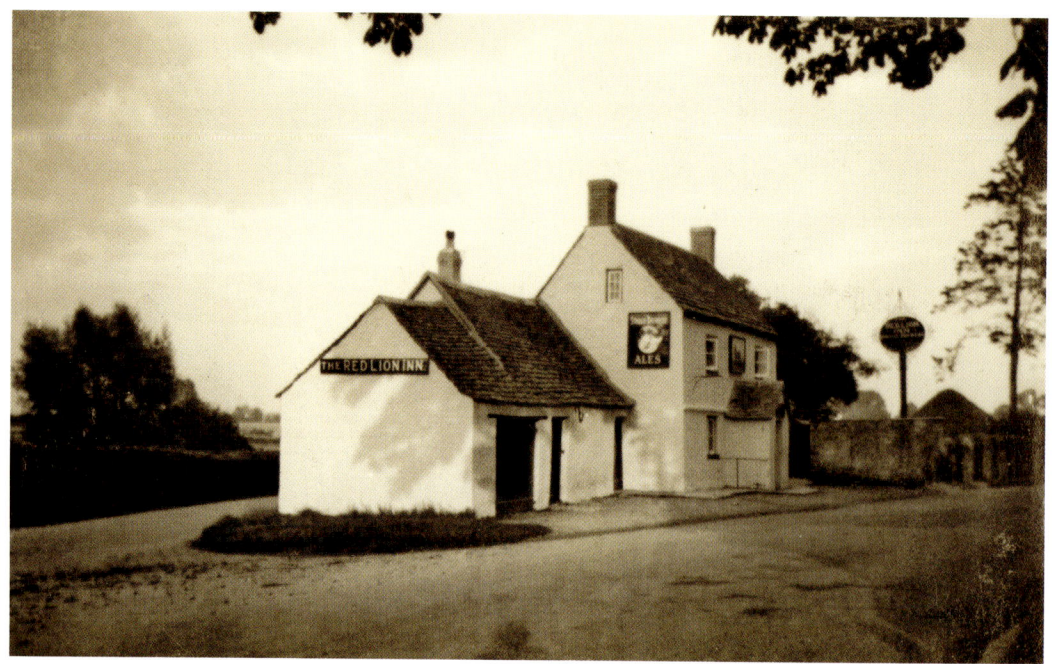

Red Lion, Ampney St Peter

The Red Lion is a living time warp, lovingly looked after by owner John Barnard who bought it from Whitbread in 1975. The Red Lion is totally unspoilt and its great strength lies in its simplicity. There are two small rooms and, uniquely, there is no actual bar. When John celebrated his eightieth birthday on 18 September 2008 he was joined by a representative from Timothy Taylors Brewery, who congratulated him on serving one of the best pints of their 'Landlord' bitter outside their Yorkshire trading area.

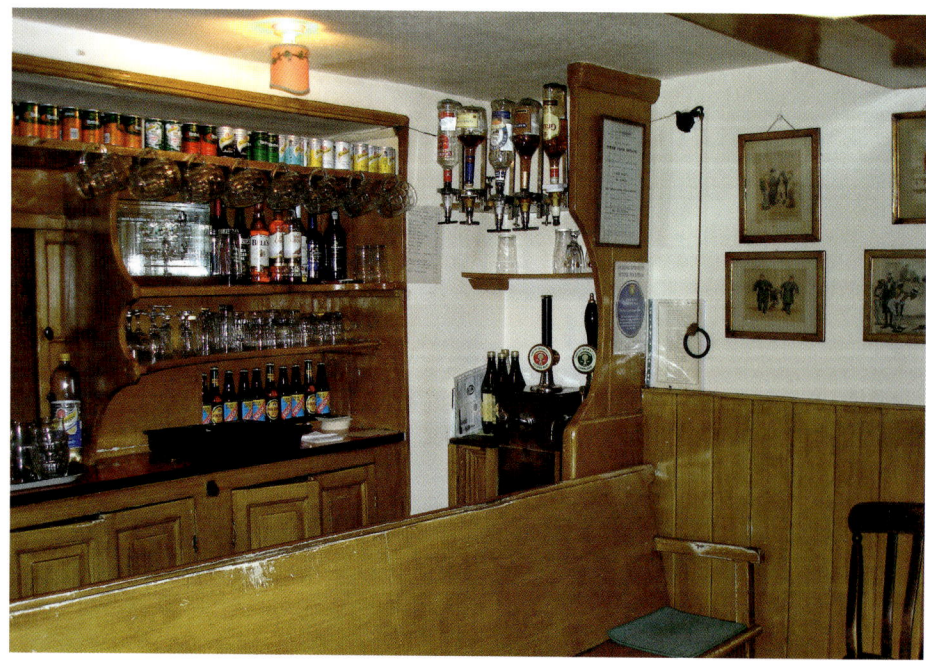

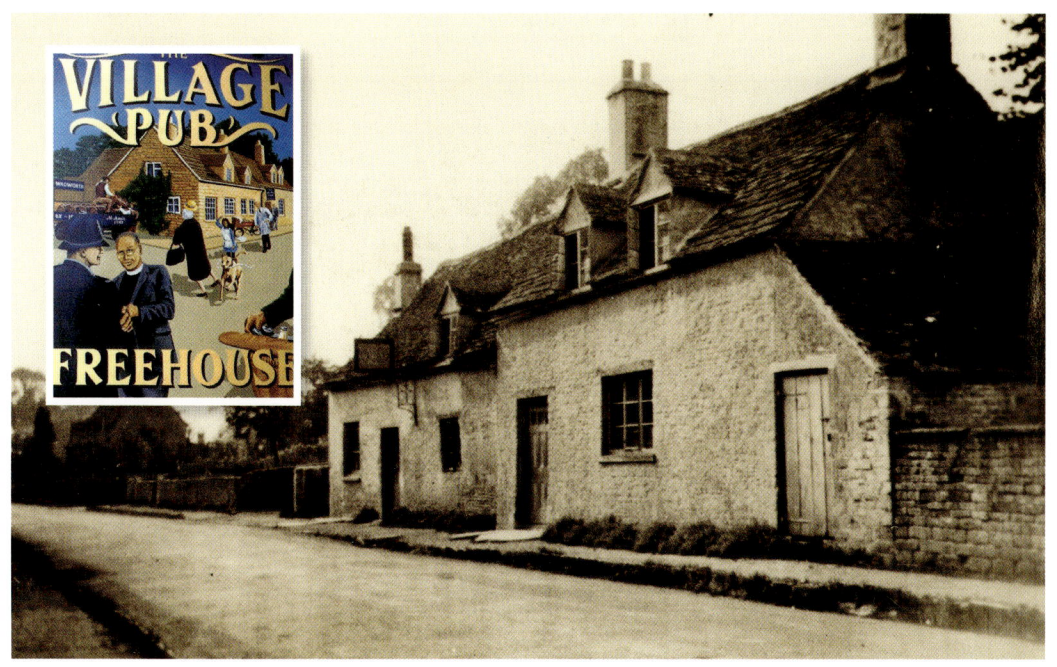

Village Inn, Barnsley

The Greyhound Inn was originally located across the road in the building that is now Greyhound Farm House. The Cirencester Brewery bought the pub on 6 September 1935 with the licence being transferred to the existing property. Known as the Village Pub since the early 1970s, and now with the emphasis strongly on fine cuisine, it was named Gastropub of the Year in 2000 by the *Guardian* newspaper.

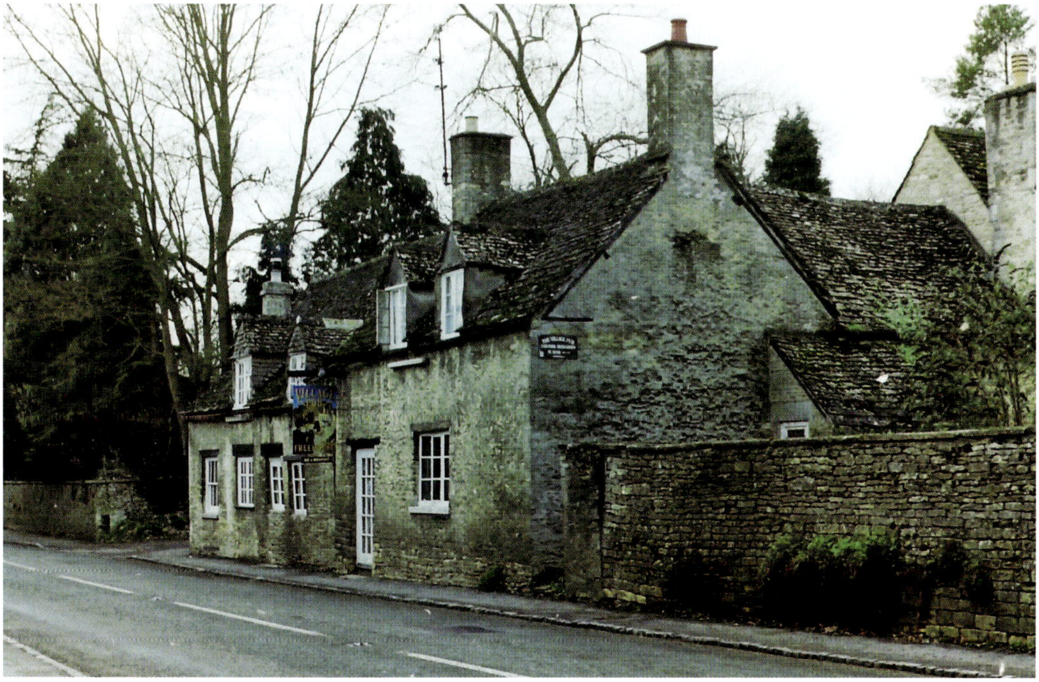

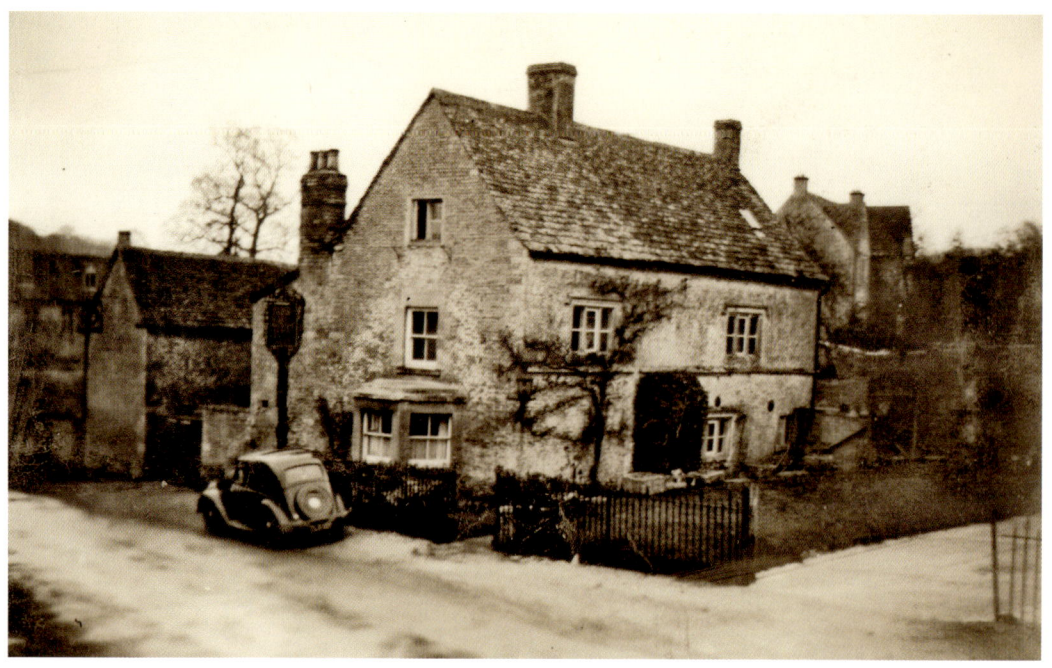

Catherine Wheel, Bibury

The landlord of the Catherine Wheel between the wars was the rotund George Mallard Adams. Nicknamed 'Damper', he was also employed as a haulier, and was a proficient heavyweight wrestler. Japanese tourists love visiting Bibury and when a famous Japanese artist painted the Catherine Wheel in 2002 after enjoying their speciality brown trout, the pub was inundated with up to 200 Japanese tourists a week all eager to sample the same trout dinners as their artistic hero.

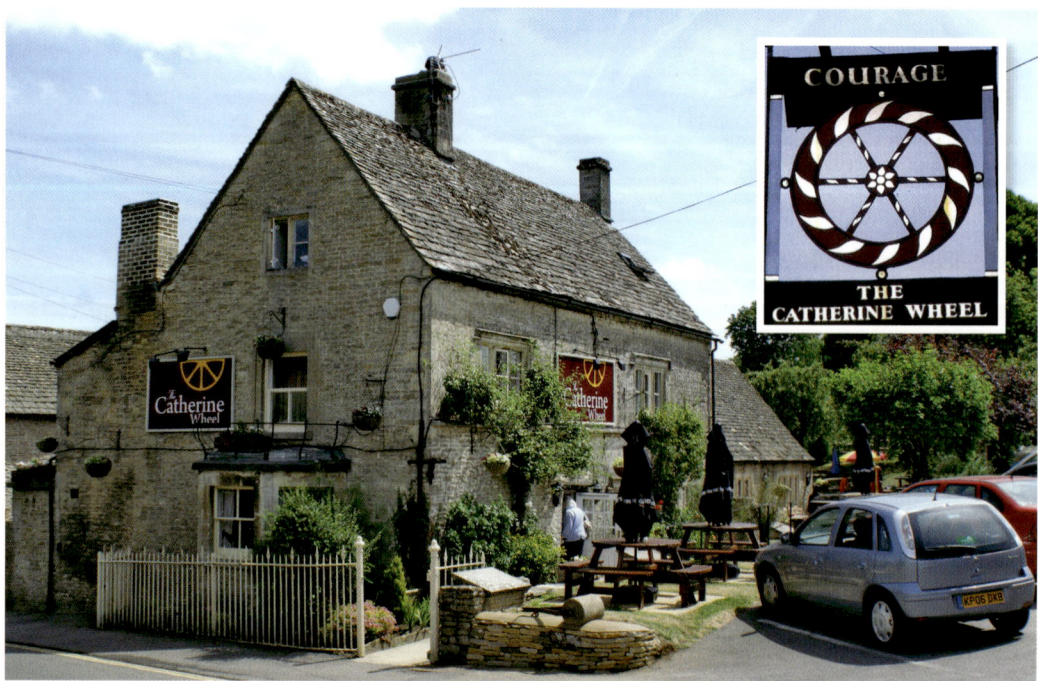

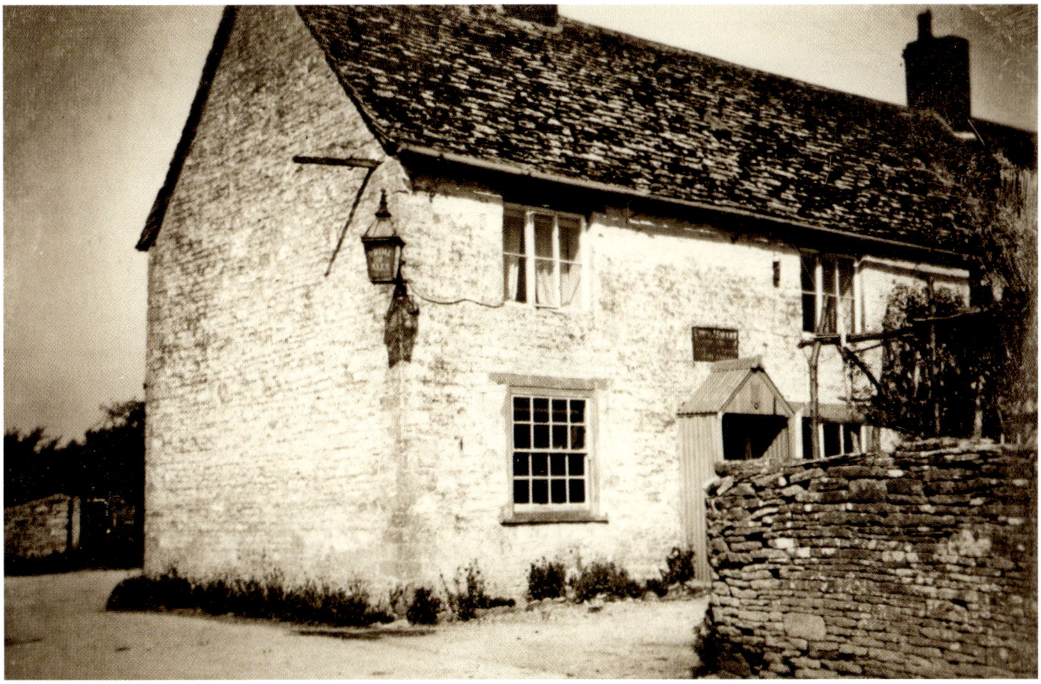

Crown Inn, Cerney Wick

A freak storm struck Cerney Wick in the early evening of Sunday 3 July 2006. The whole of the village was plunged into darkness, and a mini tornado ripped trees apart. A barman making his way to the Crown for his evening shift was so frightened that he hid in a ditch. Ten minutes later the storm had passed and customers arriving at the pub after spending the day at Cotswold Water Park, just a mile away, could not believe the devastation as they had been enjoying glorious sunshine.

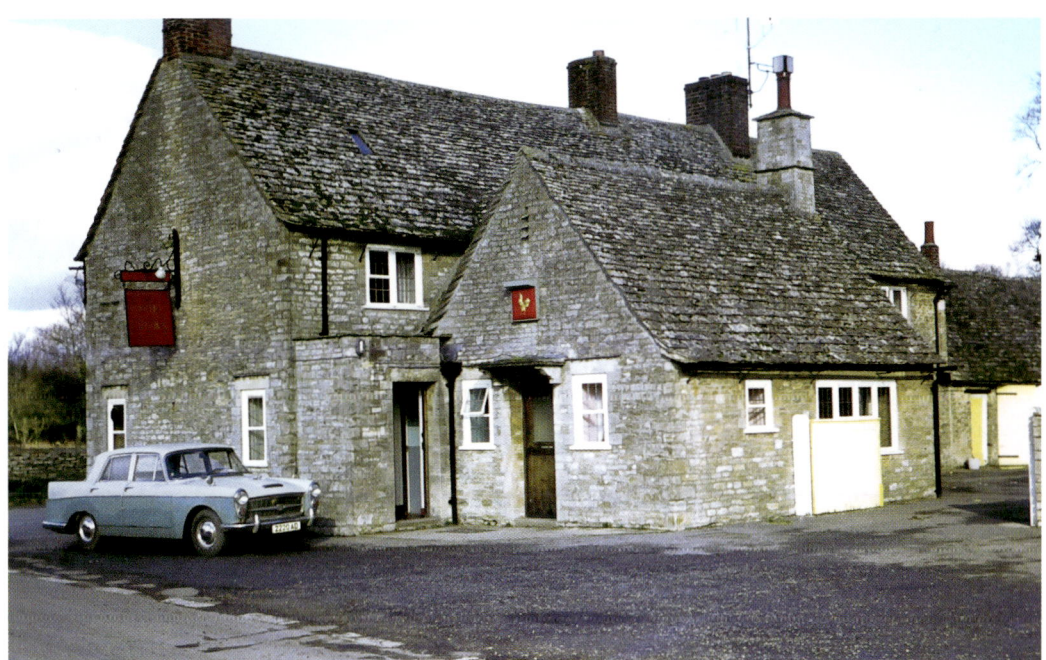

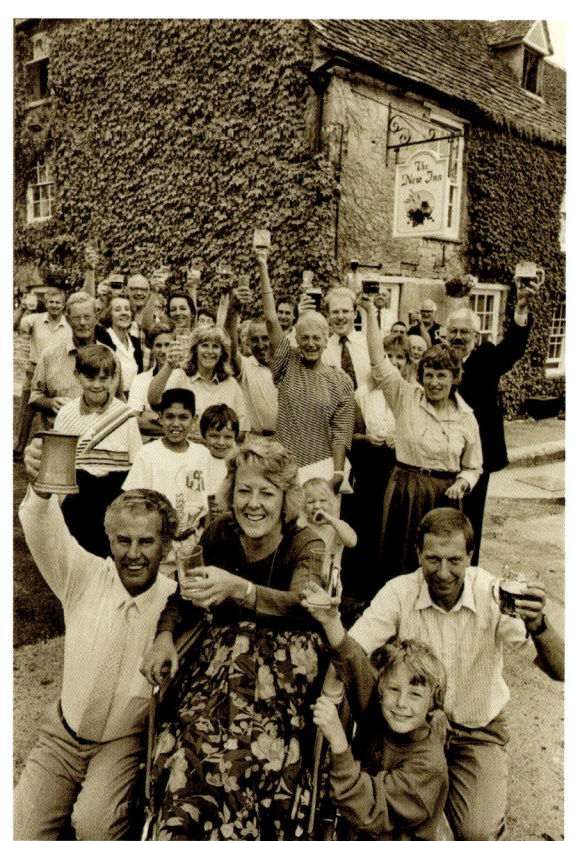

New Inn, Coln St Aldwyns

A property developer bought the New Inn in the summer of 1988 with a view to turn it into residential use. Claiming that the pub was not viable he closed it down, causing uproar in the village. After a protracted battle which led to a public enquiry, the developer eventually conceded defeat. The New Inn reopened in 1990 and has since gone on to win a string of prestigious awards including a two red star status from the AA, making it one of the top 200 inns in the UK.

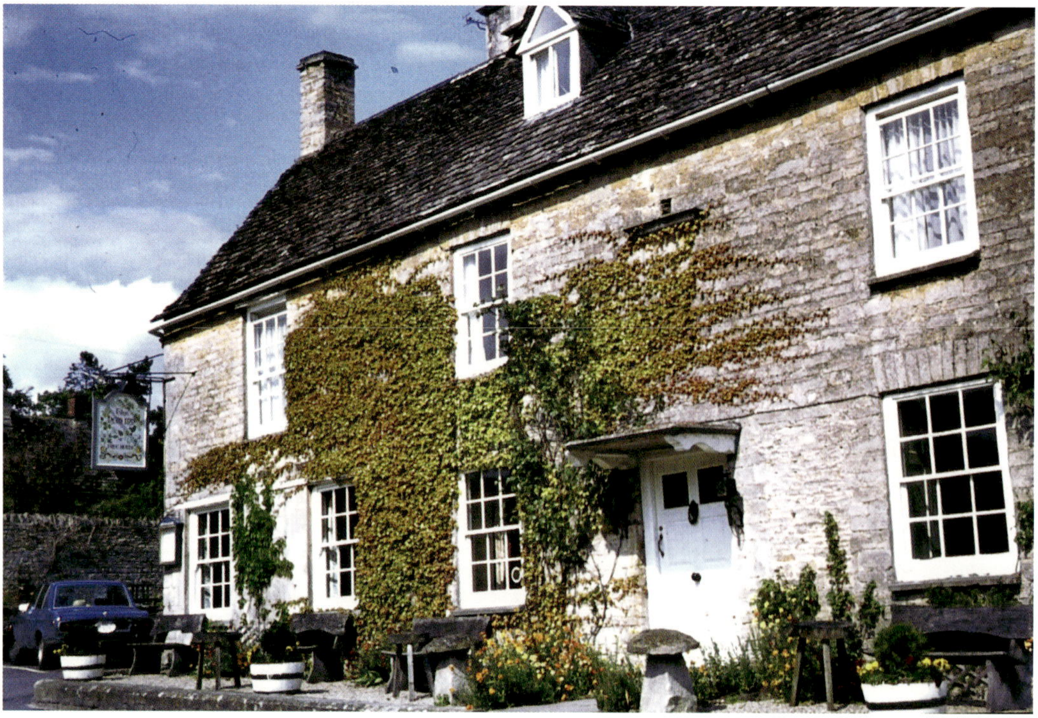

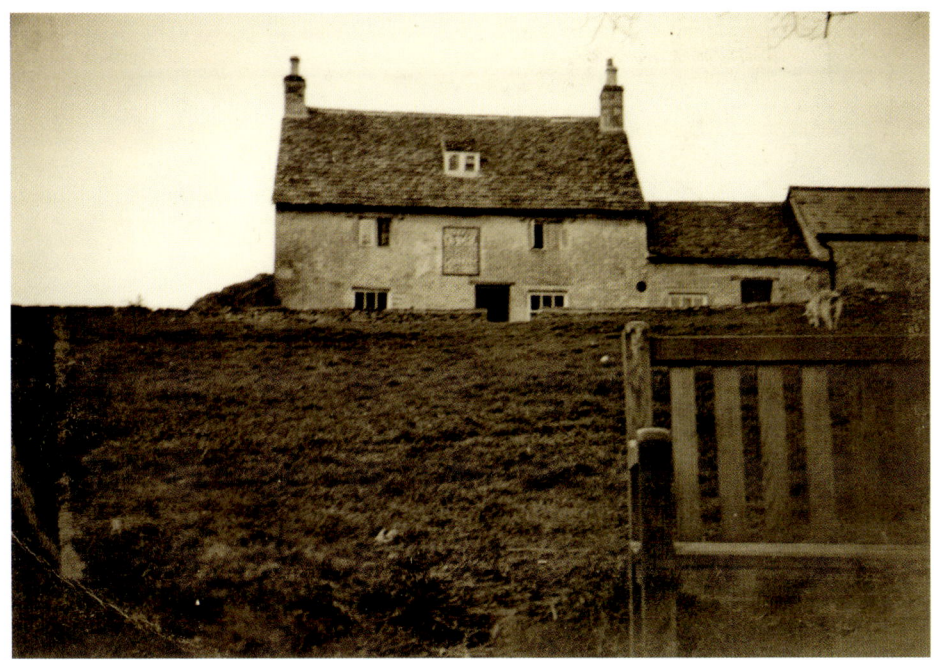

Victoria Inn, Eastleach

The picturesque village of Eastleach is actually two settlements either side of the River Leach, Eastleach Martin and Eastleach Turville. There are two Norman churches and a pretty clapper bridge straddles the river connecting the Martins with the Turvilles. The sixteenth-century village pub, the Victoria Inn, once sold beer from the Cirencester Brewery. In the 1960s it was owned by Courages and sold the likes of Tavern keg beer. Arkells of Swindon bought the Victoria Inn in 1976.

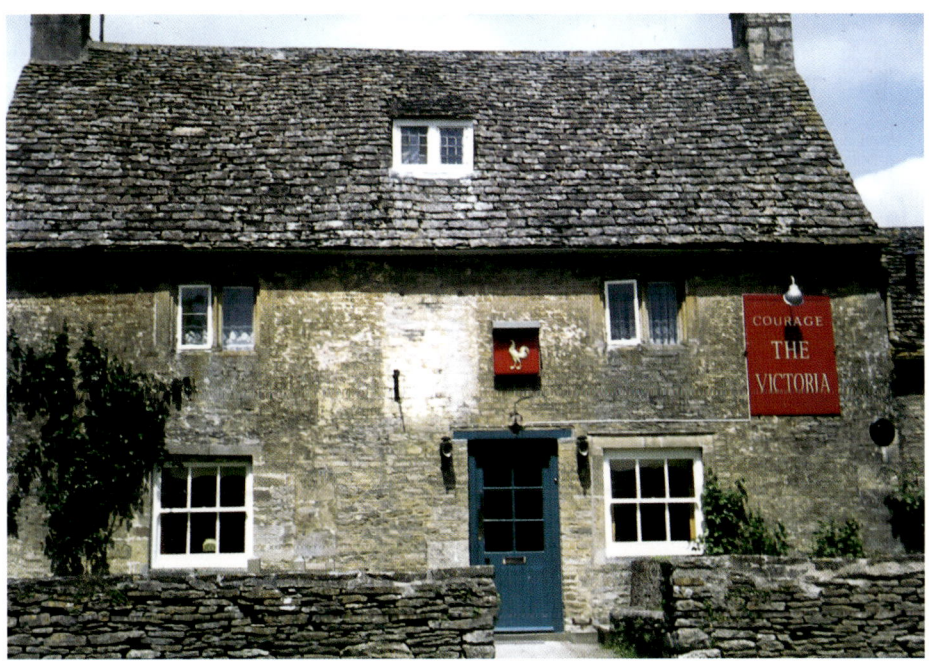

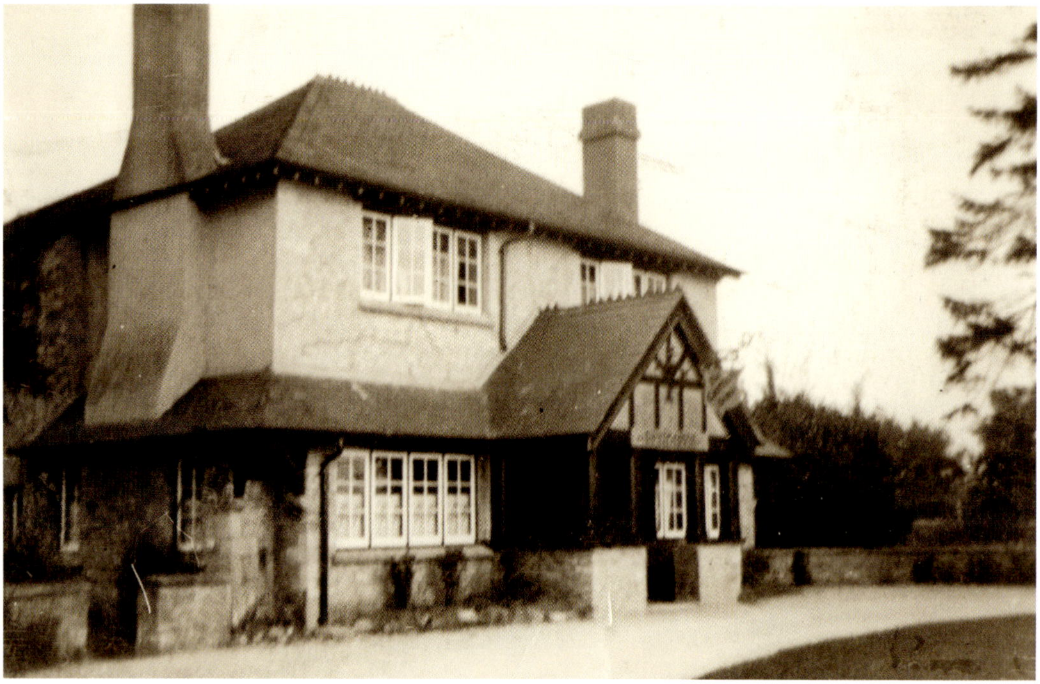

Carriers Arms, Horcott Road, Fairford

The Carriers Arms was located just before St Thomas Roman Presbytery Church as you travel along Horcott Road from Fairford town centre towards the air base. Although it was trading comparatively recently – in 1990 it was recorded as a Courage pub selling Courage Best Bitter – the Carriers Arms is one Gloucestershire pub that has eluded me. If you have any photographs or information about the Carriers Arms please get in contact with me.

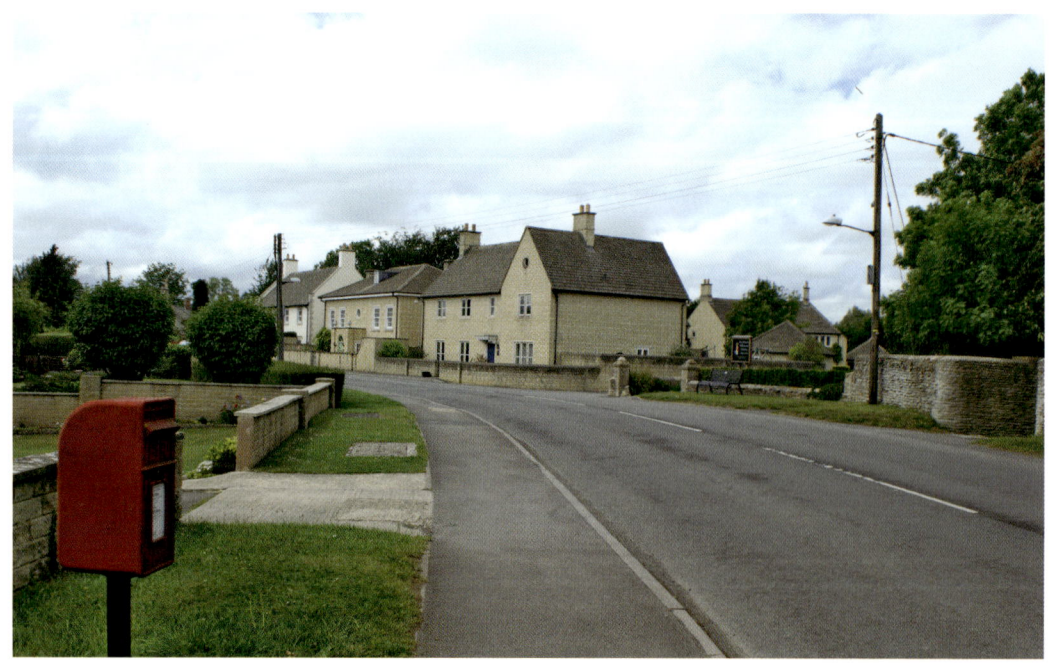

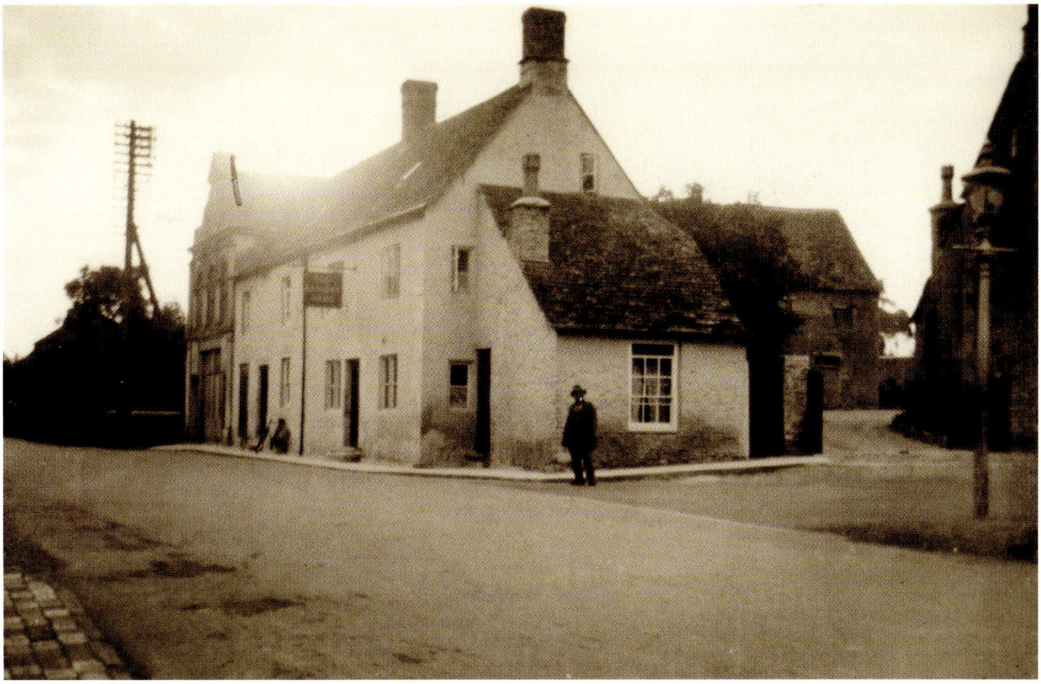

Marlborough Arms, Cirencester Road, Fairford

The Marlborough Arms, on the junction of Coronation Street and Cirencester Road, is a seventeenth-century pub. It has been recently taken over by the management of the local Halfpenny Brewery and Old Forge Breweries (at the Crown Inn, Lechlade, and Radnor Arms, Coleshill). The pub is sports orientated with a golf league, darts and bar billiard teams.

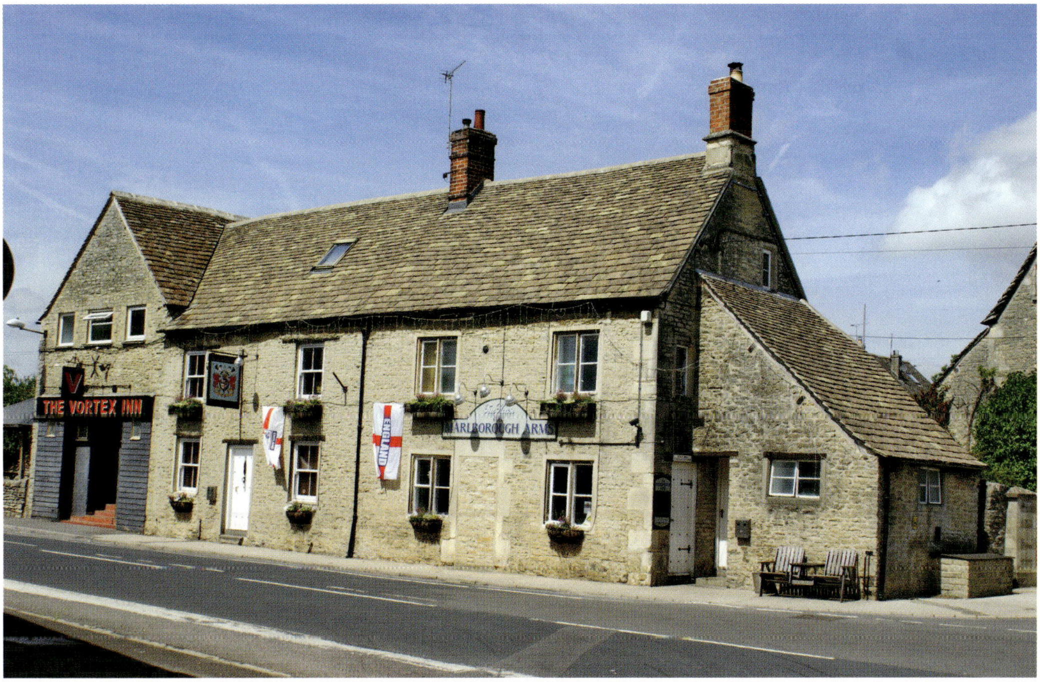

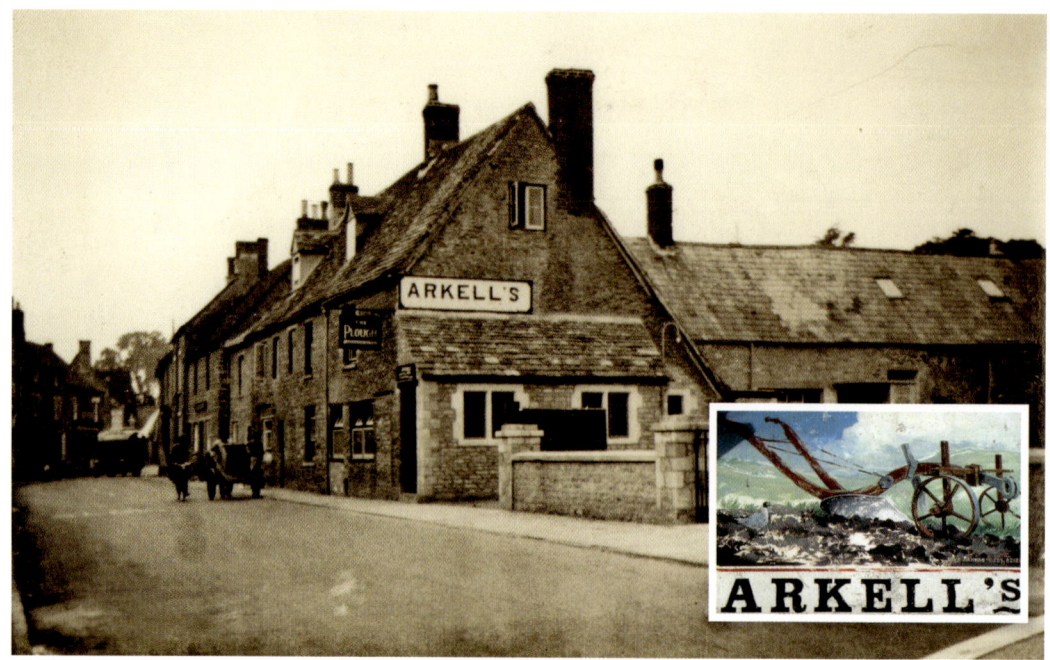

Plough Inn, London Road, Fairford

The Plough Inn has had a long association with Arkell's Kingsdown Brewery – the Swindon brewed beers have been quenching customers' thirsts at the Plough for over 150 years! Arkell's popular 3B bitter, previously known as BBB, was first brewed as Best Bitter Beer in 1910. The Plough once had a large garden, part of which was donated by the brewery to the people of Fairford in the 1930s, where Colonel A. J. Palmer built a hall for 'the enrichment of the lives of the townsfolk'.

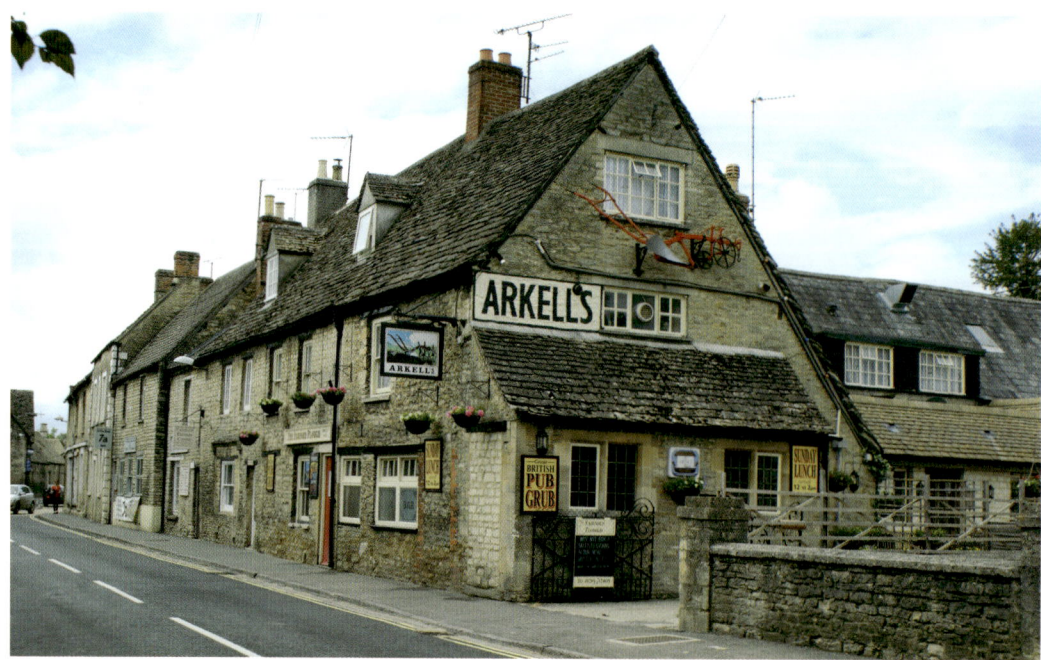

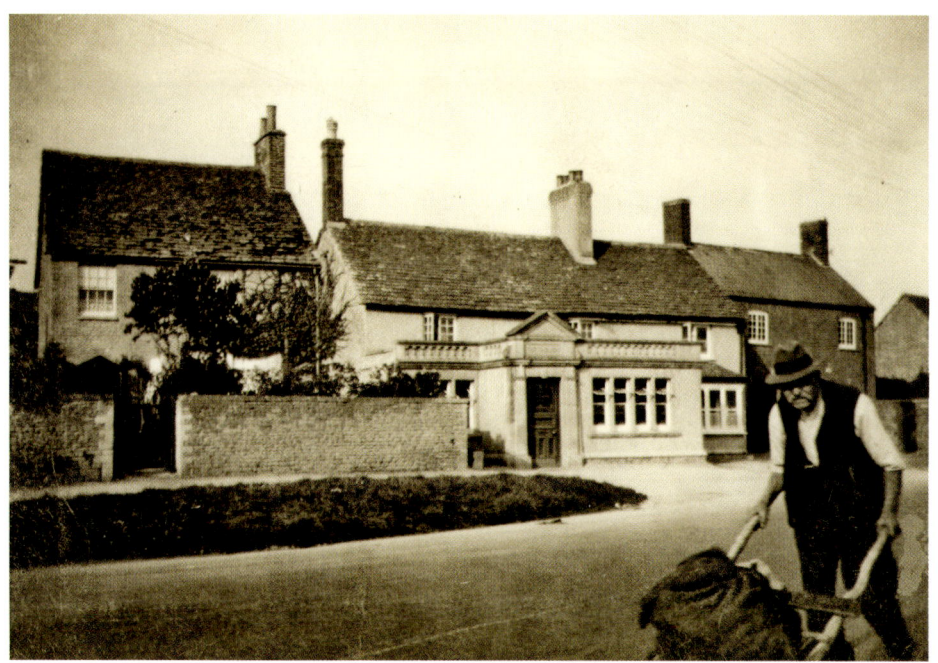

The Railway Inn, London Road, Fairford
The Railway Inn was built for R. B. Bowly & Co, North Wiltshire Brewery in Swindon to serve passengers using Fairford Railway Station, which was located nearly a mile away from the town centre. The station was the terminus of the branch line from Witney, which opened for passengers in 1873, closing eighty-nine years later in 1962. Towards the end of its life the station only served about a dozen passengers a day – hardly good business for the Railway Inn. All traces of the railway have now gone but the pub survives.

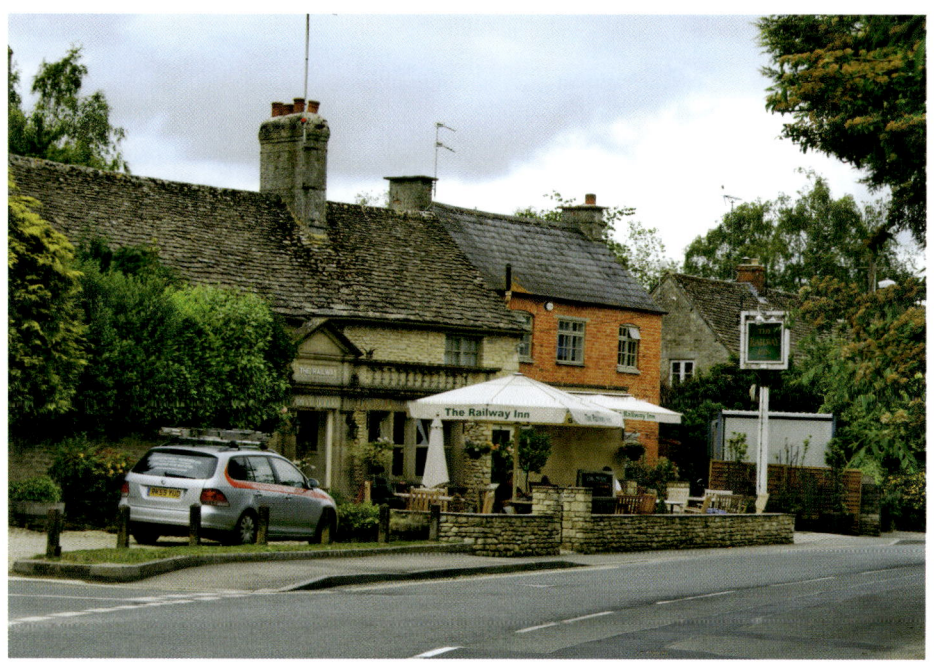

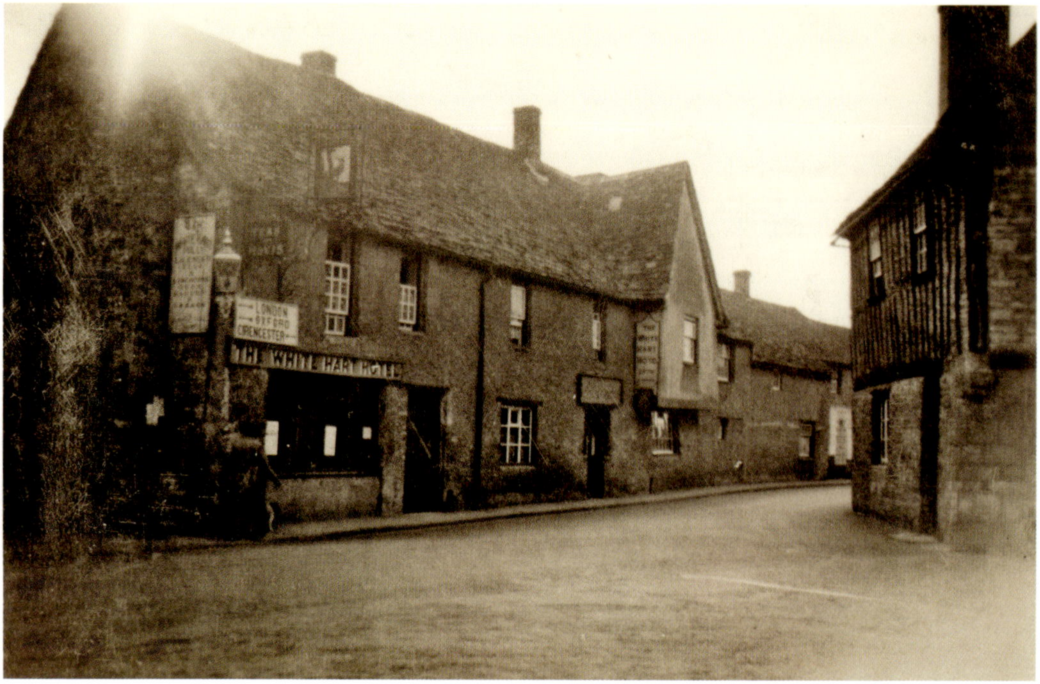

White Hart, Fairford

Spare a thought for poor George Hewer, landlord of the White Hart when it was a coaching inn in the mid-nineteenth century. The *Wilts & Gloucestershire Standard* reported on Saturday 3 July 1898 of his sudden death: 'He was seized with a fit when following his avocation at the Revd R. H. Wilmot's and died a few hours afterwards.' The Cirencester Brewery purchased the White Hart on 28 June 1920. The building is now White Hart Court.

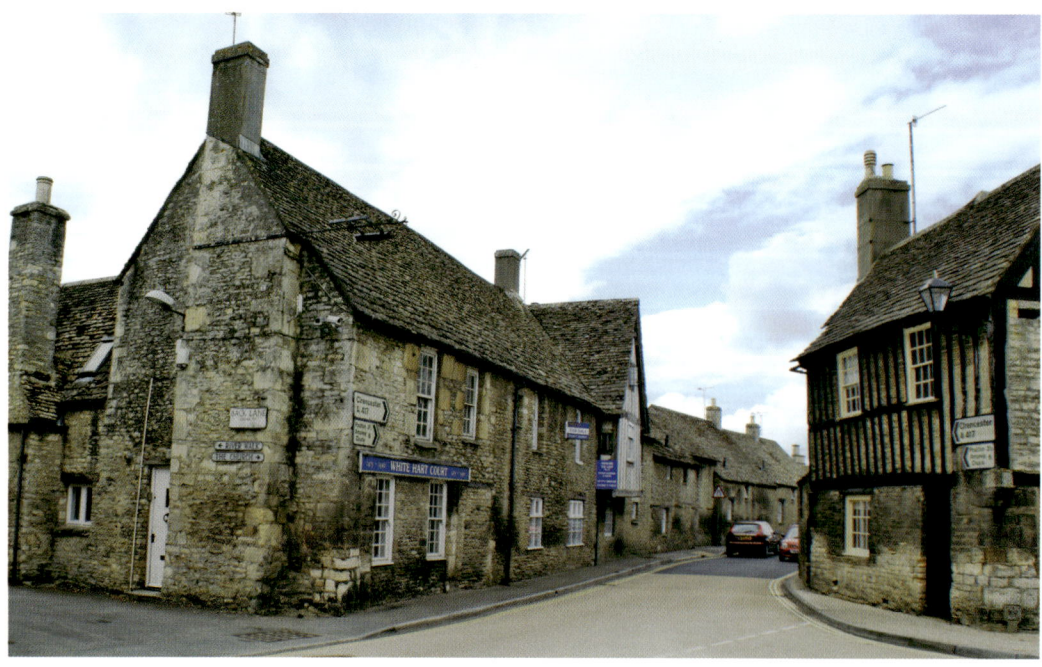

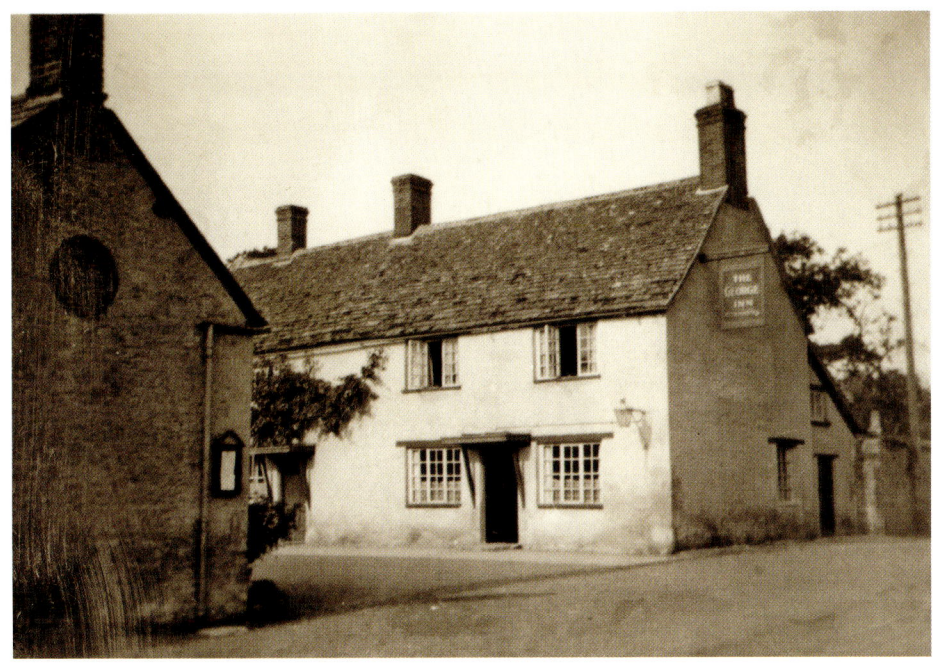

George Inn, Kempsford

Kempsford is the birthplace of brewer John Arkell, born in 1802. In 1861 Arkell's Brewery acquired the George – their first pub outside Swindon. A milestone was reached in 2011 when the nineteenth-century George Inn had been in the continuous ownership of Arkell's Brewery for an astonishing 150 years. The other pub in Kempsford, the Axe and Compass (Courage Brewery), closed in 2007.

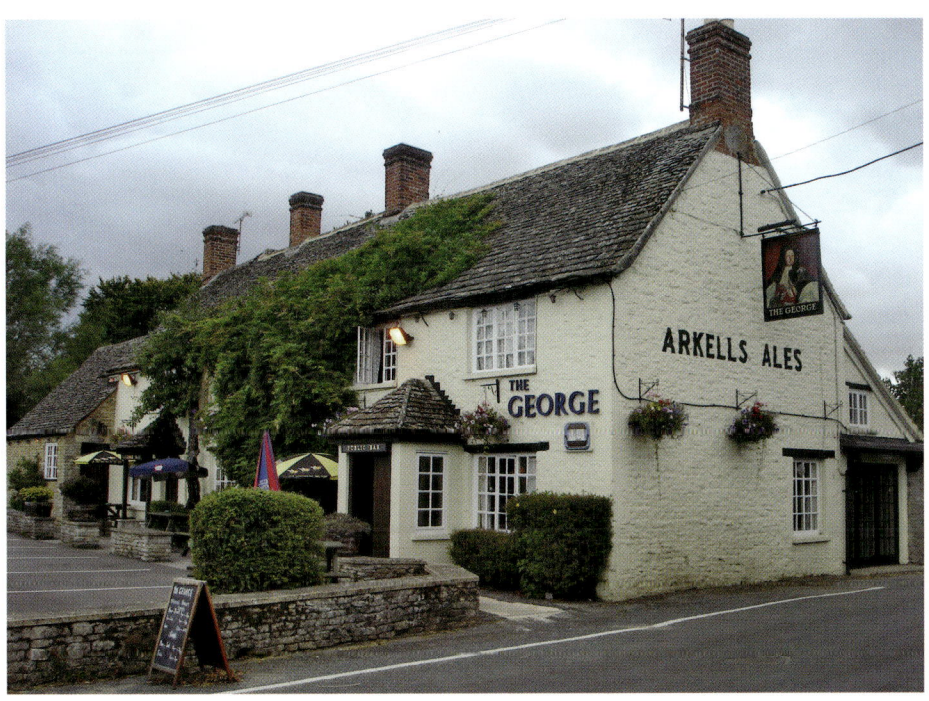

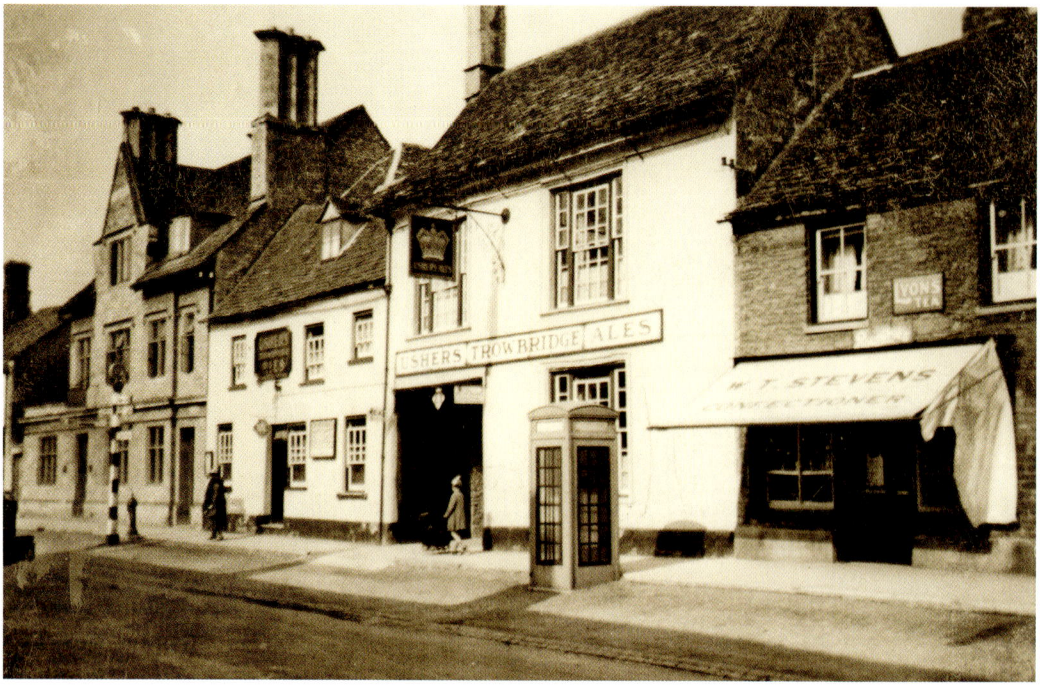

Crown Inn, High Street, Lechlade

Generations of beer drinkers at the Crown have enjoyed excellent beer. Currently the home of the Halfpenny Brewery, who brew their Ha'penny, Old Lech and Thames Tickler beer on the premises, the Crown was a pioneering Free House in the 1980s selling a good selection of real ales. Further back in time the Crown was the only pub in Gloucestershire tied to Wadley Brothers, who brewed at the Sun Brewery in Highworth supplying beer to seventeen pubs. Ushers Brewery of Trowbridge took over the Sun Brewery in 1918.

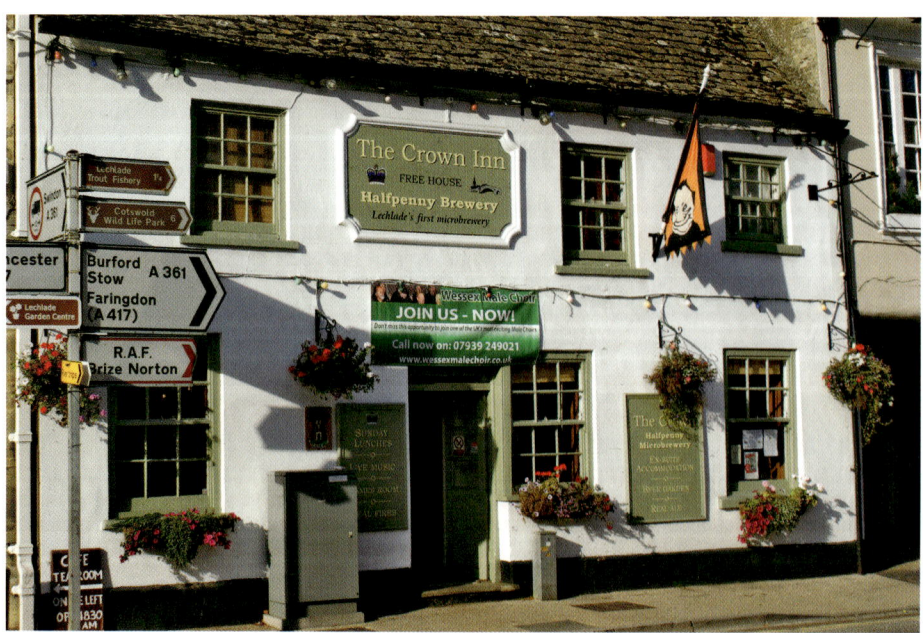

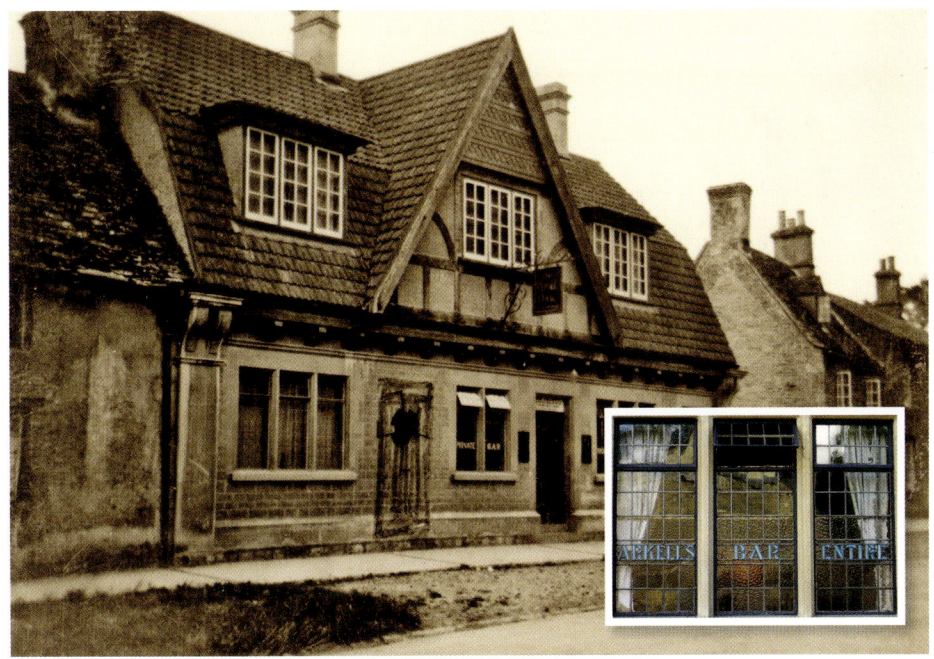

Royal Oak, Oak Street, Lechlade

The Royal Oak was originally in a small row of cottages and was leased to the Cirencester Brewery. Arkell's of Swindon bought the Royal Oak in 1922 and rebuilt the pub on the same site. Further alterations saw the addition of a second front door – as indicated by the pen scribblings on the photograph. June Turner, who retired in July 1999, was Arkell's longest serving landlady at the time, being at the pub for over thirty-five years. The Royal Oak has recently closed.

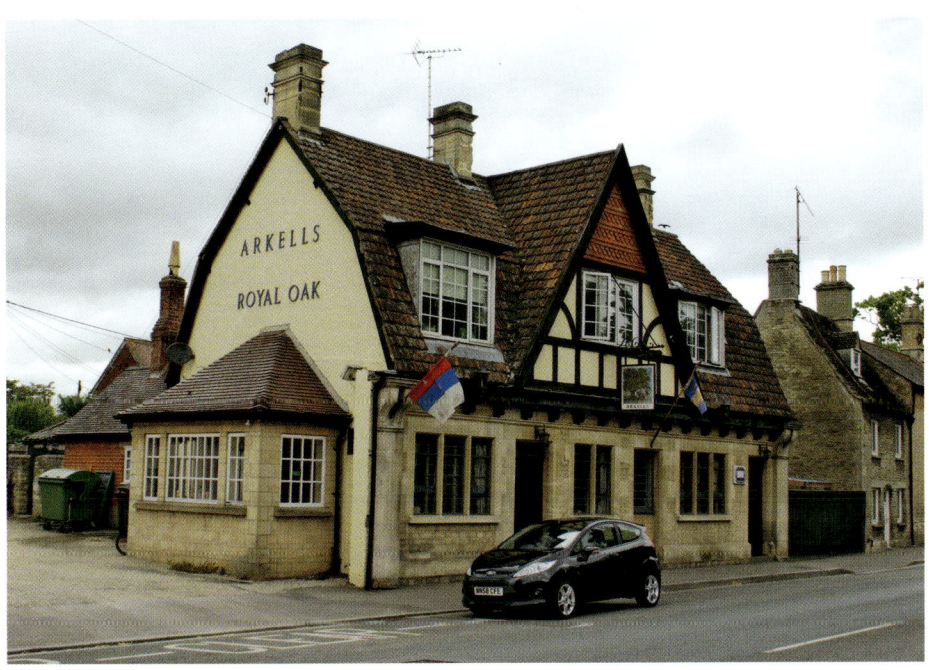

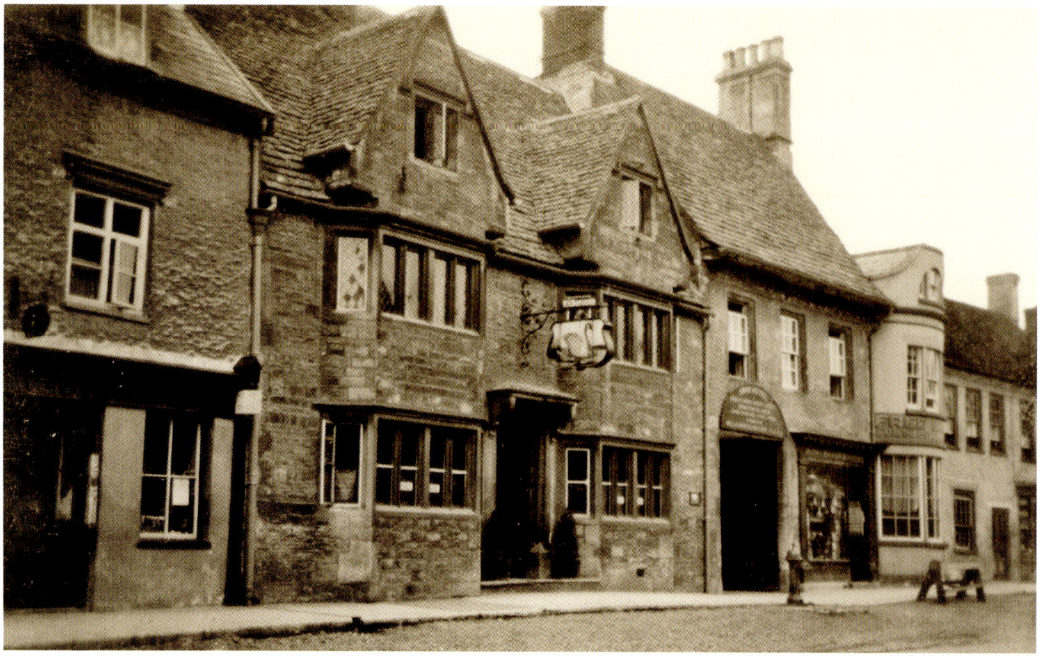

Swan Hotel, Burford Street, Lechlade

The Swan Inn can justifiably claim to be Lechlade's oldest inn. It was built in 1507 and was once a coaching inn. For a building of such antiquity the inn has little recorded history. In 1903 the Swan Inn is recorded as being a tied house of R. B (Richard Brewin) Bowly of Swindon. Bowly's also owned the Labourers Arms in the High Street, the Nags Head in St Johns Street, the Railway Tavern in Station Road and the Trout Inn at St Johns Bridge – only the Trout survives.

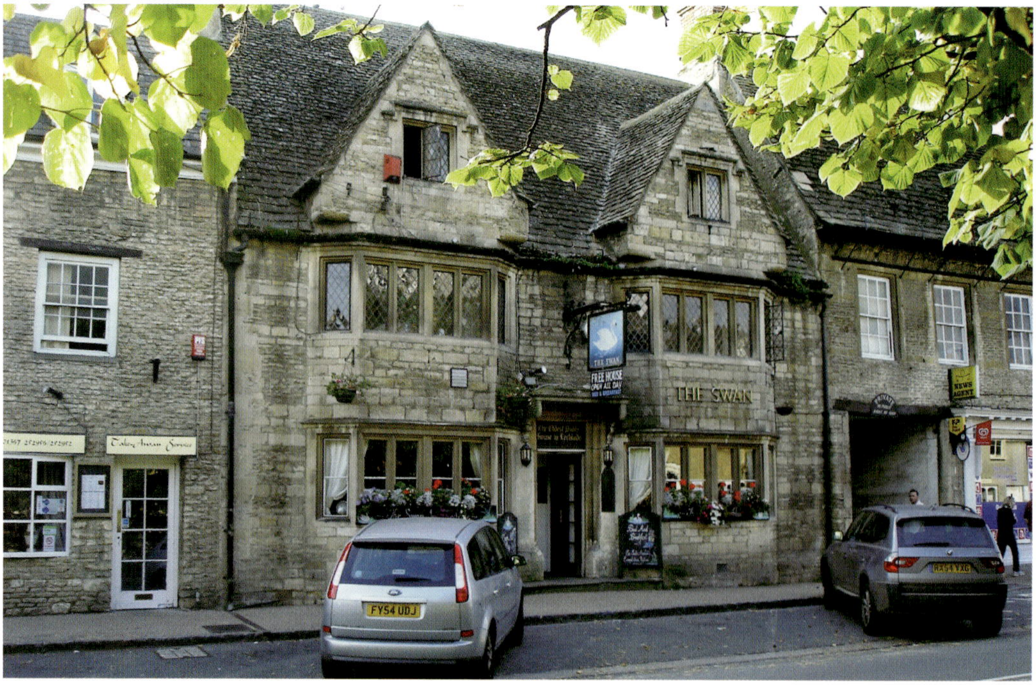

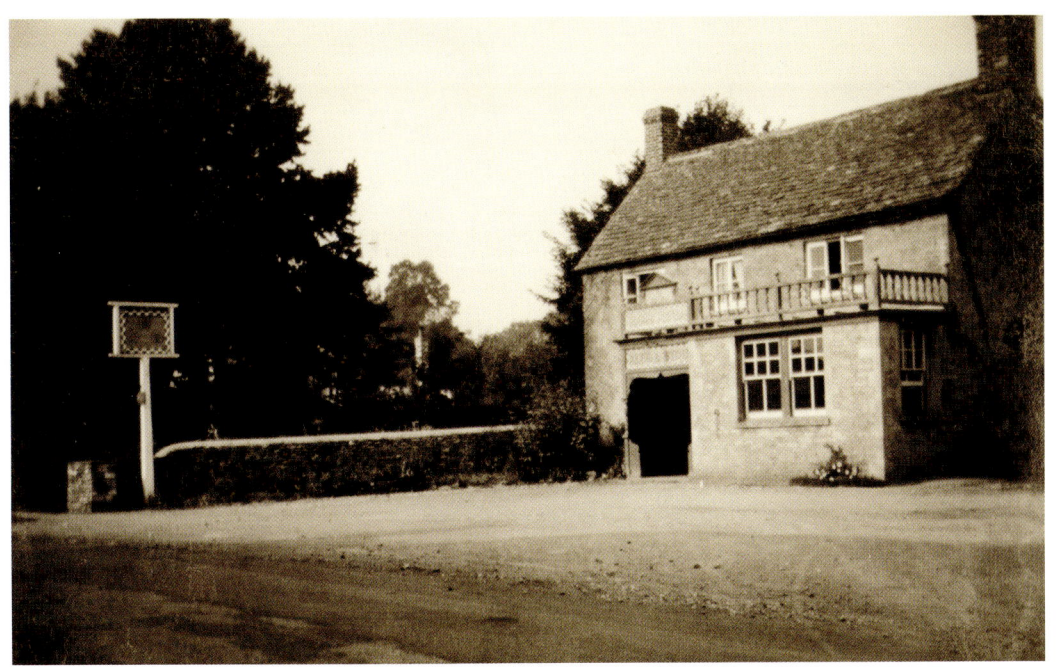

Three Horseshoes, Downington, Lechlade

The Three Horseshoes, dating from 1657, was located on the A417 Fairford road to the west of the town. Licensing records (in 1891 and 1903) show that the Three Horseshoes was the only Gloucestershire pub to be tied to Morlands Brewery of Abingdon, Oxfordshire. When the pub called 'last orders' for the final time in March 2001, Morlands Old Speckled Hen was on offer – albeit from the Greene King brewery in Bury St Edmunds.

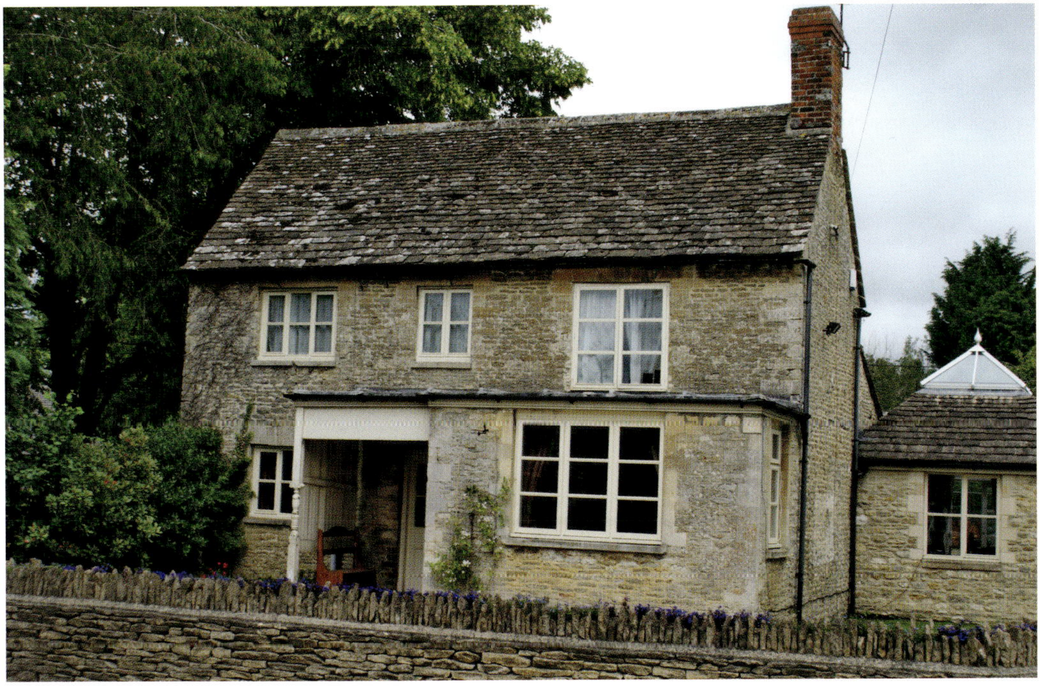

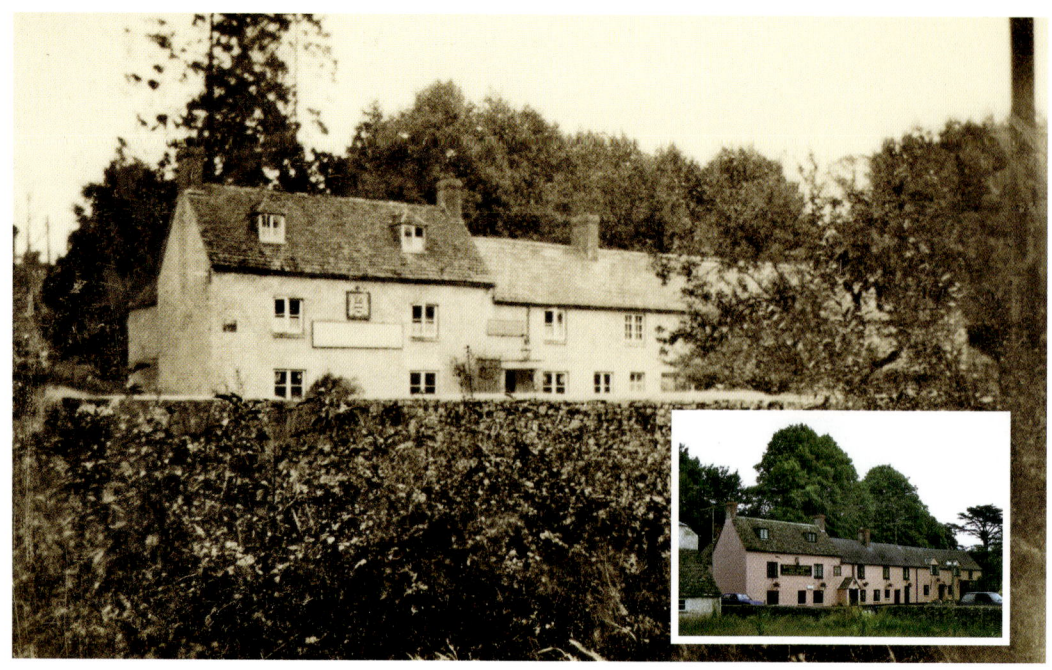

Bathurst Arms, North Cerney

The seventeenth-century Bathurst Arms is set in an idyllic setting by the River Churn. The pub has flagstone floors, settles and a stove in an inglenook fireplace. In 2011 it was given the accolade of Inn of the Year by the *Good Pub Guide*. It was also named the Gloucestershire Dining Pub of the Year in 2008 and 2011. North Cerney Primary School teamed up with the Bathurst Arms in the spring of 2005 to liven up their school dinners with fresh local produce prepared at the pub.

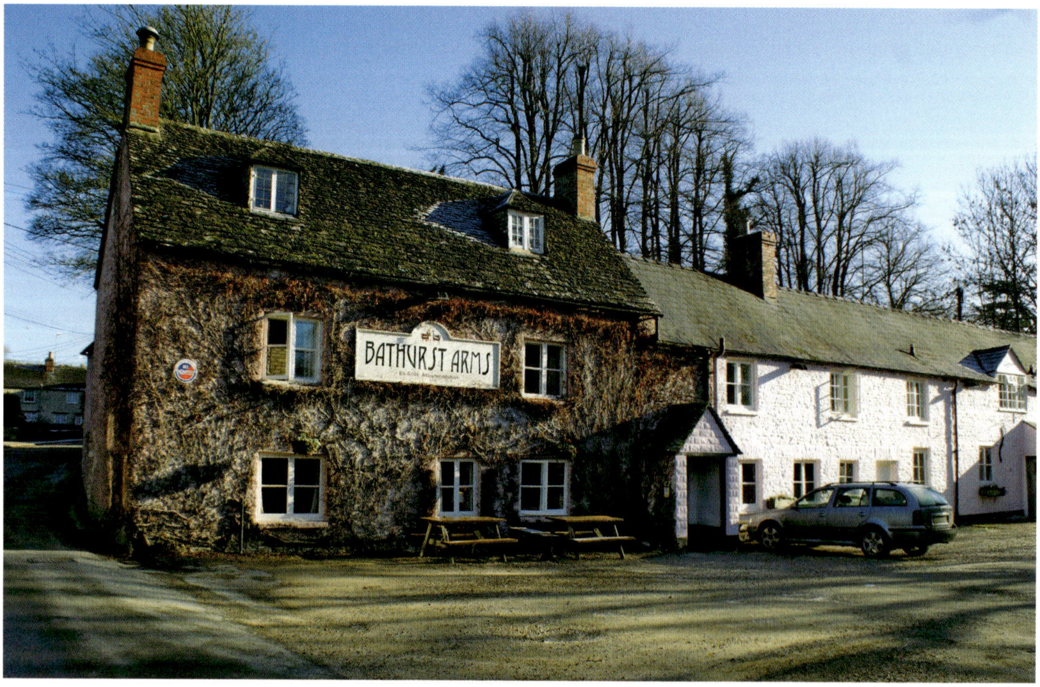

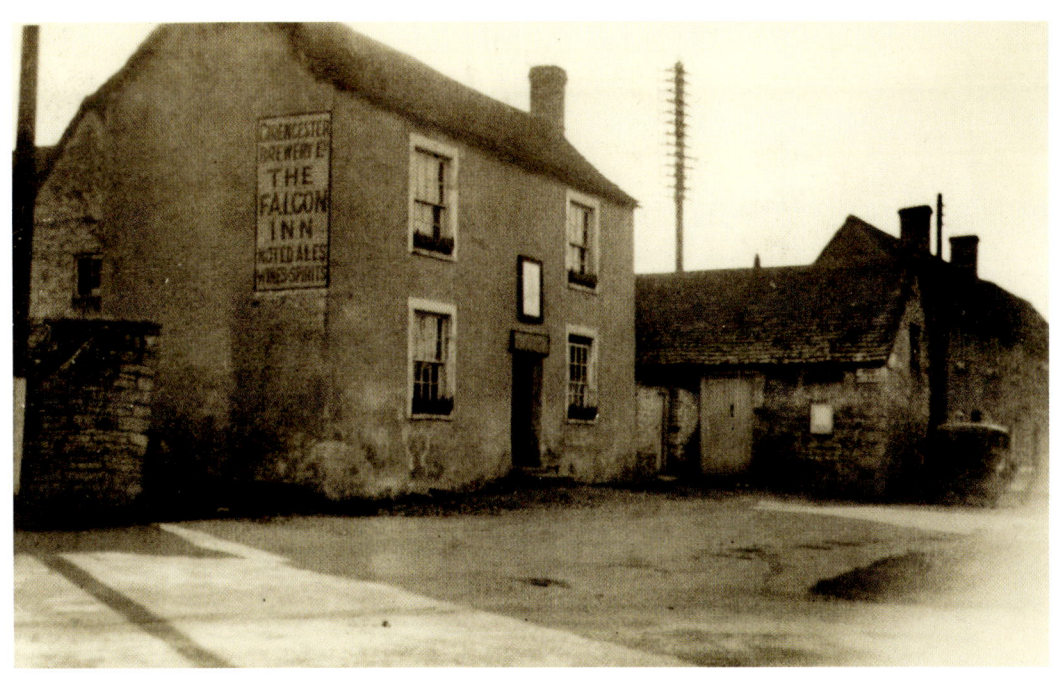

Falcon Inn, Poulton
The 300-year-old Grade II listed Falcon Inn is located on a bend on the A417 and is a prominent landmark in Poulton. Once a simple ale house owned by the Cirencester Brewery, the emphasis is now firmly on fine cuisine although the present owners are keen to stress that the Falcon should be at the heart of the community rather than an exclusive gastropub. In the 1990s the Falcon was the venue of the annual knockout conker championships, a charity fundraising event that was filmed by the BBC, HTV and Sky in 1998.

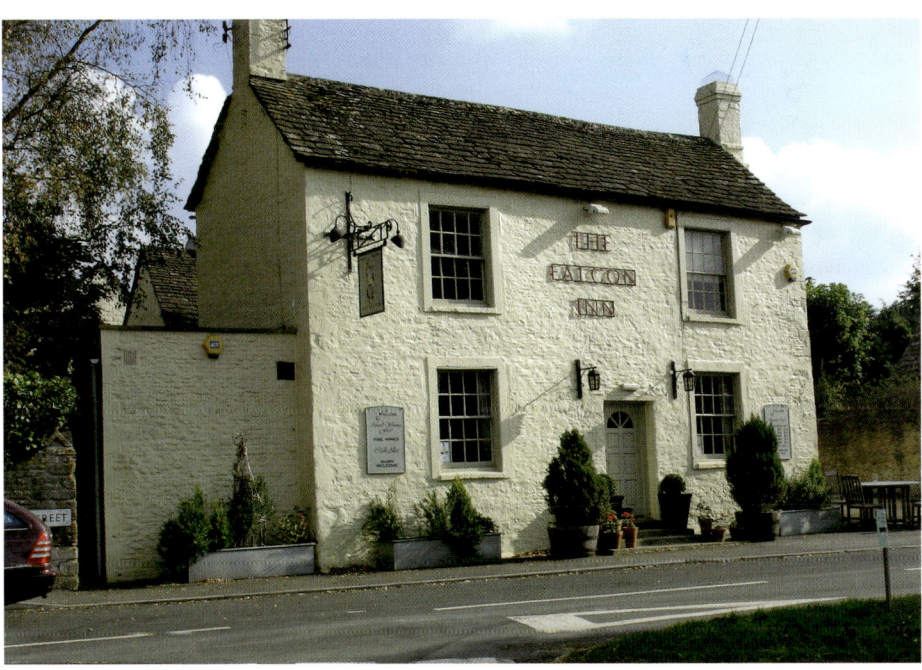

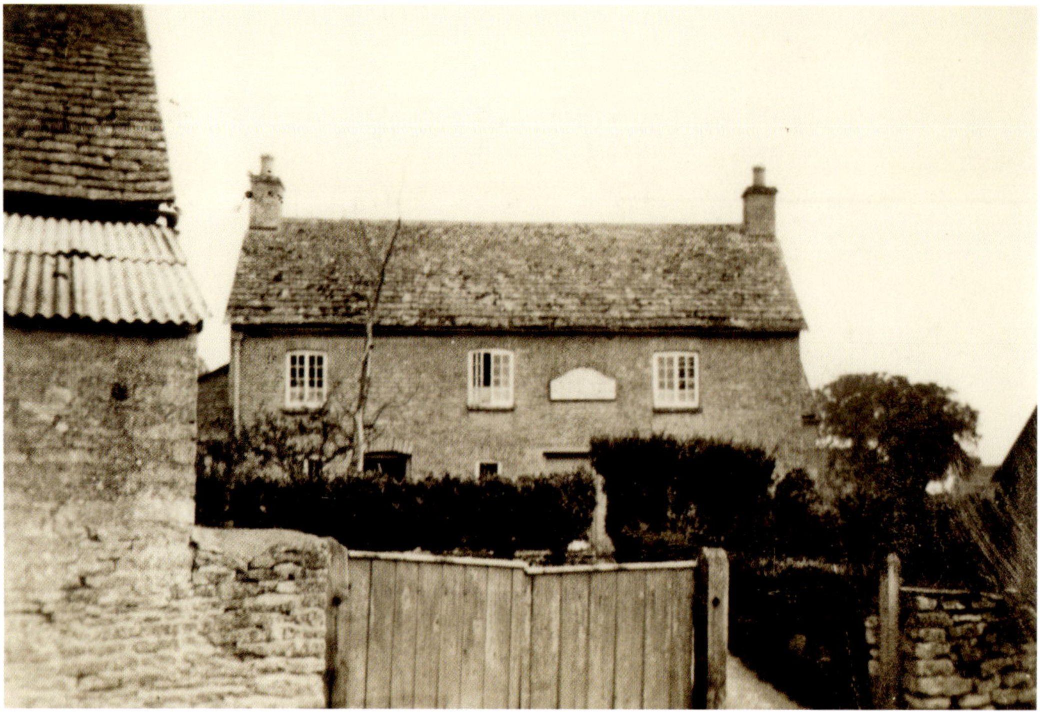

Earl Grey Inn, Quenington

The Earl Grey closed on Halloween night 1996 following the retirement of the landlady Lucie Swainson. The pub was once featured in the *Guinness Book of Records* as a contender for smallest pub in Britain. Lucie was also the village postmistress – the Earl Grey was also the home of Quenington Post Office. There was no objection to the closure as the Keepers Arms was only a few yards away.

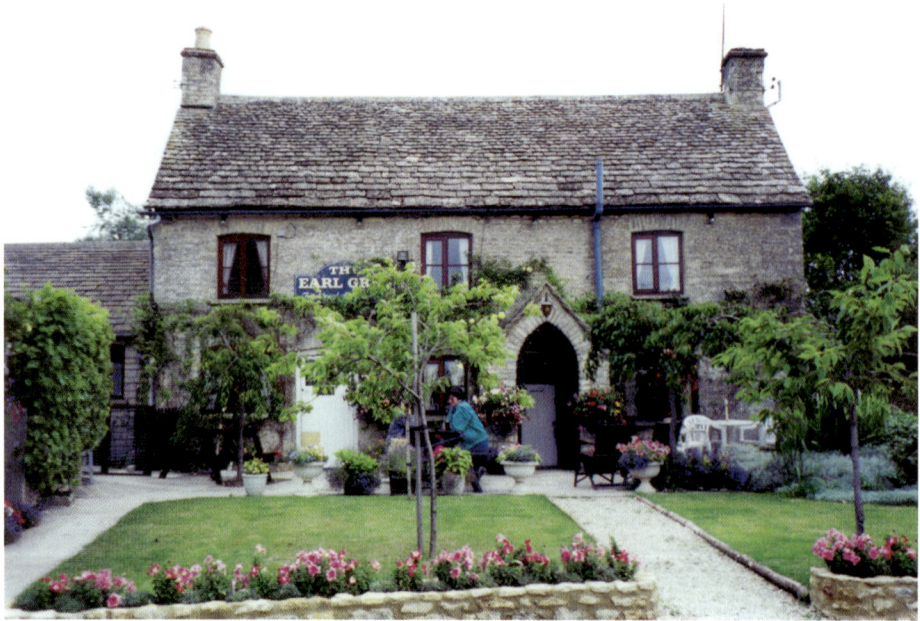

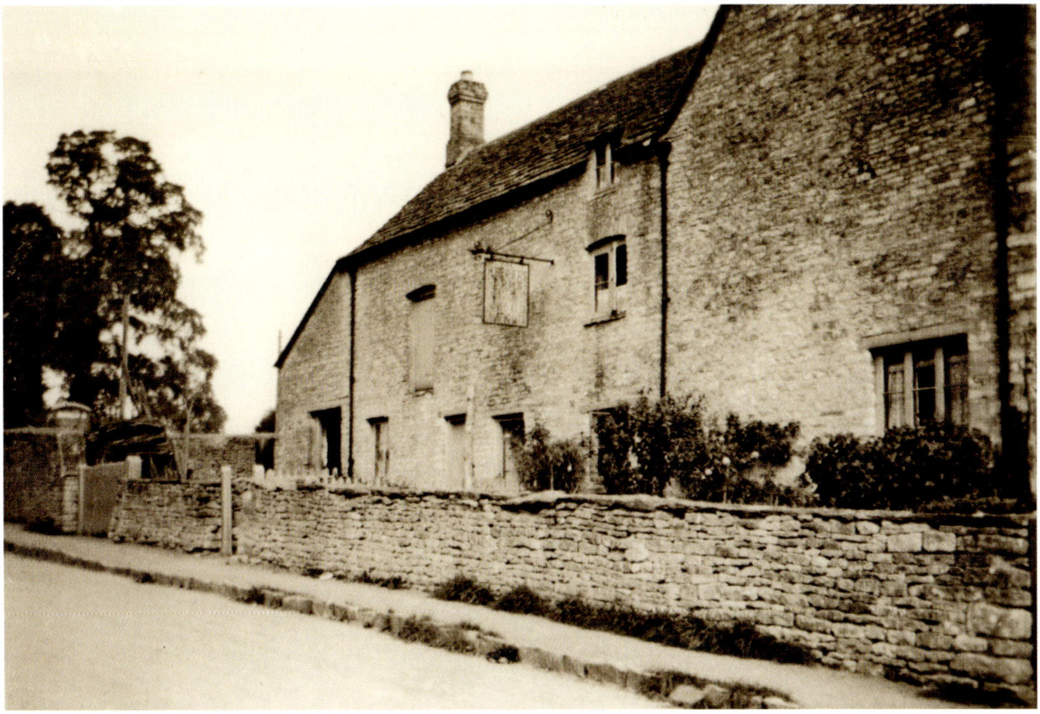

Keepers Arms, Quenington

In October 1997 the Keepers Arms was renamed the 'Liszt & Newt' and had a starring role on primetime TV. The pub was the village local in a spoof soap set in the fictional village of Crinkley Bottom in *Noel's House Party* – thankfully Mr Blobby was not a member of the cast. The Keepers Arms is a homely traditional pub selling good beer and serving delicious home-cooked food, resisting the trend to become yet another 'Country Dining Inn'.

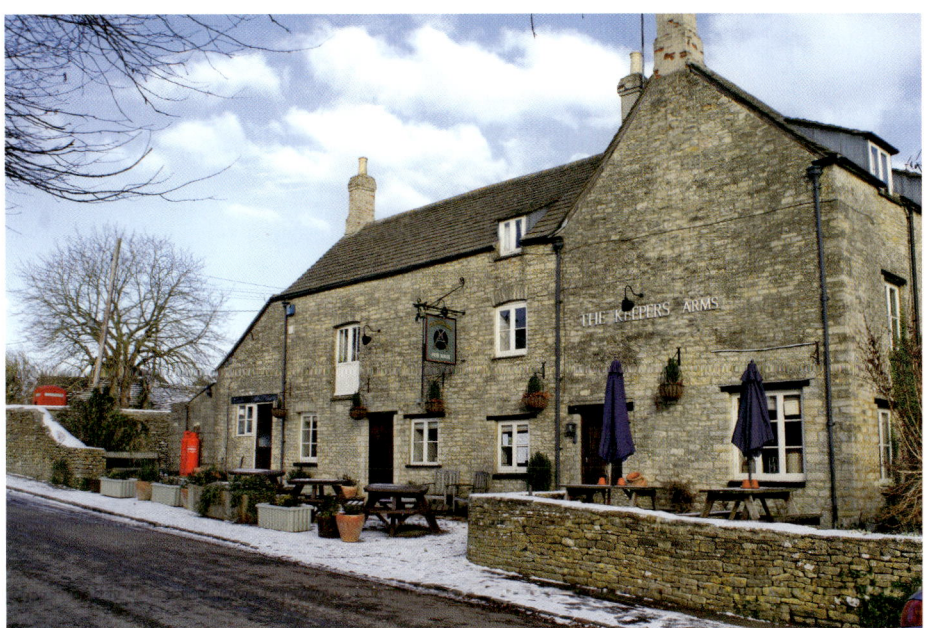

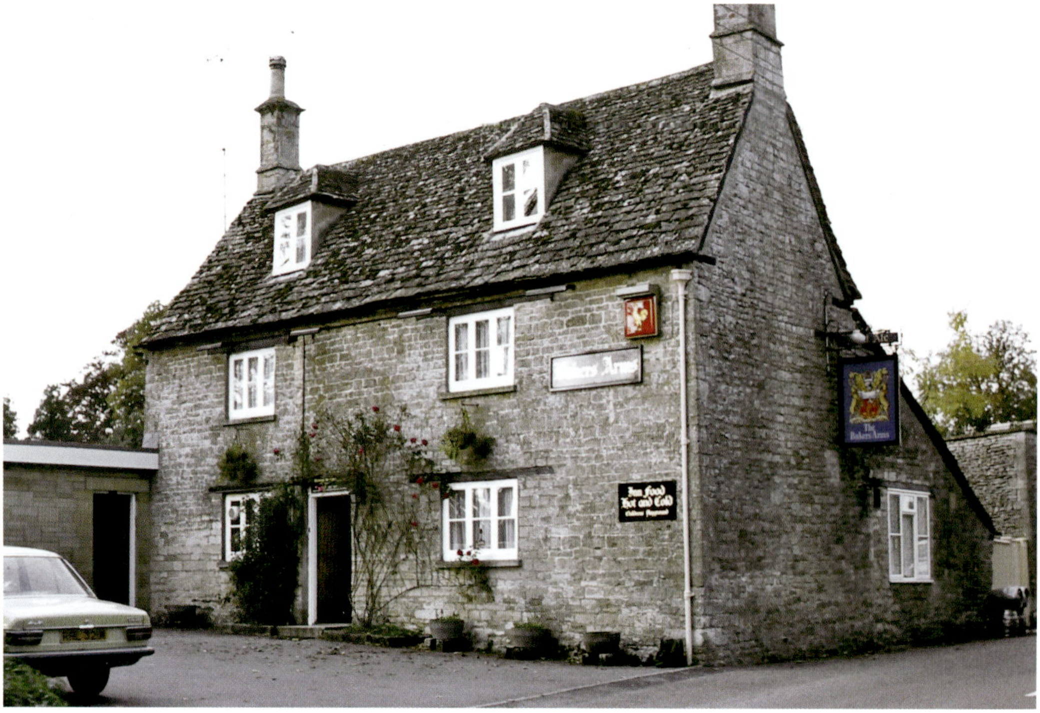

Bakers Arms, Somerford Keynes

The oldest part of the property dates back to the fifteenth century and was once a baker's shop. It has been said that there is still a baker's oven concealed behind a wall in the pub but it has never been found. The landlord in 2004, Richard Burton, was surprised to learn that one of the villagers and regulars at the Bakers Arms was called Elizabeth Taylor!

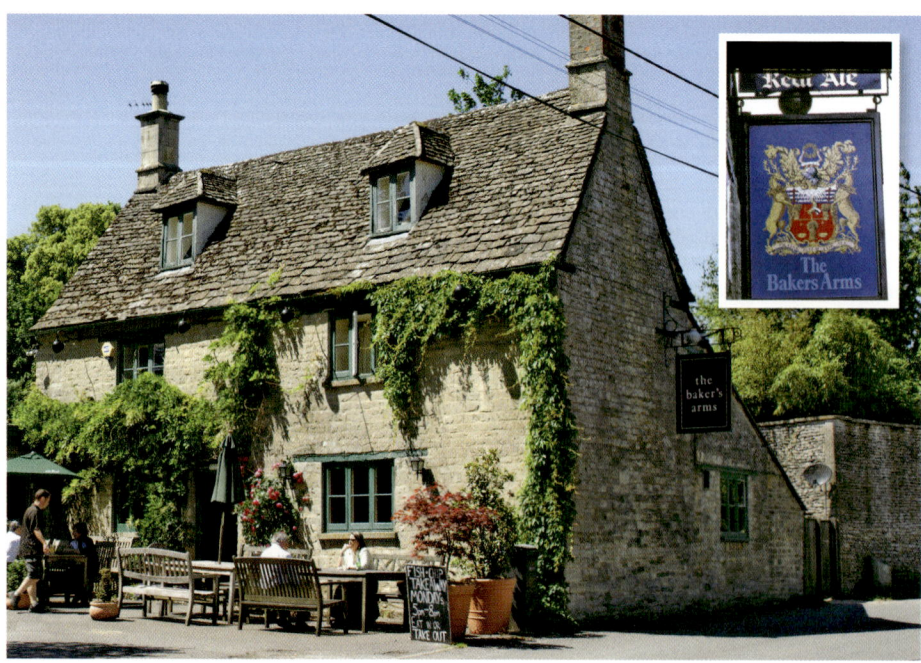

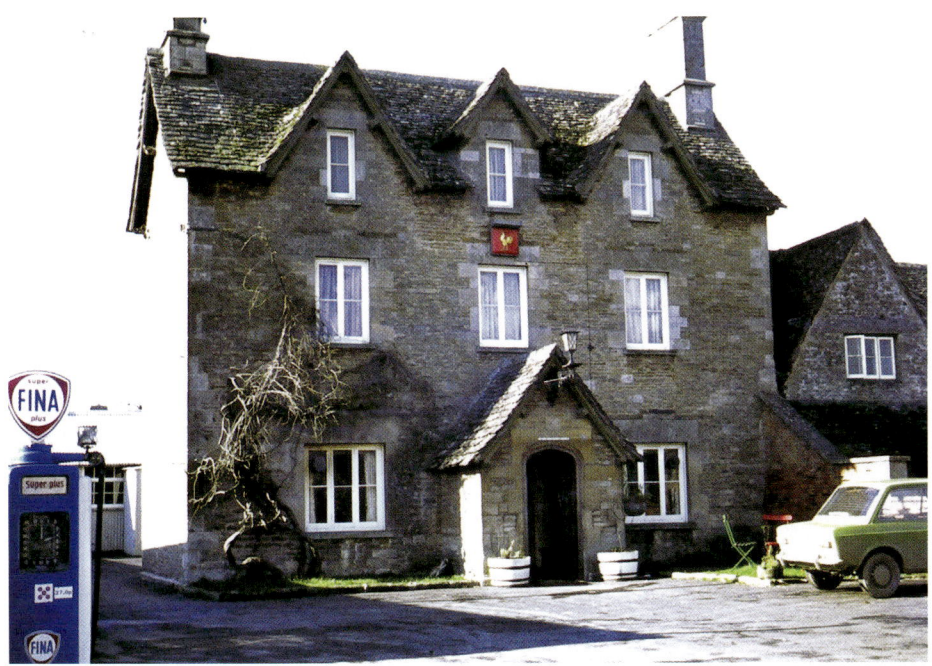

Eliot Arms, South Cerney

The first mention of the Eliot Arms is from a deed dating 30 December 1871 when Robert Stanton sold the property to Messrs Cripps & Co. of the Cirencester Brewery. The Eliot family are from St Germans in Cornwall. They owned a shooting lodge in Down Ampney where there was once a pub called the Eliot Arms. On closure, perhaps the licence was transferred to the pub in South Cerney. Their family coat of arms and motto '*Praecedentibus Insta*', as seen on the pub sign, means 'Press more closely on those that take the lead'.

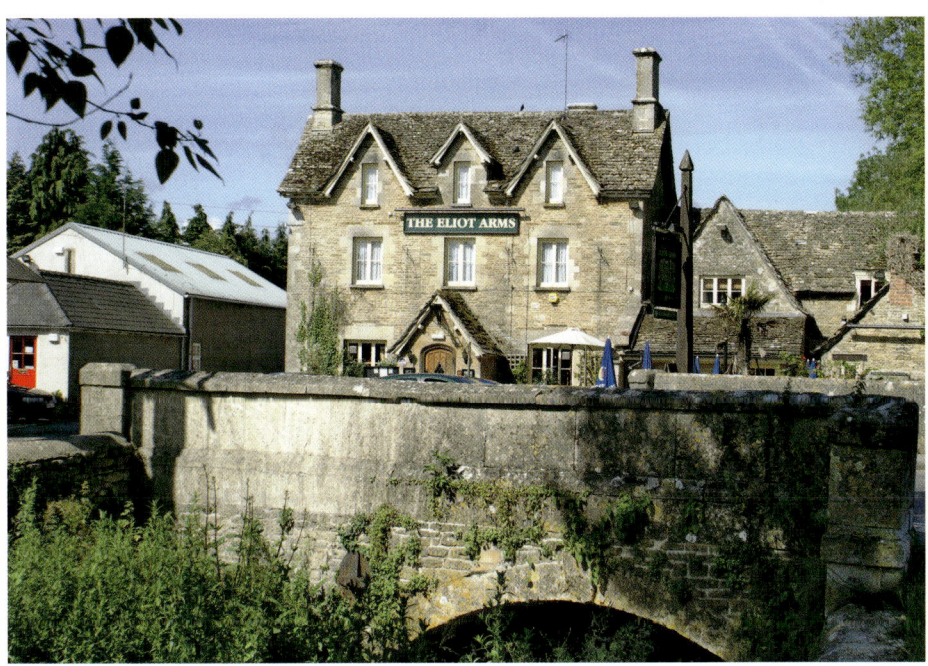

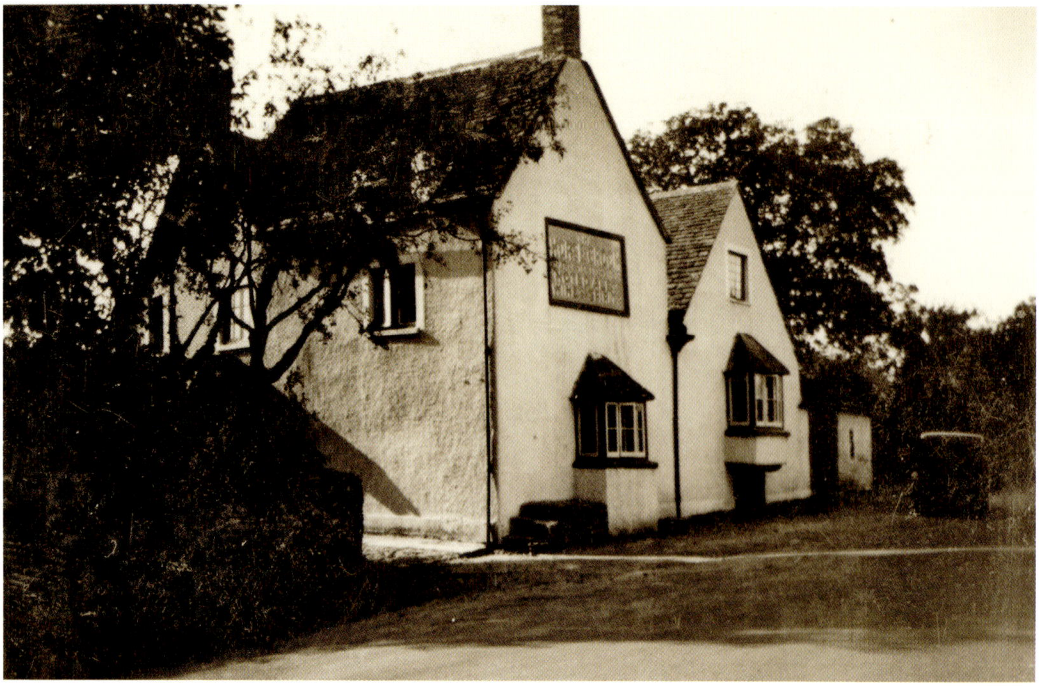

Horse & Groom, Cricklade Road, South Cerney

The Horse & Groom was purchased by the Cirencester Brewery with 'land in Cricklade Road adjoining' on 25 March 1919. The eighteenth-century pub once stood on the busy A417 Cirencester to Swindon road but the Cirencester bypass constructed in 1997 left it isolated. A twelve bedroom motel was built on the site of a barn at the back of the pub in an attempt to gain custom. However, permission was granted to convert the pub and adjoining motel into residential use in the summer of 2004.

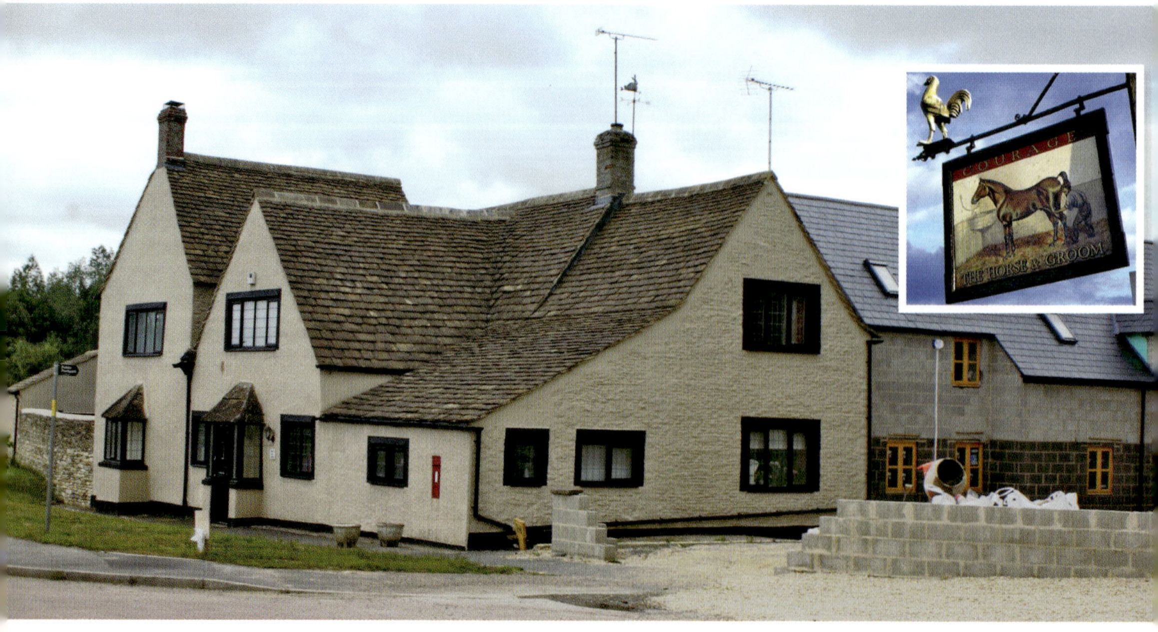

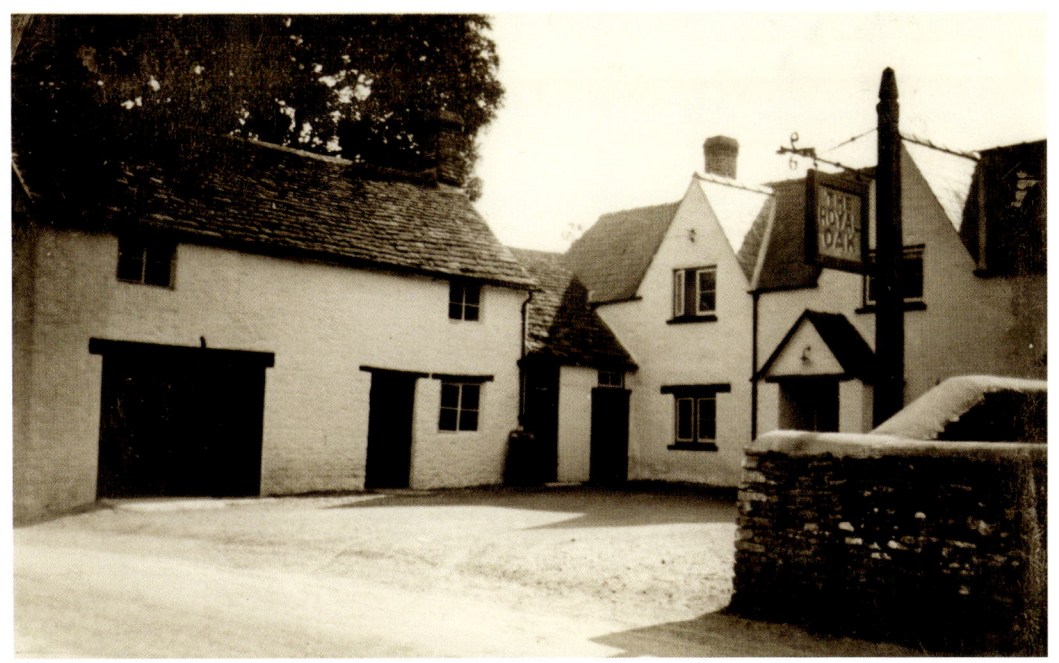

Old George, Clarks Hay, South Cerney

In about 1900 Mr Isaac Howell owned Barston House (now Tanners) at Upper Up, and also operated a brewery. He also owned the Old George Inn which he sold in 1903. The Old George was transformed into a trendy young persons' venue called 'Walter Mitty's' in the 1980s, but the pub reverted back to its true identity in the mid-1990s. Jamie Cullum entertained locals here before he was famous and former Sex Pistol Glen Matlock played a charity gig at the pub in January 2012 in aid of the Alzheimer's Society. Anarchy if it's OK!

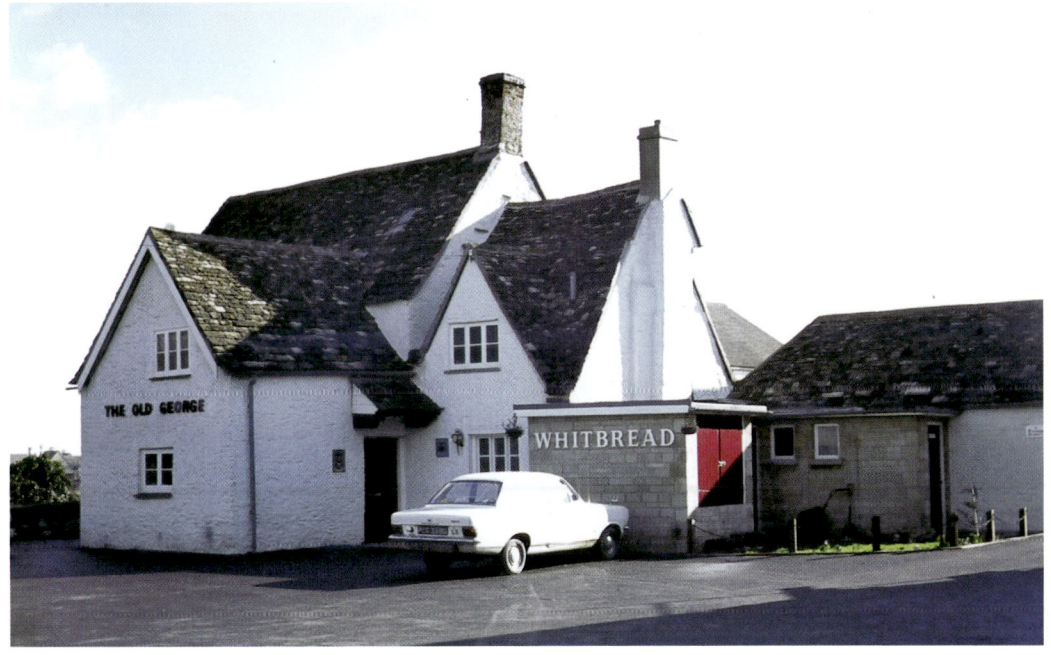

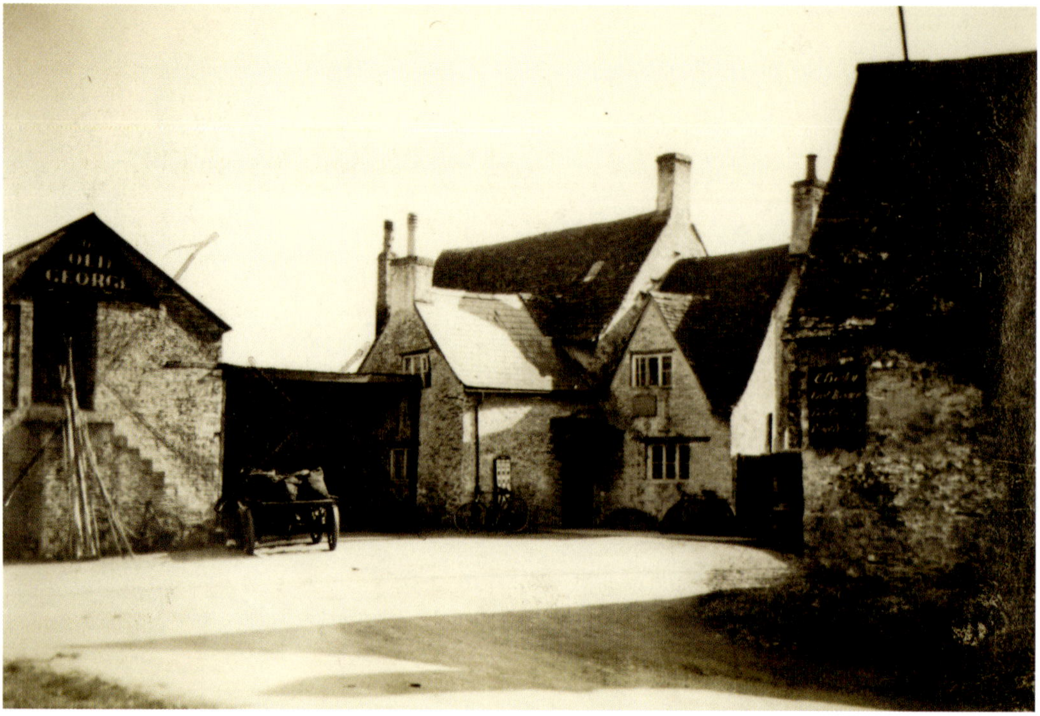

Royal Oak, High Street, South Cerney

The Royal Oak is a 300-year-old listed building. The 1856 reference is simply The Oak, South Cerney. When excavations were being made in 1997 to lay pipes for a new cellar human remains were found which necessitated a police enquiry. No criminal investigations were necessary on that occasion but police were called again in July 2008 to solve the mysterious disappearance of four hanging flower baskets.

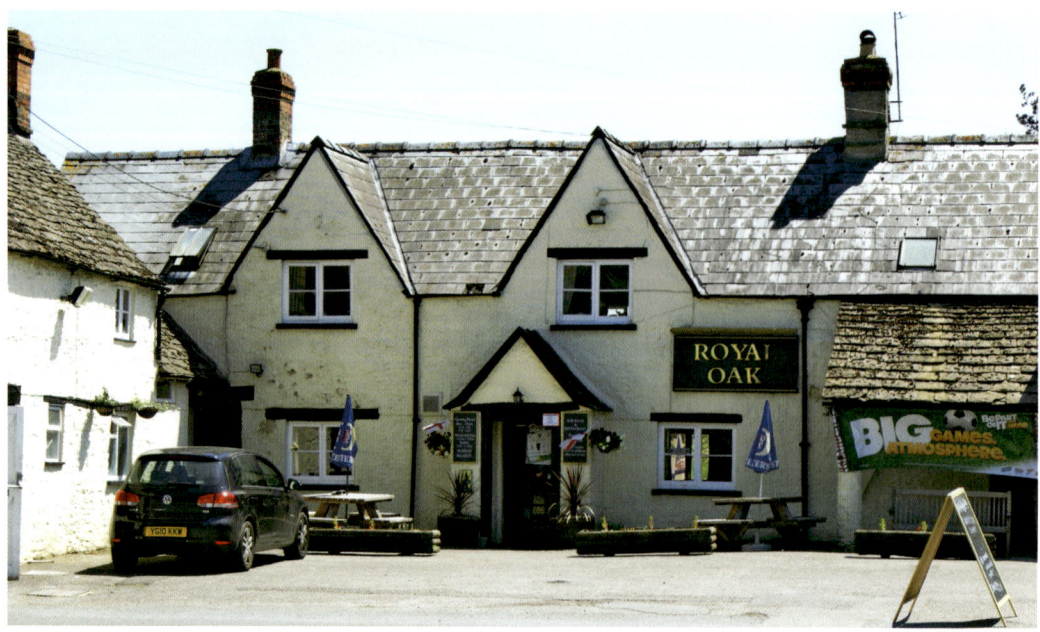

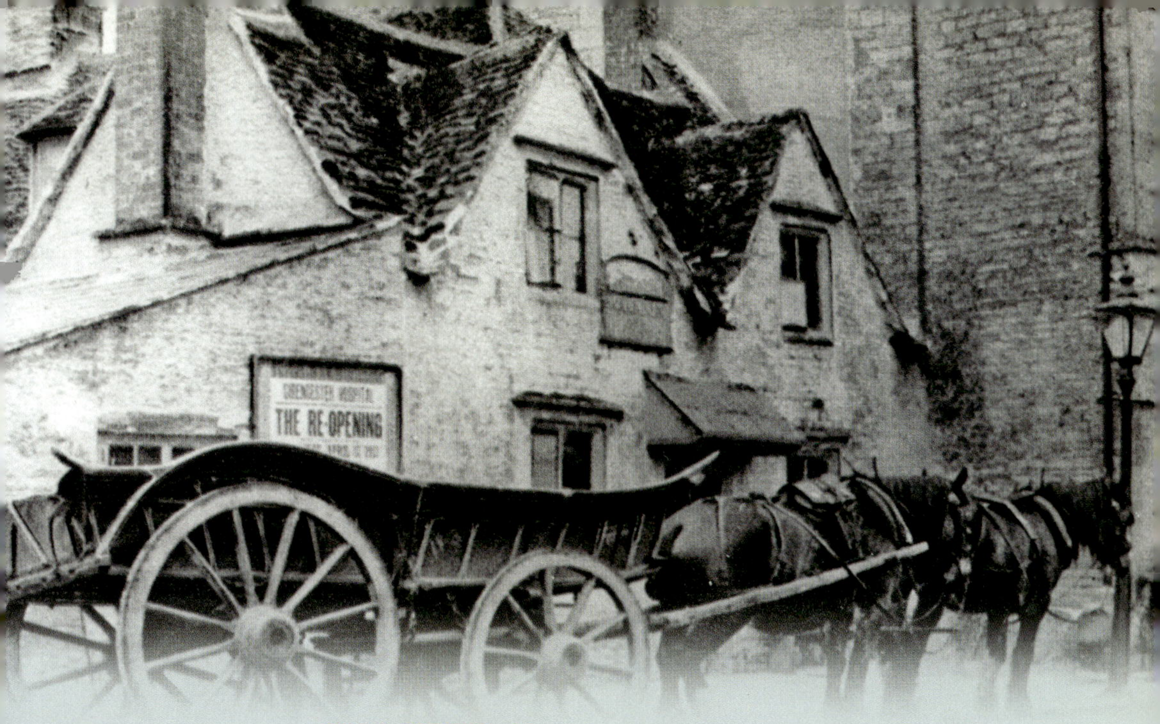

CHAPTER 2

Cirencester

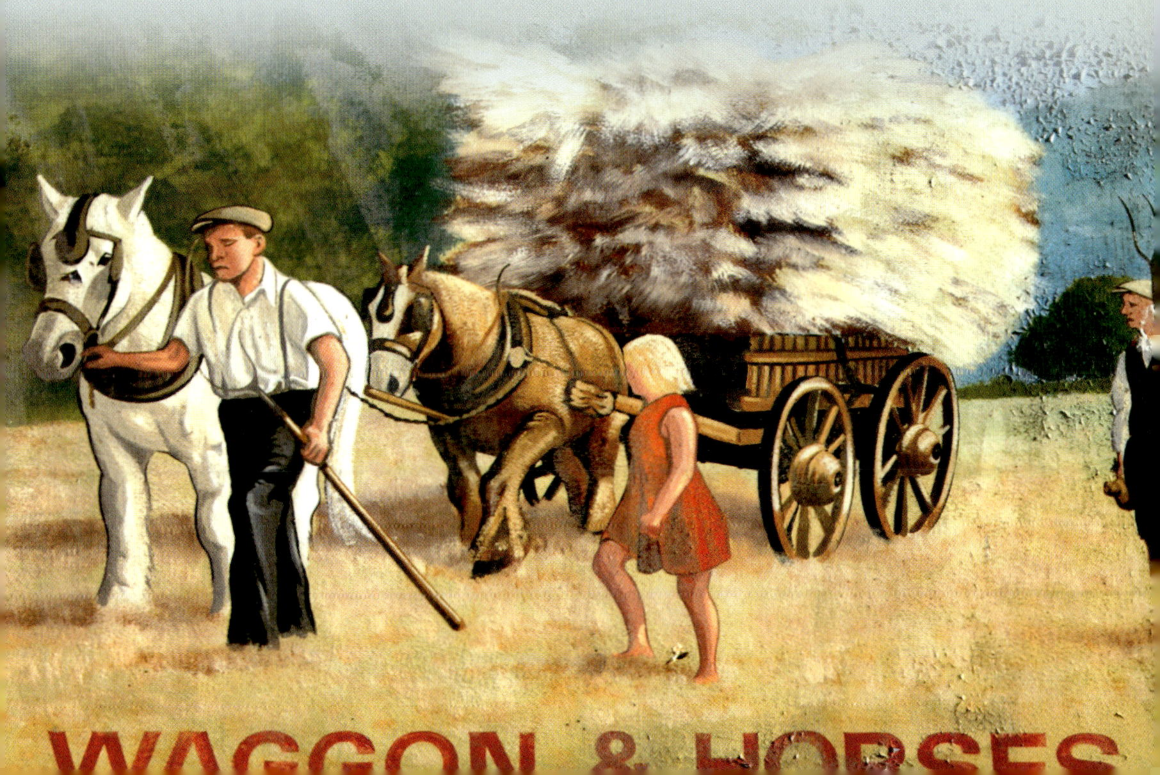

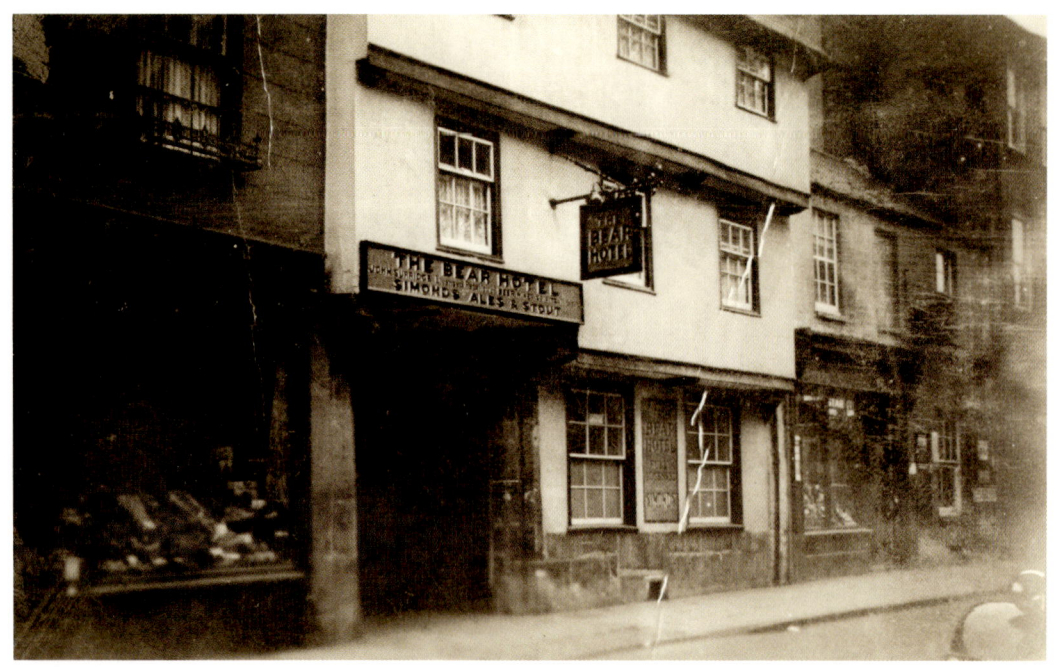

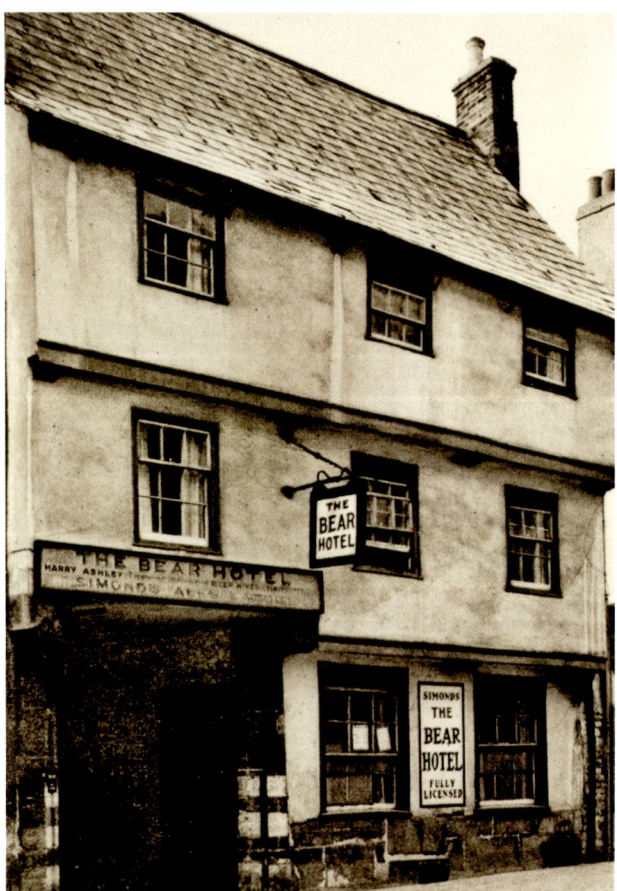

Bear Hotel, Dyer Street, Cirencester

When W. St Clair-Badderly wrote his *History of Cirencester* in 1924 he made some disparaging and somewhat oblique remarks about the Bear Hotel: 'This house was formerly of more importance than it is now, being a famous market inn frequented by many of the chief farmers in the district, including the leading Cotswold ram dealers such as the Garnes the Lanes, the Hewers and the Bartons, and the like.' Today the Bear Inn is simply described as a 'busy town centre pub with a traditional welcome'.

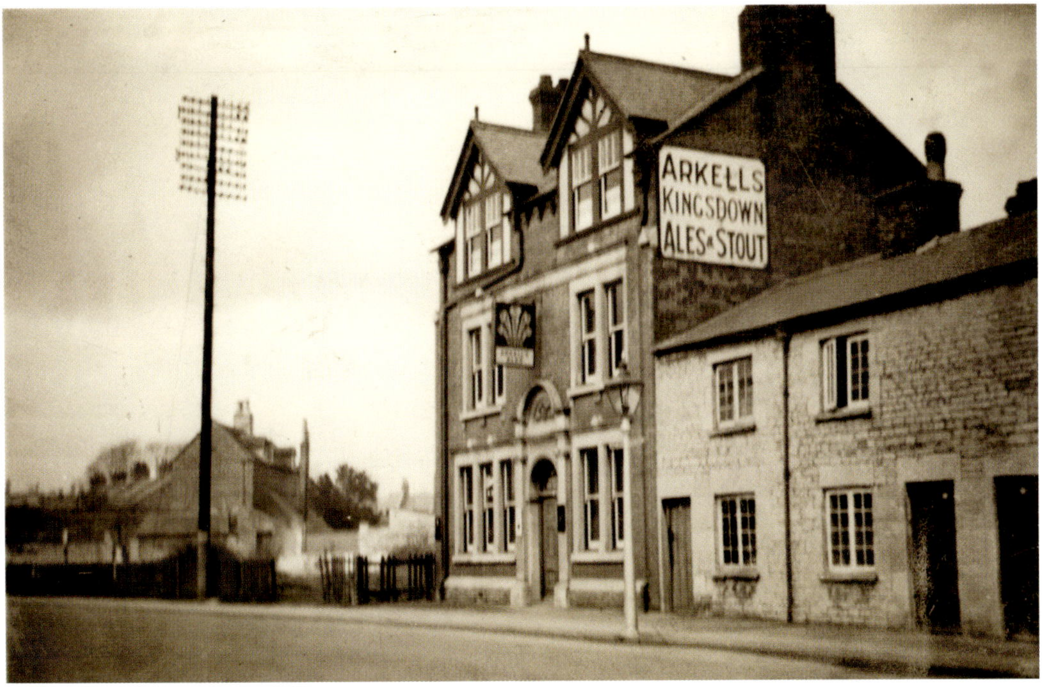

Bees Knees, Watermoor, Cirencester

Arkell's Brewery of Swindon has owned the Bees Knees since 1871, although for the first 129 years (until September 2000) it was known as the Plume of Feathers. The pub was once convenient for passengers using the Midland & South Western Junction Railway station at Watermoor and, until the Cirencester ring road was built, the Plume of Feathers was on the main road from Cheltenham to Swindon. Today the Bees Knees is a popular sports orientated pub in a quiet *cul-de-sac*.

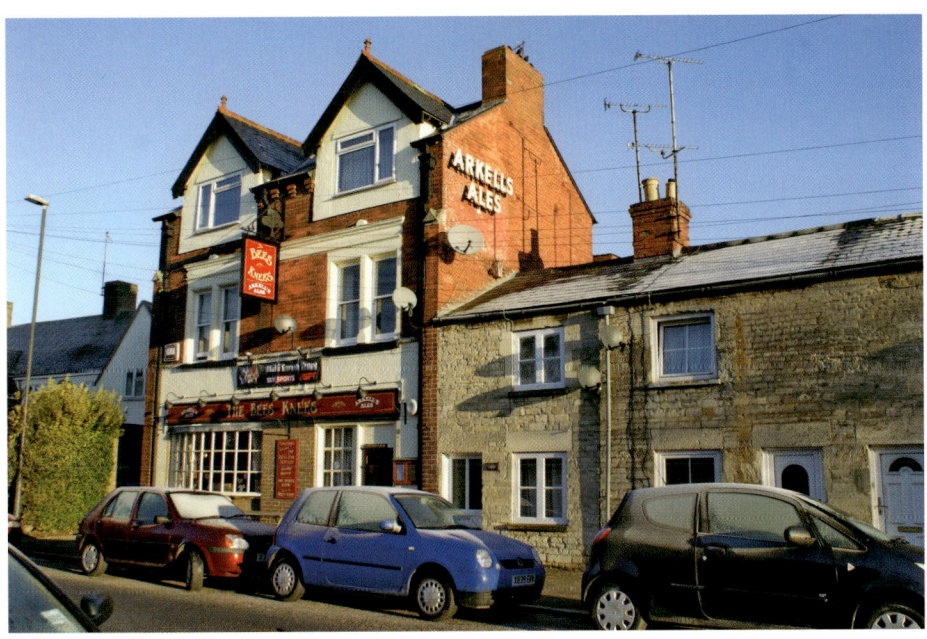

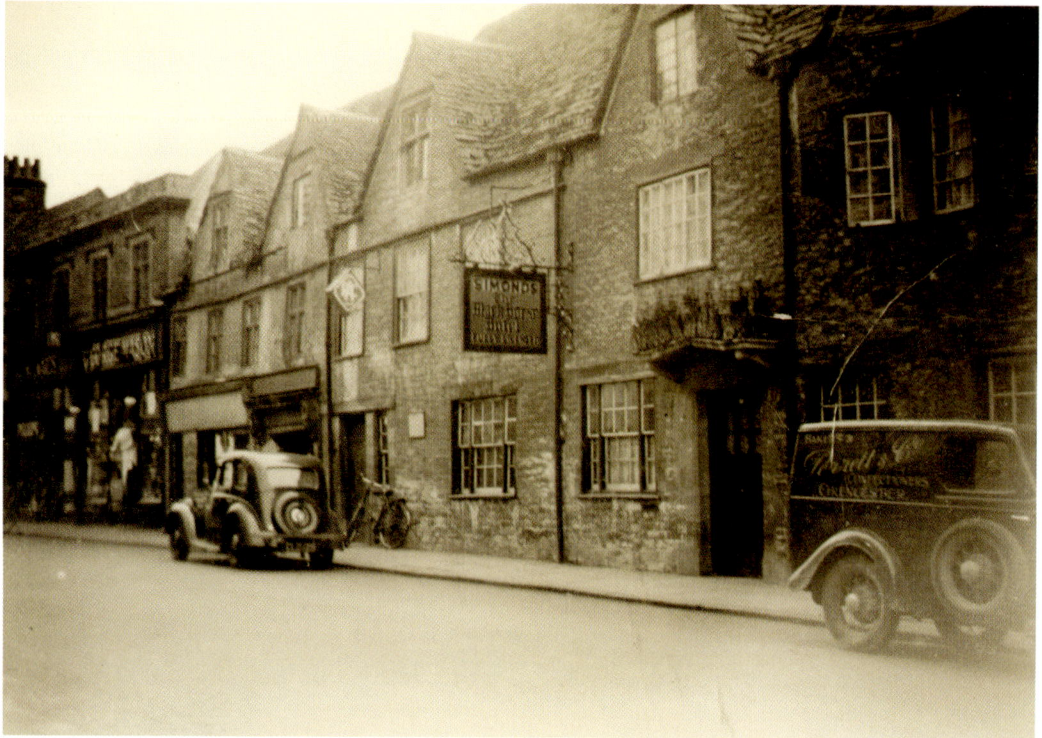

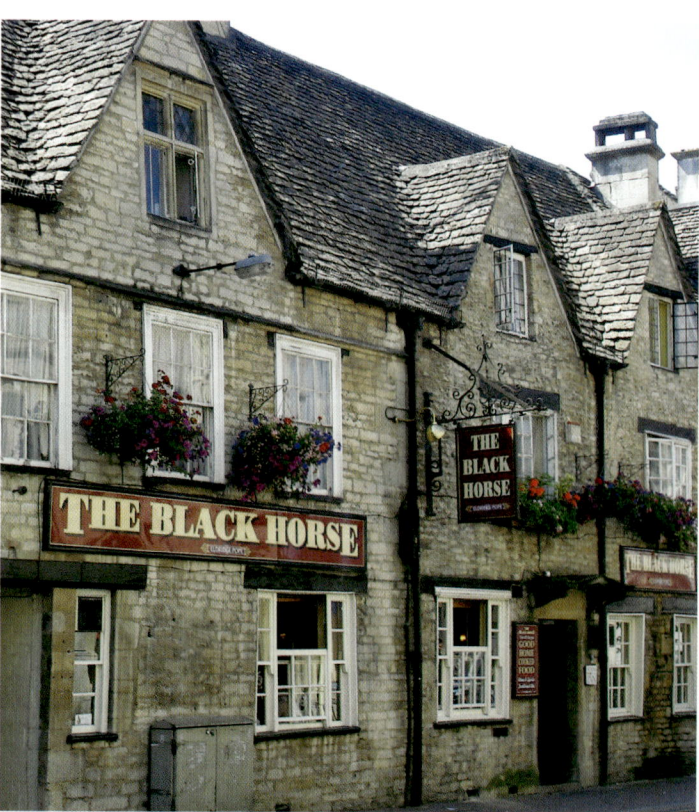

Black Horse, Castle Street, Cirencester

There were once two Cirencester Brewery pubs side by side in Castle Street, the Black Horse and Kings Arms, which amalgamated to form the Black Horse Commercial Hotel in 1927. British novelist and playwright Graham Greene stayed overnight at the Black Horse with his brother, Hugh, on 3 October 1932. Graham and Hugh had lunched in Northleach earlier in the day and, finding there was no bus, walked the considerable distance to Cirencester. Greene's diary noted that they had baths, supper and went to bed to read and sleep.

Bull Inn, Dyer Street, Cirencester

Don Cole, landlord of the Bull Inn during the Second World War, was a keen pigeon breeder. One of his hen pigeons named Kenley Lass was recruited by the National Pigeon Service and in October 1940 she was dropped by parachute with a secret agent who travelled nine miles in enemy territory collecting information with the pigeon 'concealed about his person'. Kenley Lass was then released and successfully flew back to England with the information. The pigeon, NURP 36 JH 90, was awarded the Dickin Medal – one of fifty-four animals to receive the award.

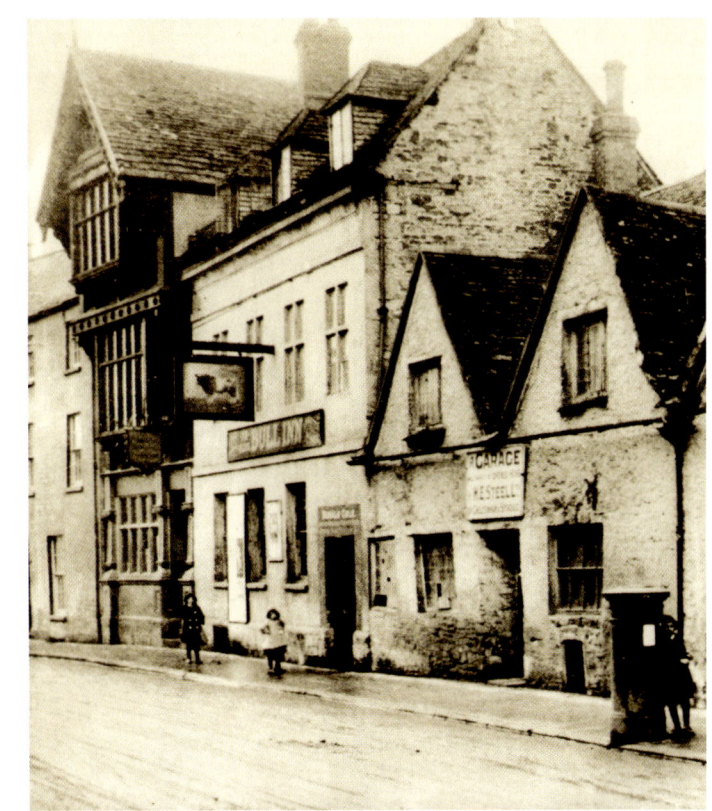

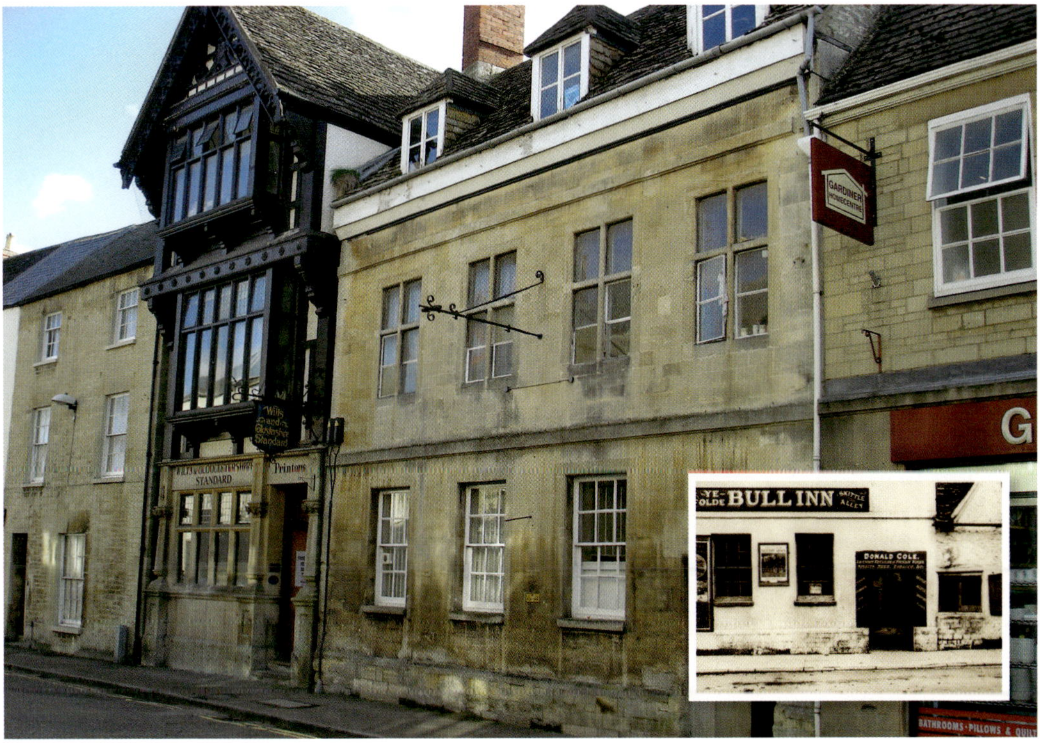

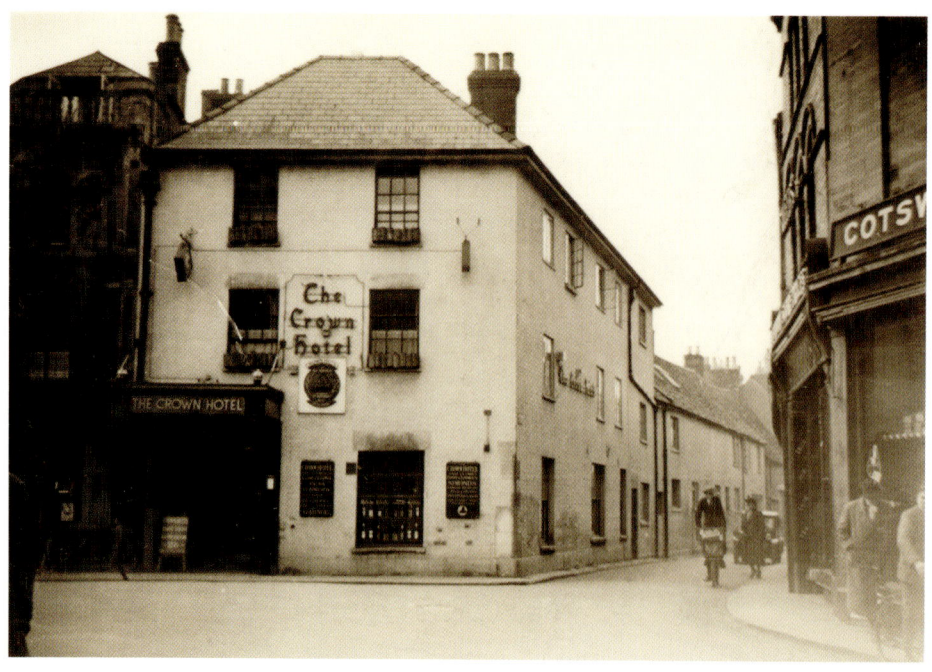

Crown Inn, West Market Place, Cirencester

The Crown Inn was severely damaged by a devastating fire that took hold in the building in June 1914. Firemen were called to the inn after closing time when the bar area was seen to be well alight. The fire was apparently extinguished by three o'clock and the firemen left. Mr Oliver Quin, the proprietor, then went to bed only to be awakened by smoke penetrating his bedroom at 6.30 a.m. The fire bell summoned the brigade but the hotel was practically burnt out by eight o'clock. £2 worth of coppers left in the till were saved.

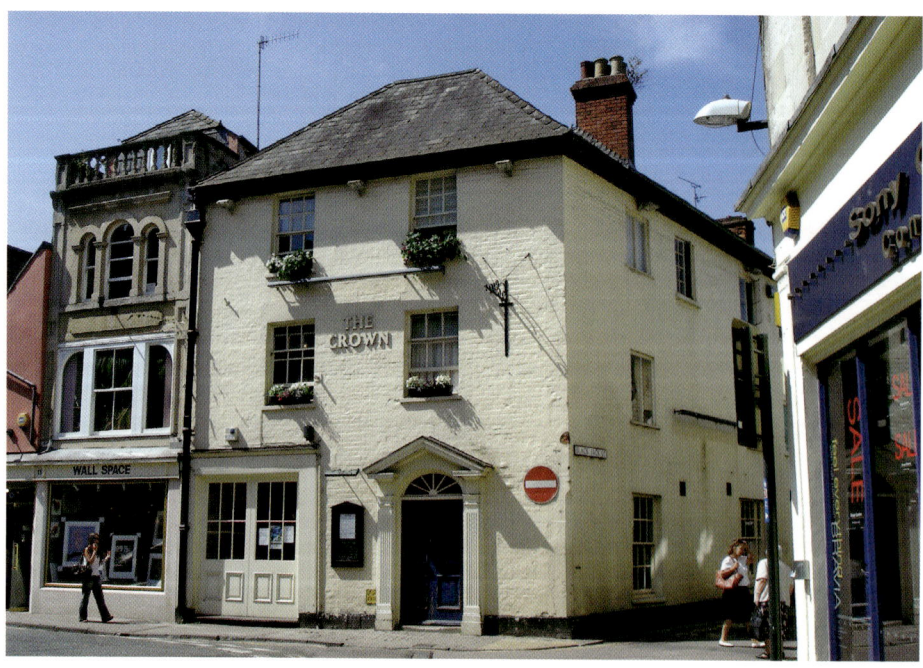

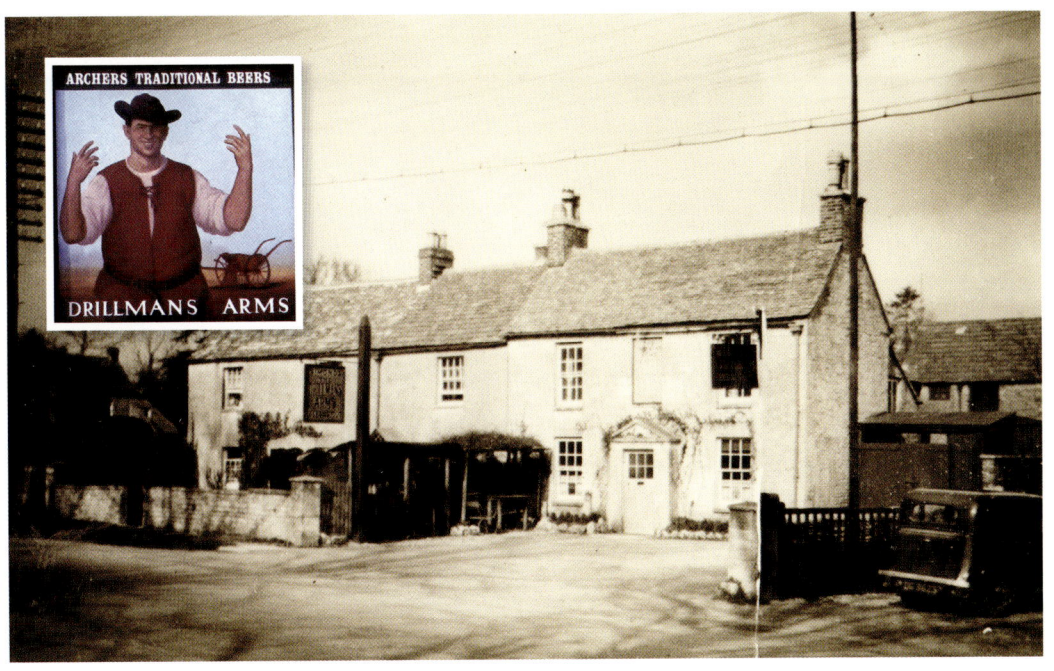

Drillmans Arms, Stratton, Cirencester

The Drillmans Arms is just outside the Cirencester town boundary at Stratton. Being a 'rural pub' closing time used to be at 10 p.m. There must have been a temptation to walk the short distance to the Royal Oak in Gloucester Street which did not call 'time' until 11 p.m. The Drillmans Arms is a true community pub, with ten skittle teams, three darts teams and a cribbage team. The pub holds a beer festival every August Bank Holiday and they even recently held a pickled onion and chutney competition. A pub sign in the bar depicts the Mandrills Arms.

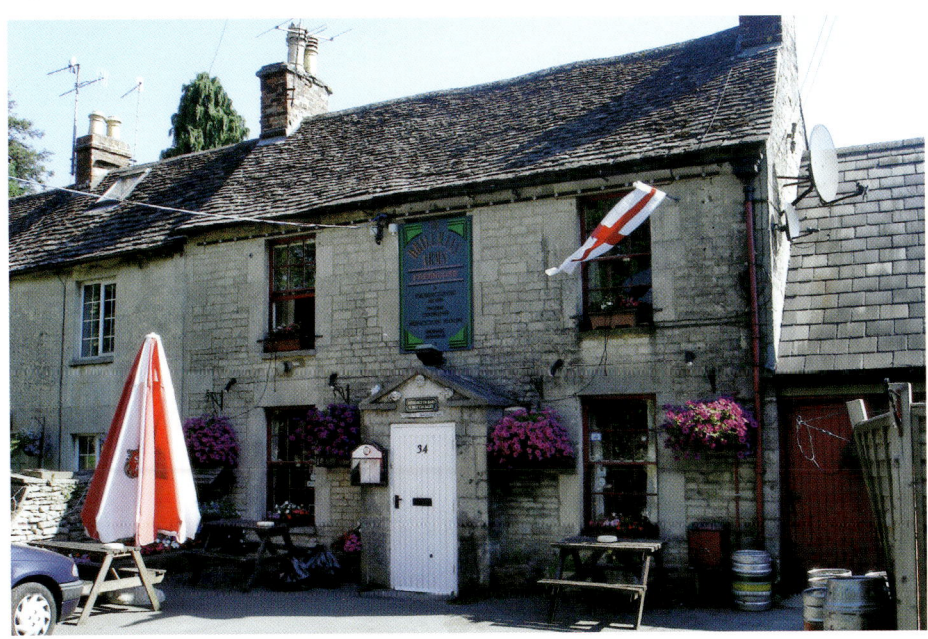

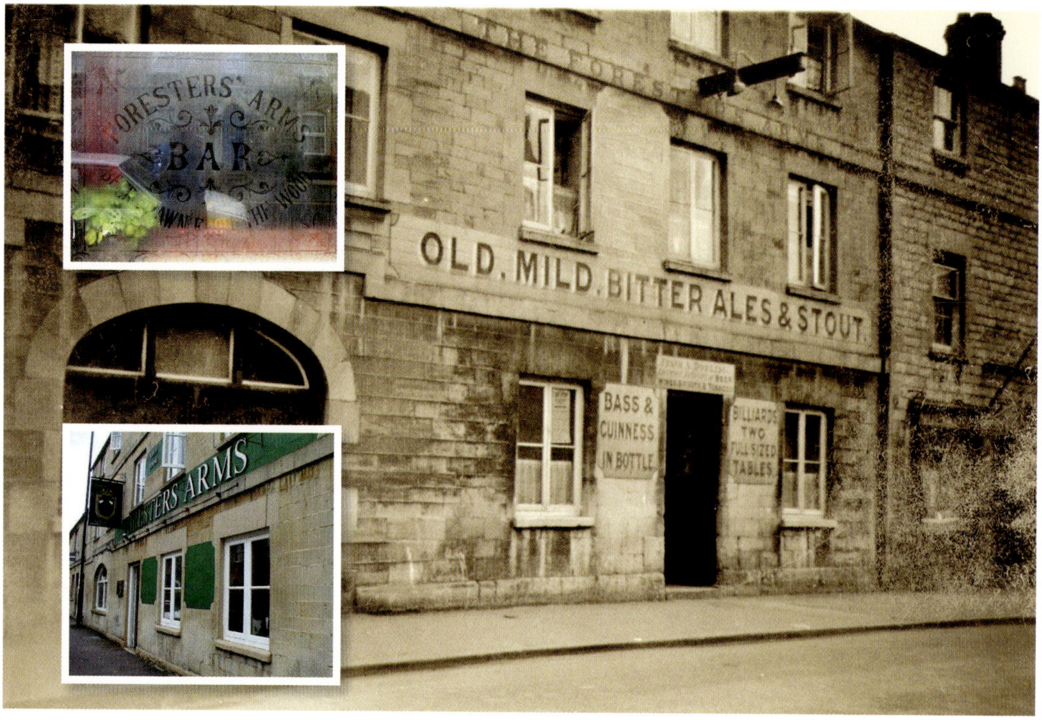

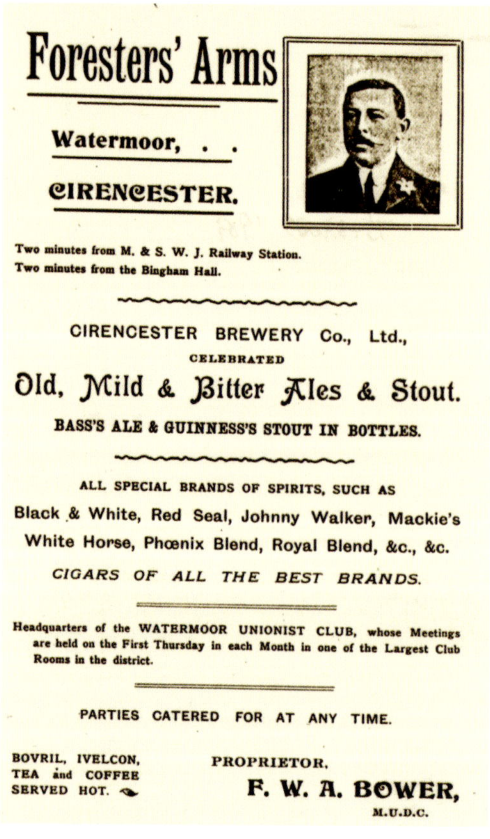

Foresters Arms, Queen Street, Cirencester

The Foresters Arms became a freehouse in 1975 when it was purchased from the Courage Brewery. Before closure in 2003 the Foresters had a superb etched window which advertised 'beers drawn from the wood', which presumably dated to the years when the Foresters Arms sold beer from the local Cirencester Brewery. The Foresters has now been converted to residential use. Unfortunately, the etched window did not survive the redevelopment.

Golden Cross, Black Jack Street, Cirencester

The eighteenth-century Golden Cross has been under the ownership of the Arkell's Kingsdown Brewery since 1864 – an amazing 148 years. It was the first pub bought by Arkell's in Cirencester. If the pub sold an average of four casks of Arkell's ales per week that equates to 30,784 barrels. If those casks are assumed to be of 18 gallons capacity that means that nearly four and a half million pints of Arkell's beer have been consumed in the pub – that's enough beer to fill an Olympic sized swimming pool!

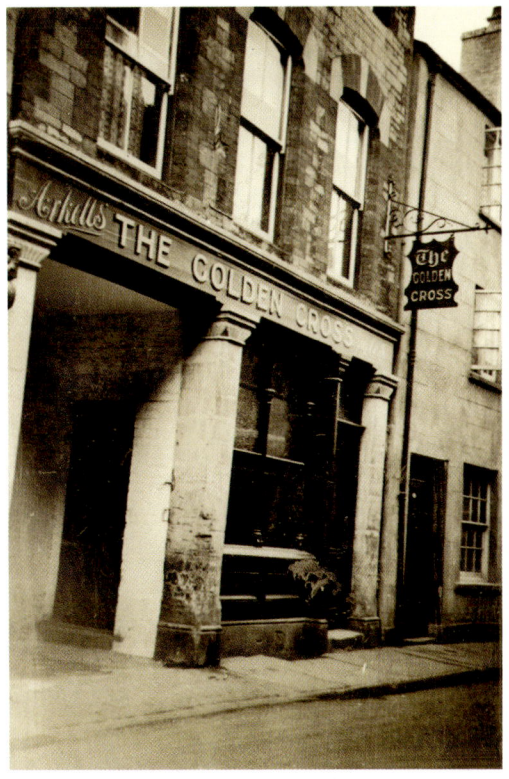

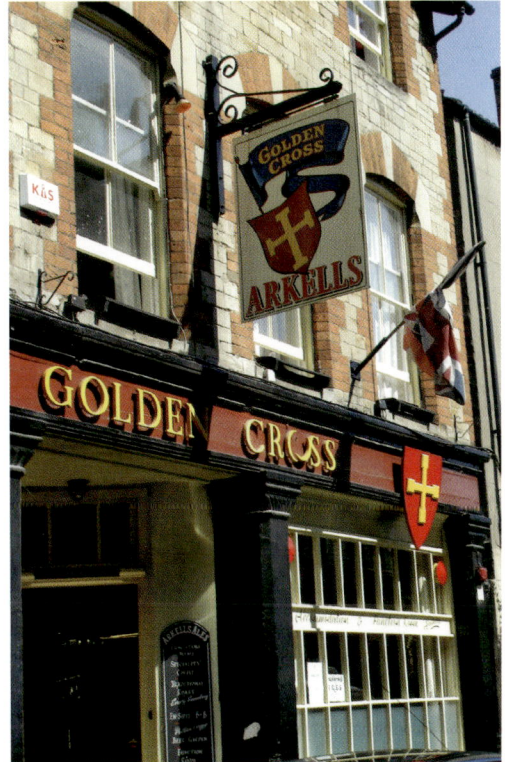

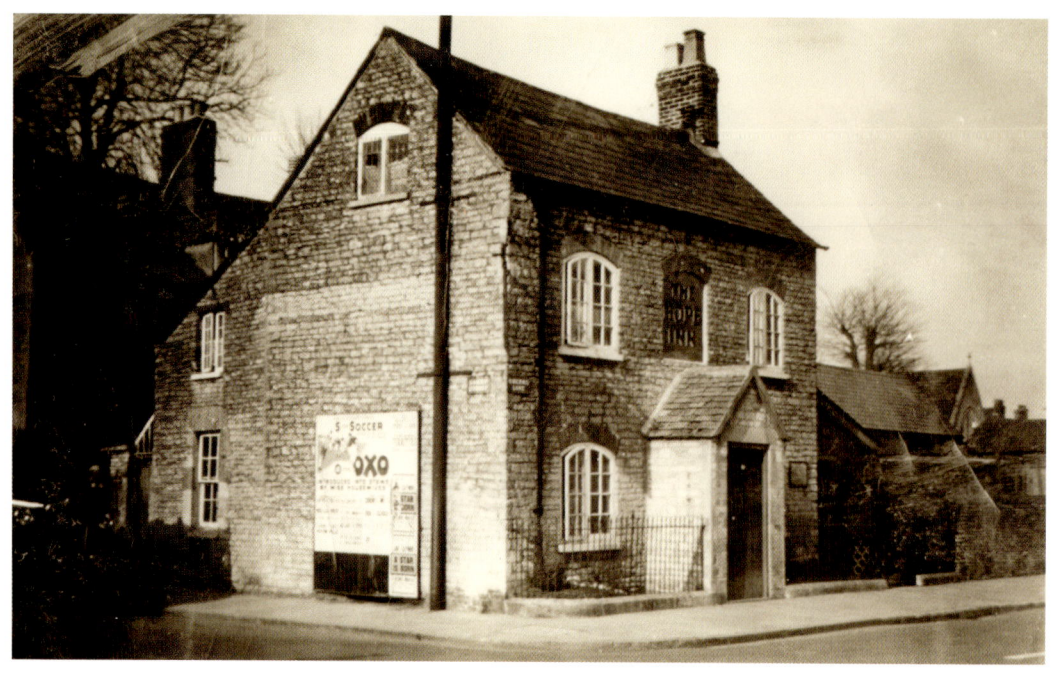

Hope Inn, Querns Lane, Cirencester

The Cirencester Brewery Company purchased the 'Hope Inn beer house and garden in Querns Lane' on 24 December 1904. The building is now in use as 'Sydney Free Saddlers and Country Clothing'. A modern sign on the side of the building obscures the wording of an original wall painted pub sign which used to advertise Simonds Brewery Ales & Stouts.

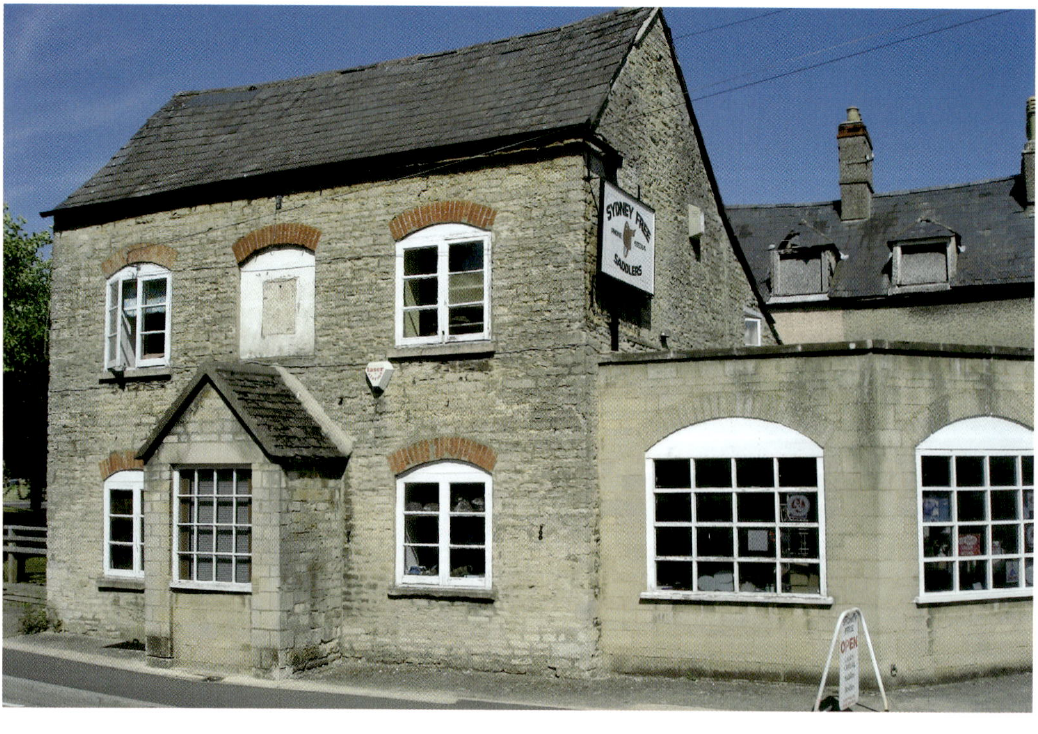

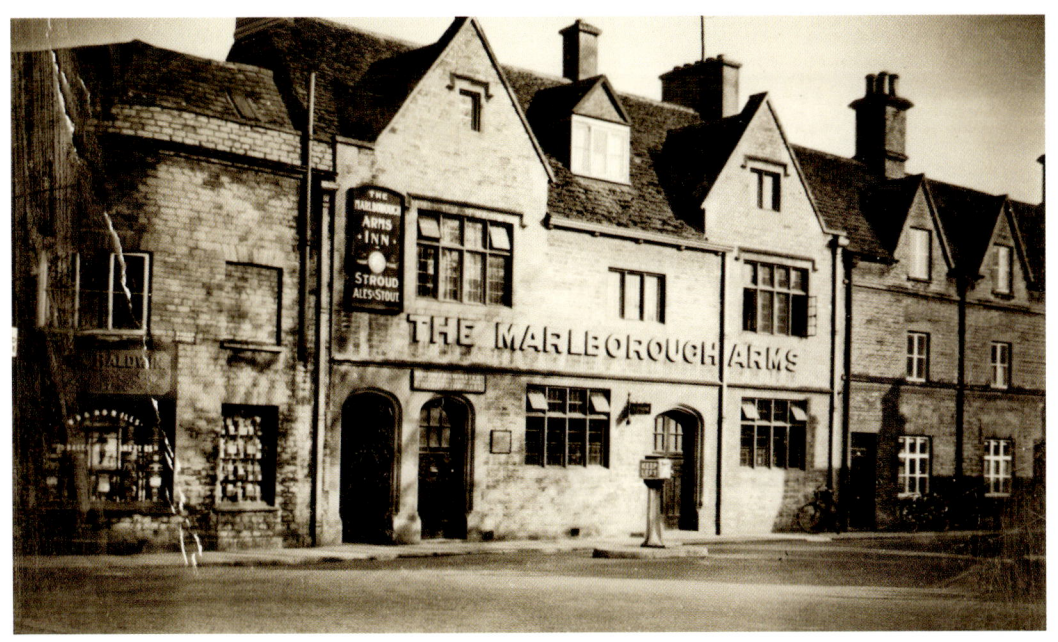

Marlborough Arms, Sheep Street, Cirencester

The Stroud Brewery Courier announced in June 1948 that 'Mr J. H. L. Newman, after several years employment finding suitable persons to conduct the Company's licensed houses, resigned from his position at the end of March, having found a pub for himself, becoming the landlord of the Marlborough Arms in Cirencester. On behalf of the Directors and Staff, the Managing Director presented Mr Newman with a silver tea set, and expressed their best wishes for every success and prosperity in his new venture.'

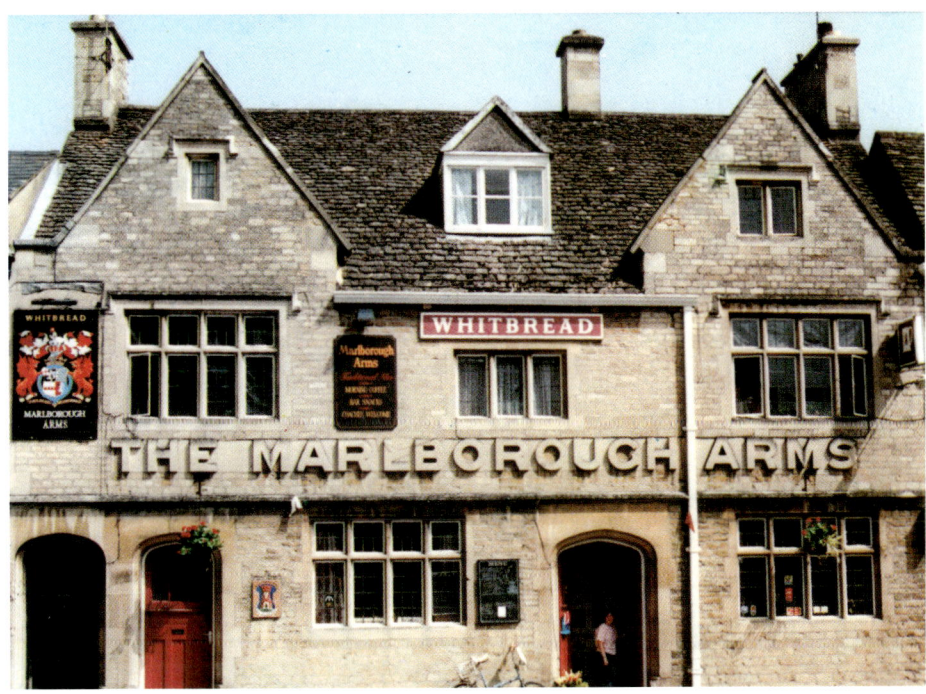

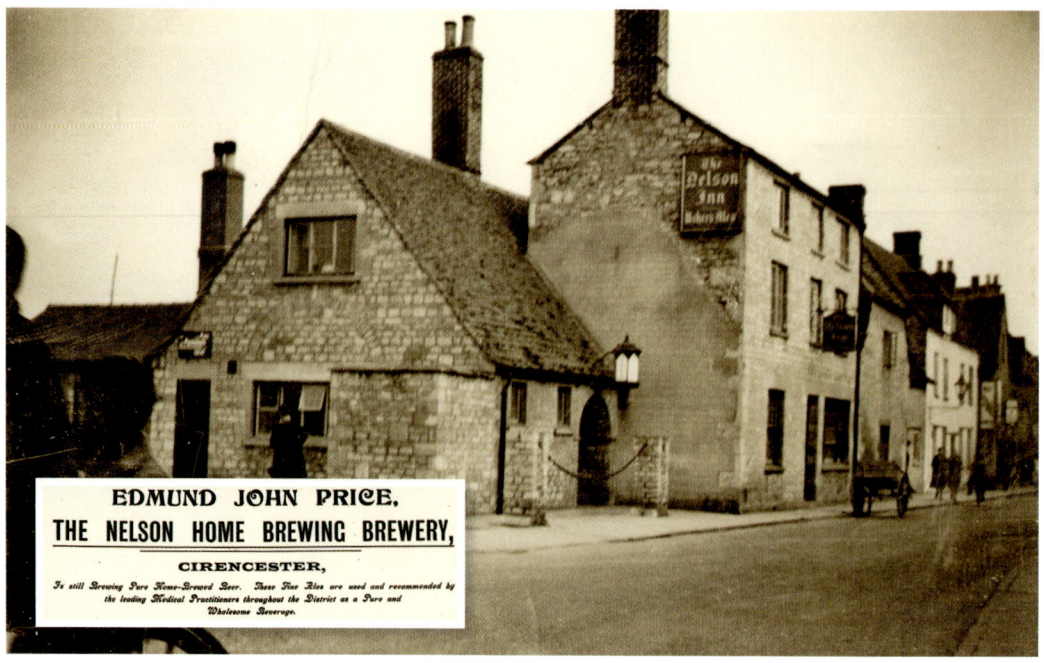

Nelson Arms, Gloucester Street, Cirencester

The Nelson Inn once boasted its own brewery and may have been the last of its kind to operate in Gloucestershire. An advertisement in Bailey & Woods town directory of 1909 states that the 'Nelson Home Brewery (established over a century) is still brewing Pure Home Brewed Beer. These fine ales are used and recommended by the leading medical practitioners throughout the district as a pure and wholesome beverage.' The large chimney that dominates the pubs skittle alley is probably part of the old brew house.

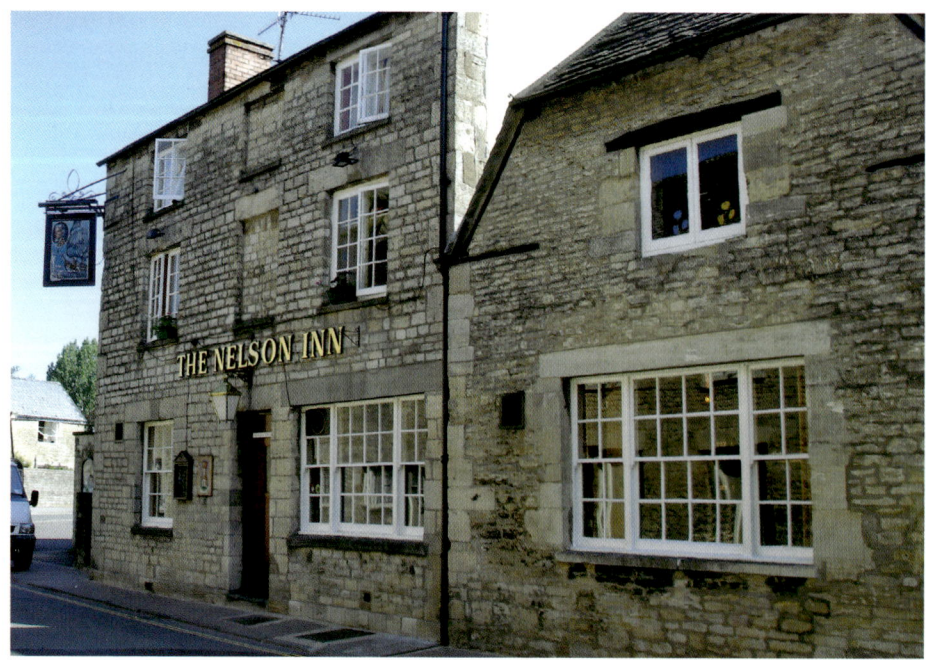

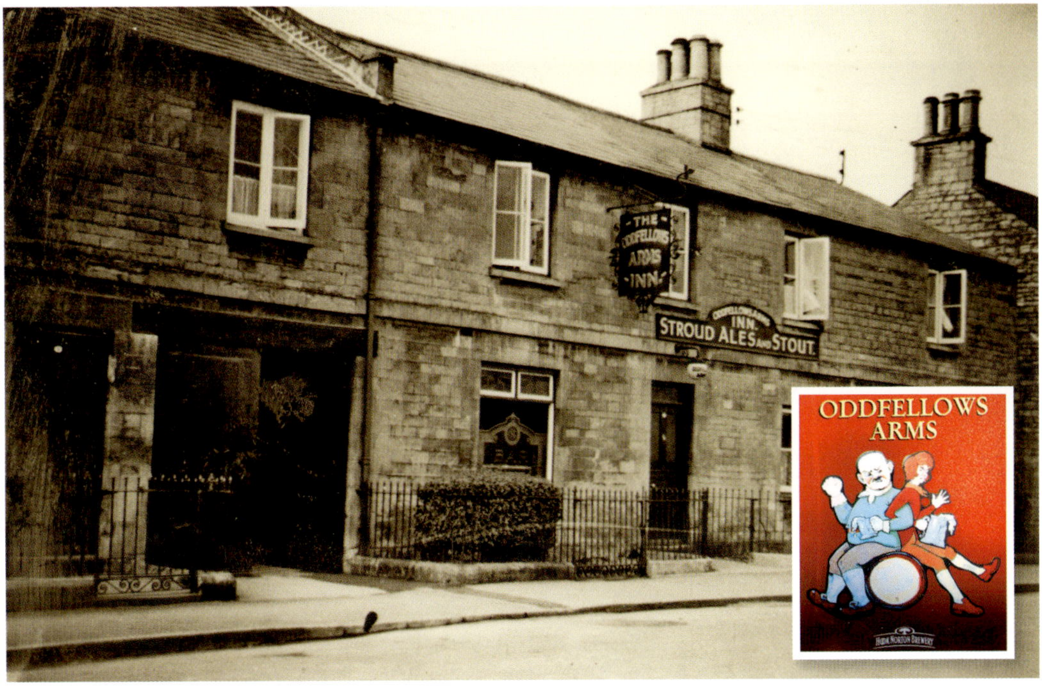

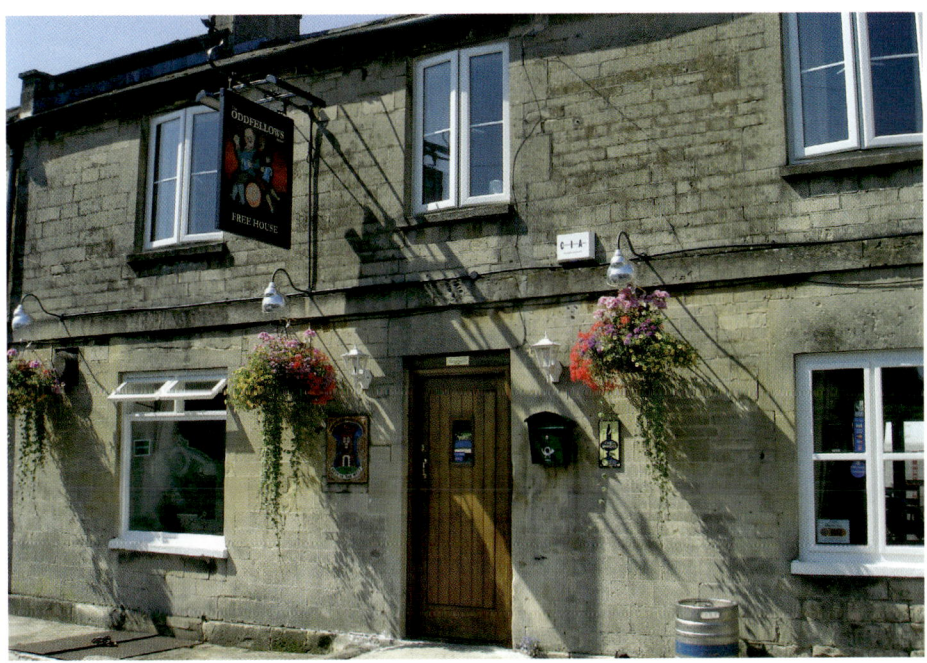

Oddfellows Arms, Chester Street, Cirencester

After several years operating as a Free House, the Oddfellows Arms was purchased by the Hook Norton Brewery of Oxfordshire in the Autumn of 2007. Stroud Brewery once owned the pub and one of their decorative etched glass windows survives at the pub to this day. There are only two other pubs in Gloucestershire with Stroud Brewery etched windows – the Berkeley Arms at Cam (page 56) and the White Hart in Cinderford.

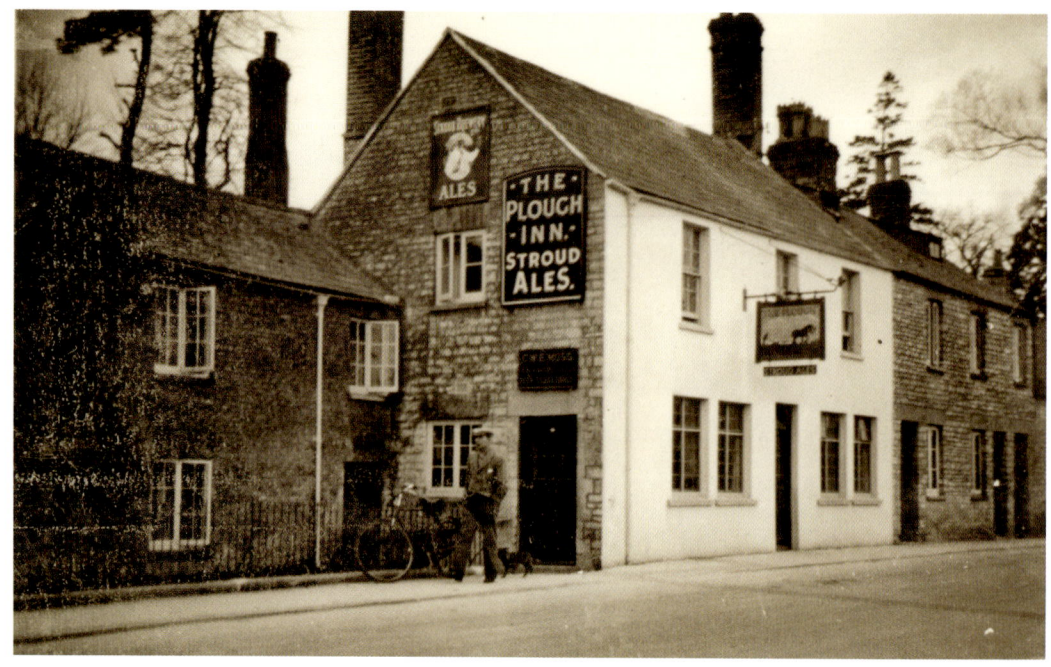

Plough Inn, Stratton, Cirencester

During the Second World War the New Zealand Expeditionary Force 11th Forestry Company were billeted at Stratton House next to the Plough. Reg Grundy won a competition to see who could chop up trees the fastest. A brass plaque commemorating his achievement was attached to a log and was displayed in the pub for many years. Lightning struck a tree at the rear of the Plough in April 1948 which fell onto power lines causing a black out, and in October 2002 a large tree fell onto a car parked in the pub car park.

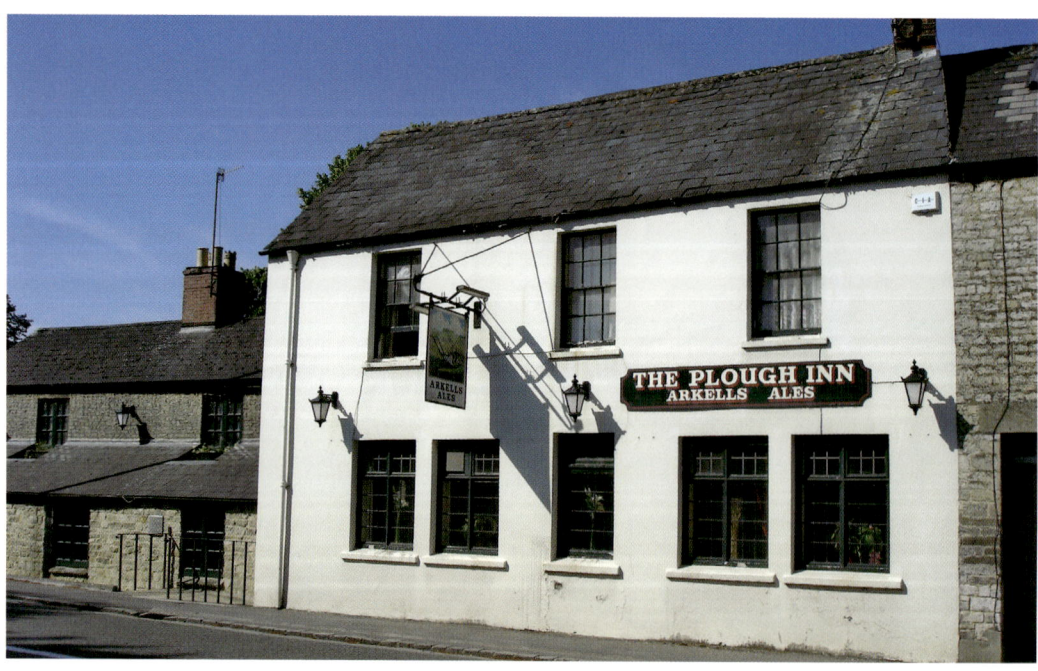

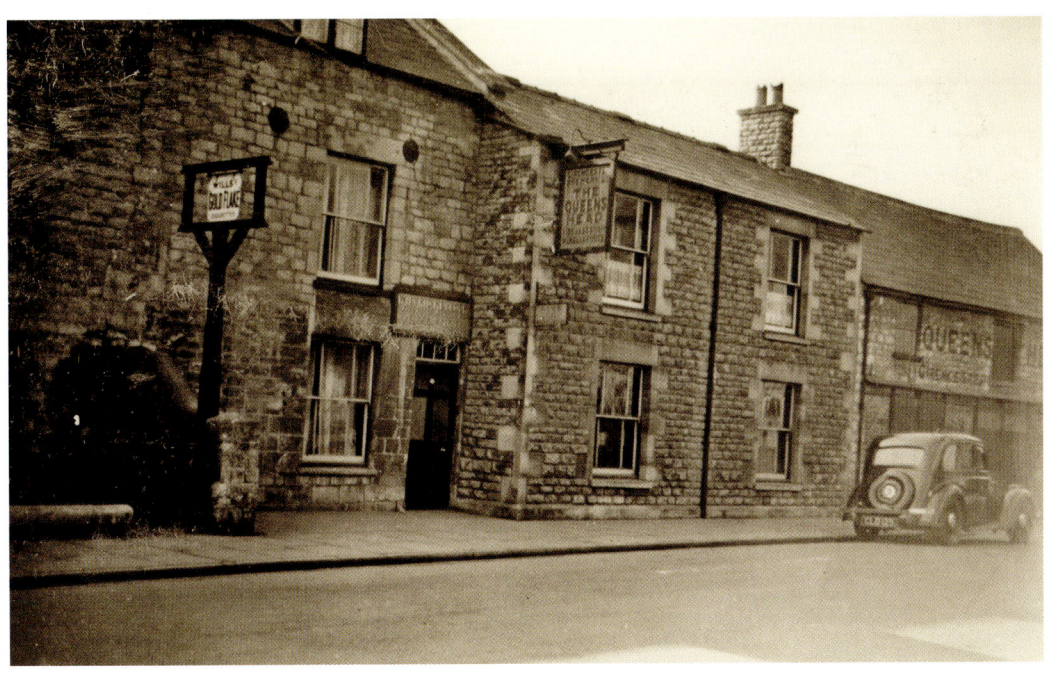

Queens Head, Watermoor Road, Cirencester

When the Queens Head closed in September 2008 a spokesman from Enterprise Inns expressed a view that it could be 're-opened in the near future'. However the property was on sale for £298,500 in July 2012 as a converted three bedroom mews house. The 1993 edition of 'Real Ale in Gloucestershire' (CAMRA) described the Queens Head as a 'two bar pub on the outskirts of town with skull-crushing noise from the juke-box in the public bar.' Not surprisingly there were no concerted campaigns by local residents to stop the pub from closing.

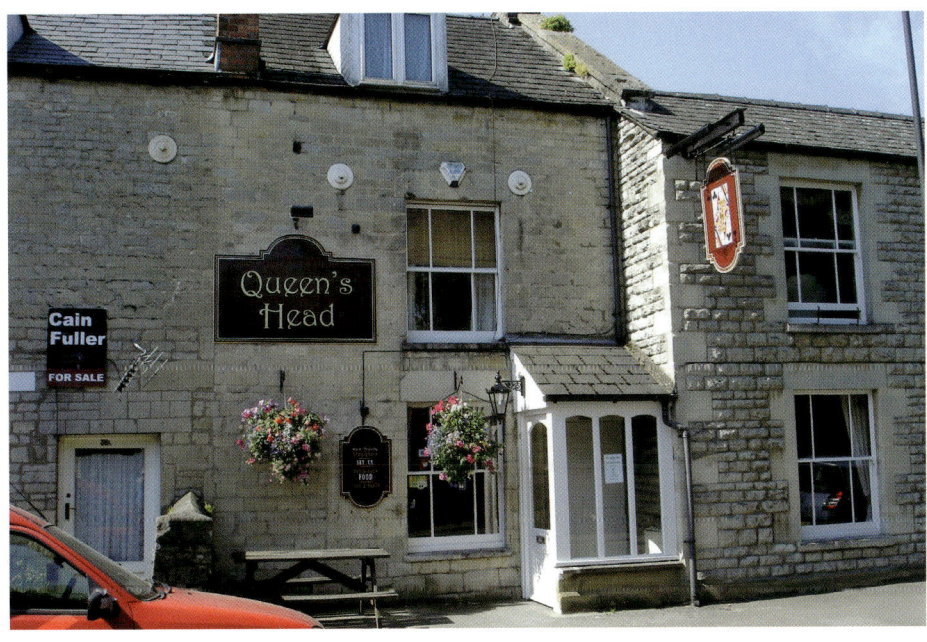

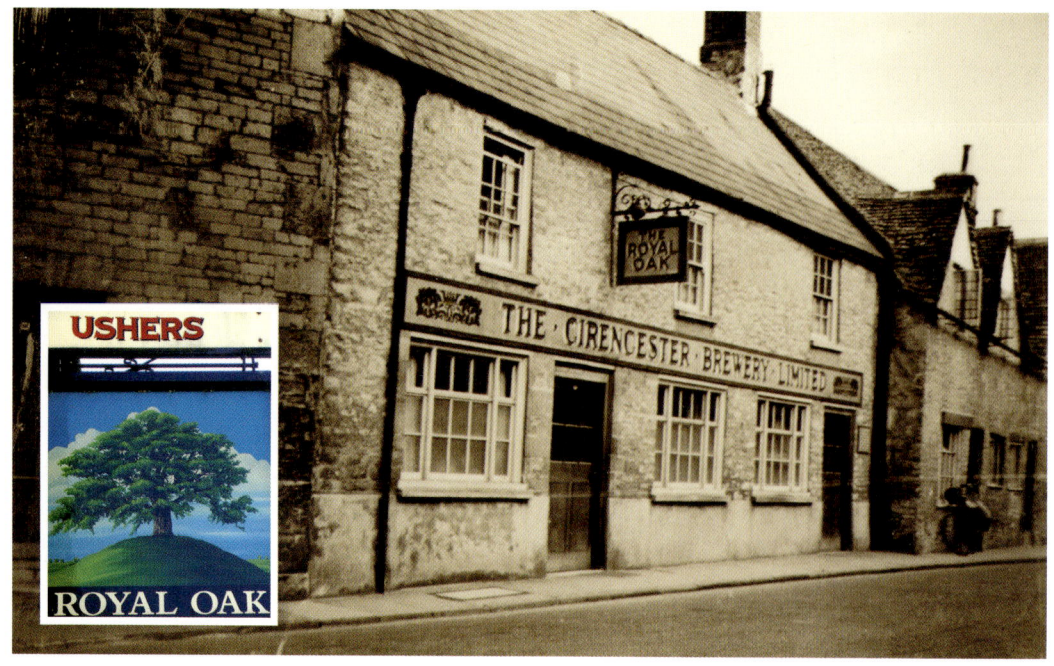

Royal Oak, Gloucester Street, Cirencester

Mr Job Sheppard had nearly fifty years service as landlord at the Royal Oak when, on the afternoon of Saturday 28 February 1948, Job called 'time' at 2 p.m. and left drinkers alone in the bar to drink up while he attended matters in another part of the house. When he returned shortly afterwards the men had gone along with approximately £20 in cash from the till. Needless to say the Cirencester police were not impressed. The Royal Oak closed in the summer of 2007.

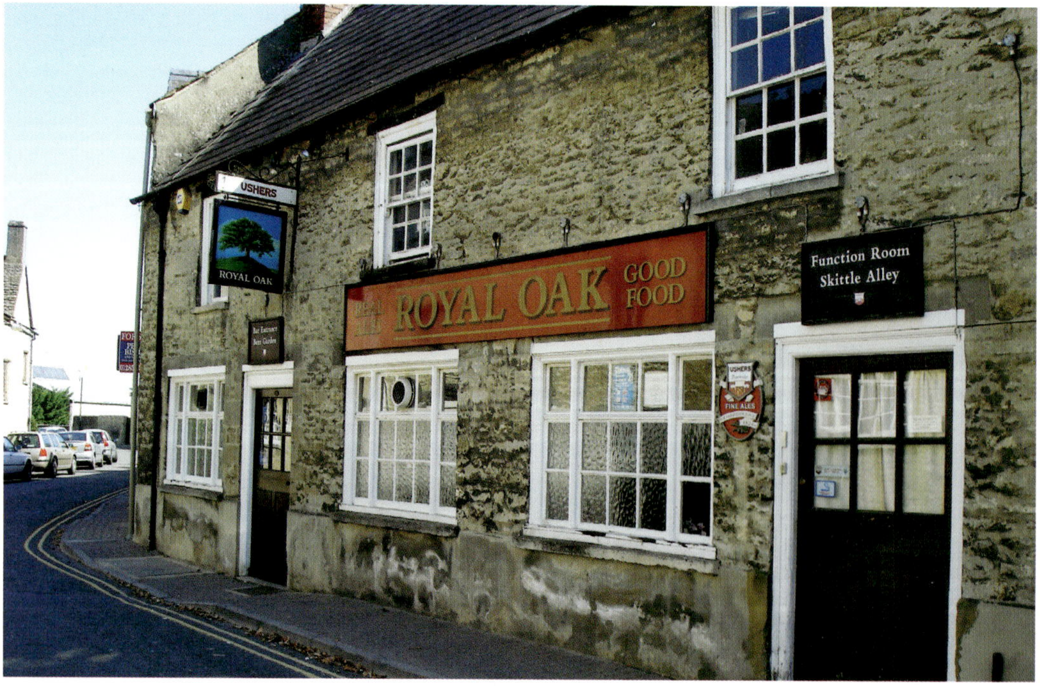

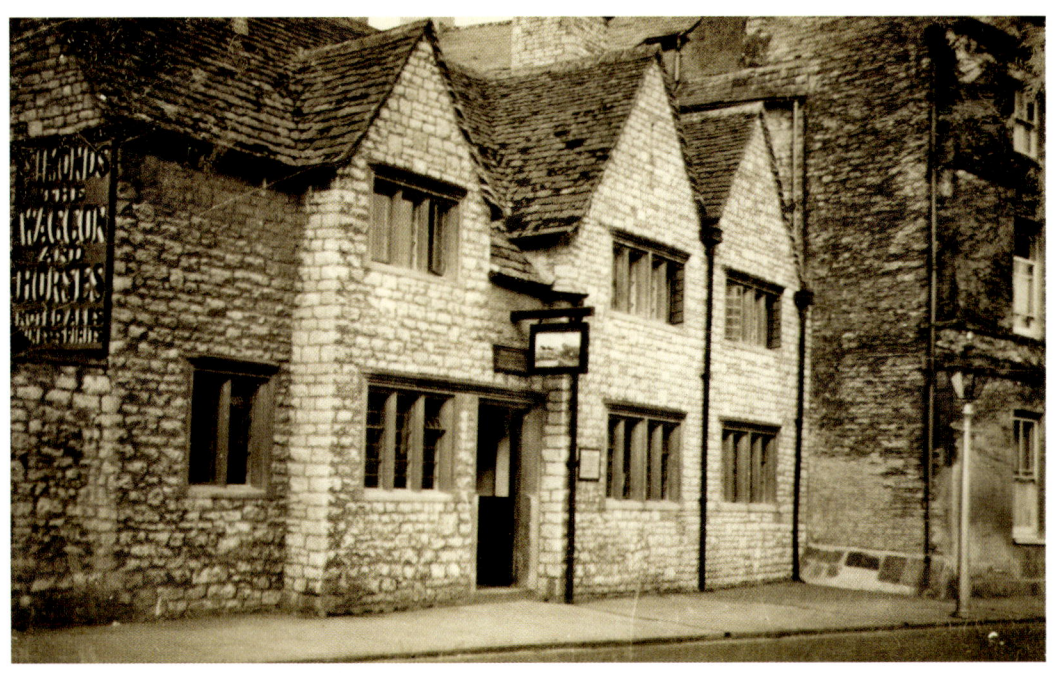

Waggon & Horses, London Road, Cirencester

The original Waggon & Horses was a tiny twin gabled alehouse. It was substantially rebuilt in 1920 in a similar style on the same spot by the Cirencester firm of R. A. Berkeley. The Waggon & Horses was purchased by Gibbs Mew of Salisbury in 1997, the year that they ceased brewing. The pub estate of Gibbs Mew was acquired by Enterprise Inns in February 1998. The Waggon & Horses now sells a varied selection of real ales and specialises in Thai cuisine.

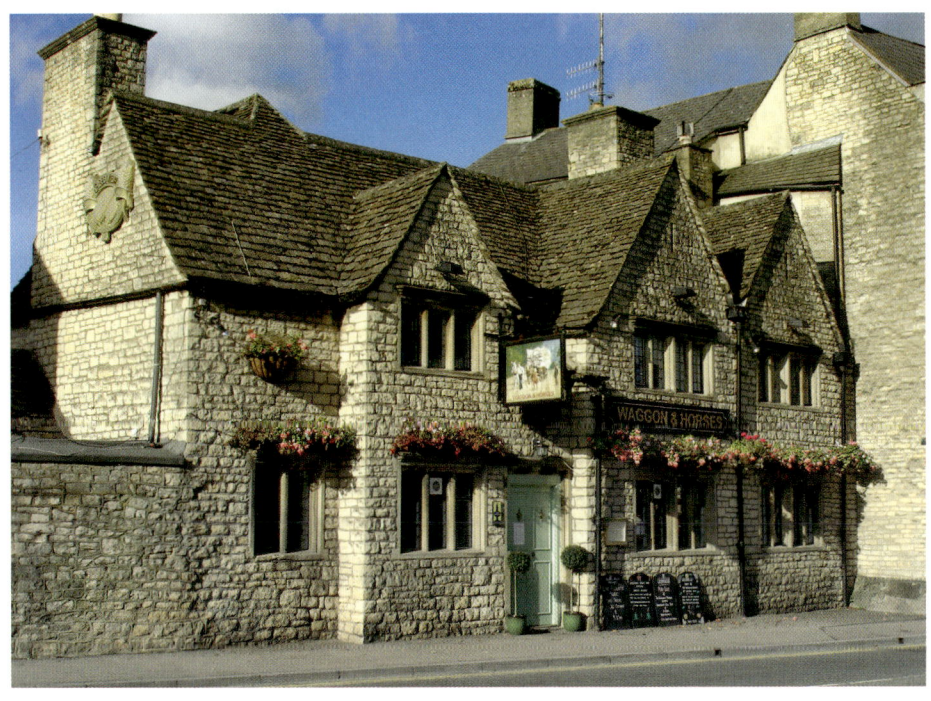

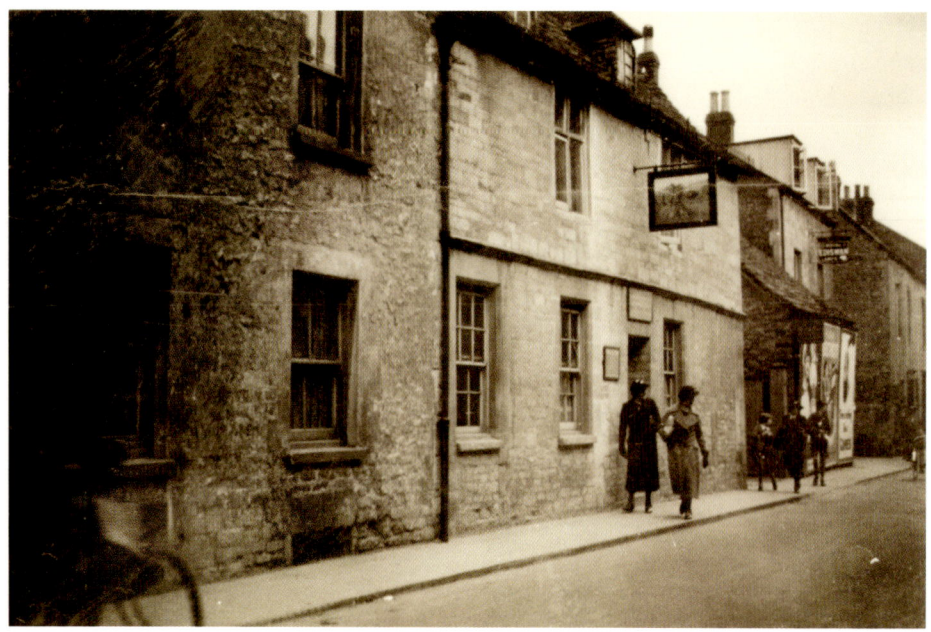

Wheatsheaf Inn, Cricklade Street, Cirencester

In 1999 the Wheatsheaf was runner up in the Sports Bar of the Year award, a national competition run by the trade magazine *Licensing and Morning Advertiser*. When the World Cup was hosted in Japan and South Korea in the summer of 2002 time differences meant that some of England's games started early in the morning. A special licence was granted by Cirencester magistrates that enabled the Wheatsheaf to open outside the normal licensing hours. About 200 fans watched England draw with Sweden 1–1 and many ordered breakfast and settled down with a pint in front of the big screen.

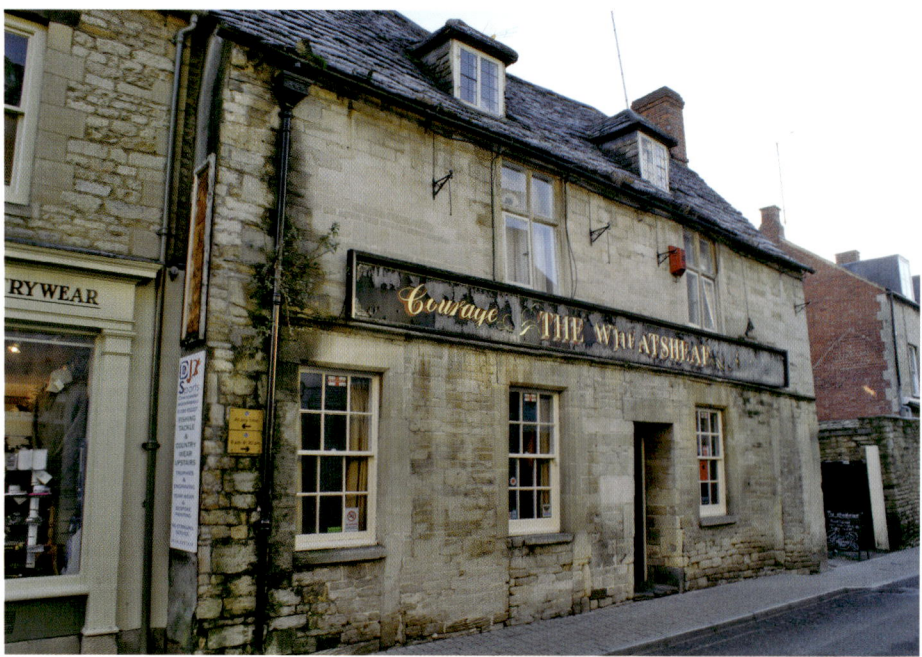

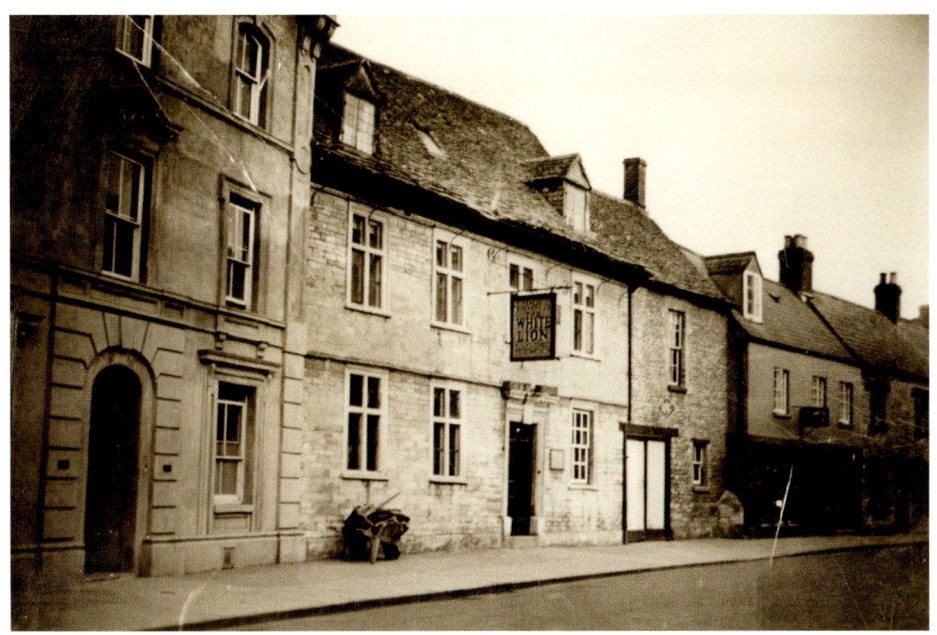

White Lion, Gloucester Street, Cirencester

The seventeenth-century White Lion was owned by the Cirencester Brewery and the pub passed into the ownership of H. & G. Simonds of Reading in 1937. In the 1990s the White Lion was a free house offering bed & breakfast accommodation. An advertisement in November 2001 noted that 'just recently two of the three rooms have been converted into delightful four poster rooms, ideal for honeymoon couples or anniversary celebrations'. In February 2010 a planning application was submitted to Cotswold District Council for change of use to two residential dwellings and first floor rear extension. The application was permitted.

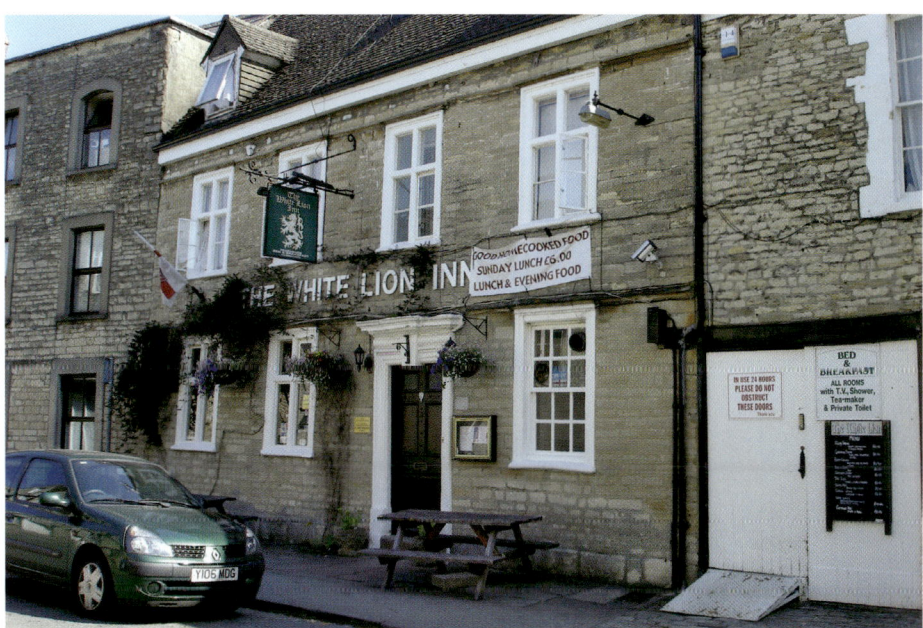

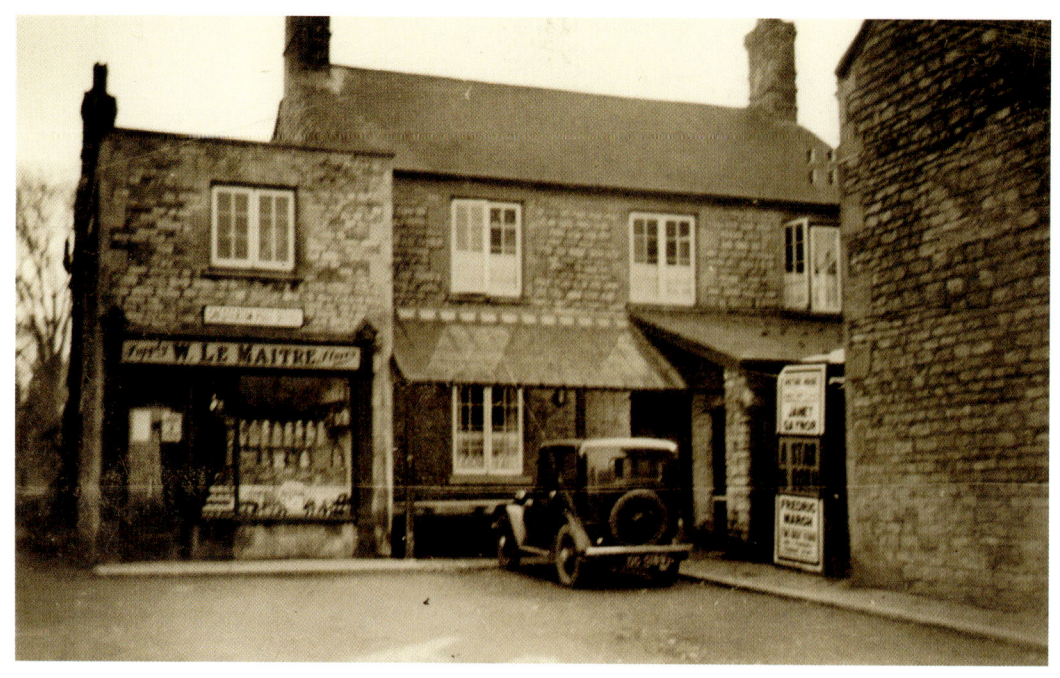

Woodbine Inn, Chesterton Lane, Cirencester

In the 1990s the Woodbine Inn was a friendly family orientated pub. In the garden was a children's play area, pet's corner and even a crazy golf course. In the summer of 2004 the Woodbine Inn was 'refurbished' which saw the traditional two-bar layout being replaced by a single bar. Four years later the Woodbine had closed and was boarded up. An application was submitted to Cotswold District Council in May 2009 for demolition and replacement with six new houses on the site. Permission was granted.

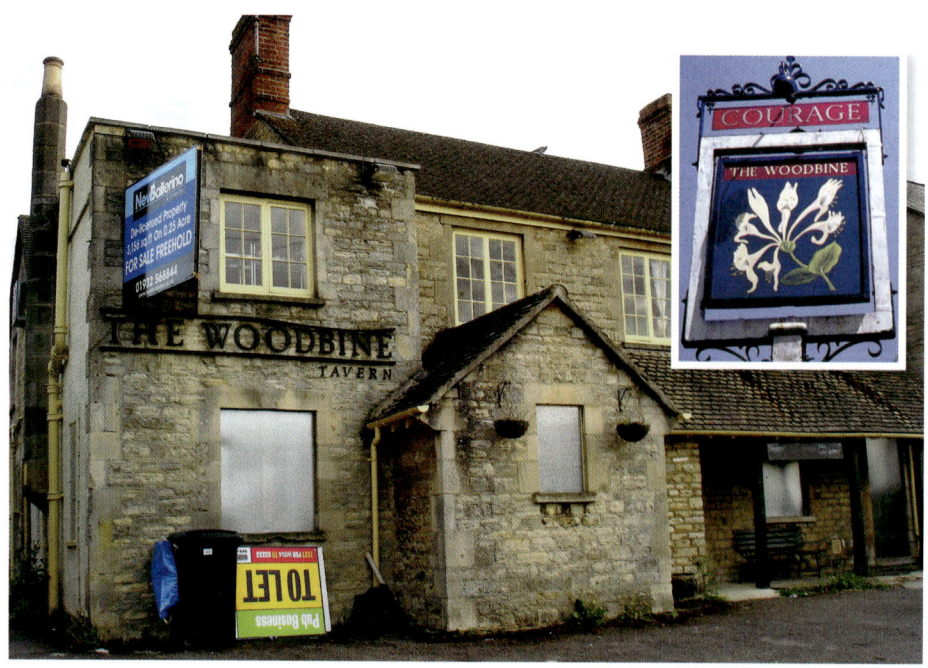

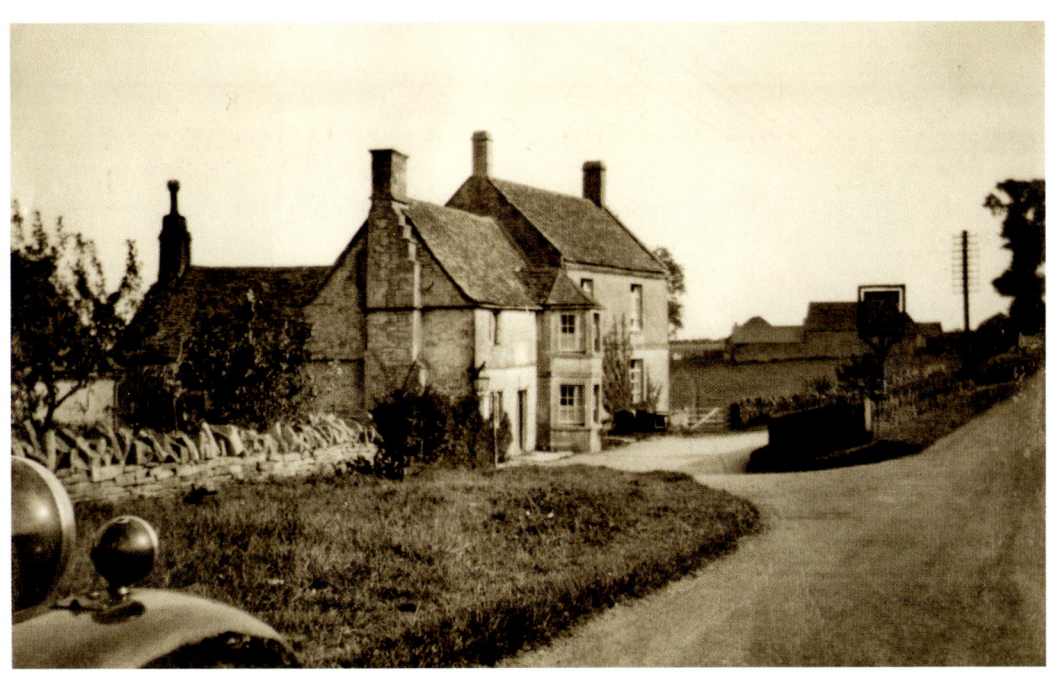

Five Mile House, Duntisbourne Abbots

When landlady, Ivy Ruck, died in 1995 there were fears that this totally unspoilt pub would close forever. The Five Mile House had been in the Ruck family since the 1930s and had hardly altered in the intervening sixty-five years with bare wooden floors, high-backed settles and wood burning stoves. Thankfully the classic country pub was saved when the Carrier family bought the Five Mile House and re-opened it again after a sensitive refurbishment in 1997. In November 2011, to the surprise of many, it was decided to stop serving food at the Five Mile House.

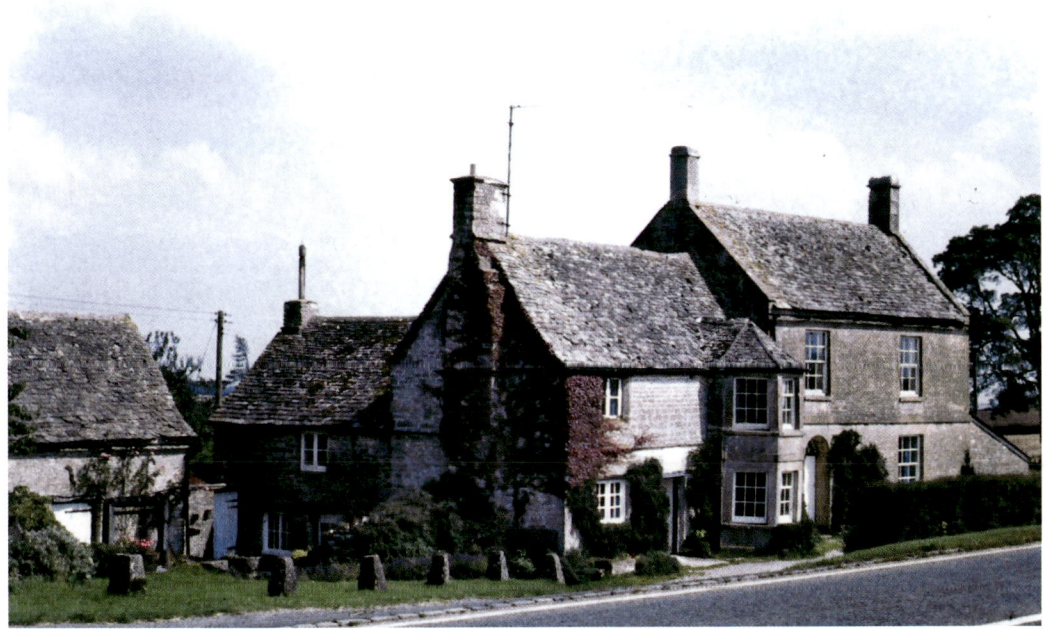

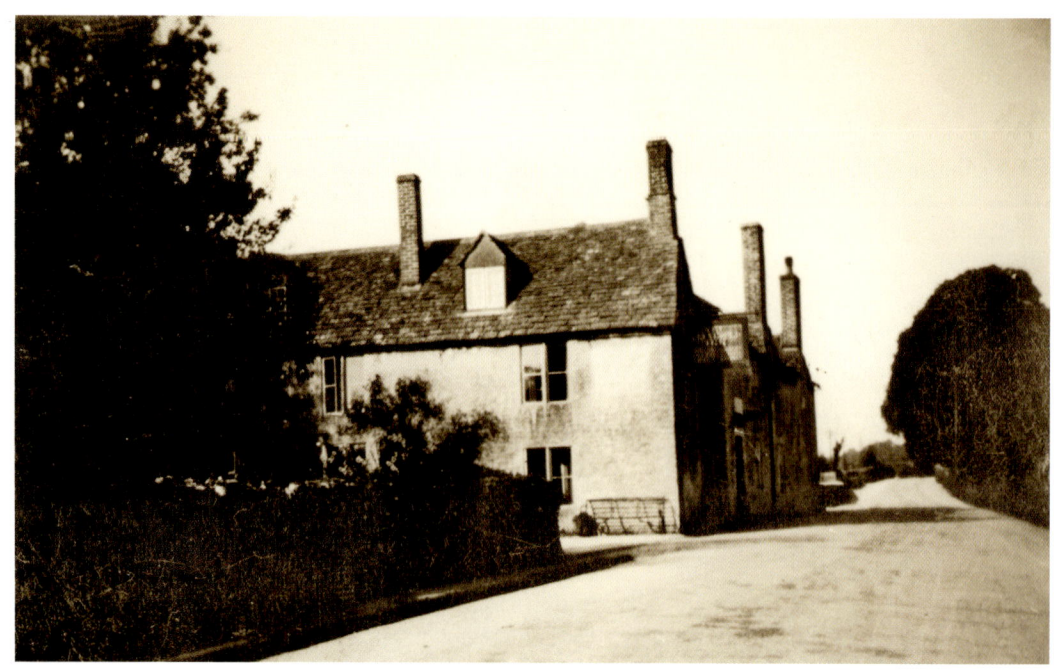

Greyhound Inn, Siddington

On Monday 1 October 1900 Edmund Wall, a labourer aged seventy-four, had a pint or two at the Greyhound and headed for home along the towpath of the Thames & Severn Canal. The night was very dark and it is thought that he fell over the canal wall, struck his head against the brickwork and then rolled down the rather steep declivity into the water. His body was found the following day. An inquest was held at the Greyhound Inn which recommended that the canal authorities should take steps immediately to heighten the wall near the pub.

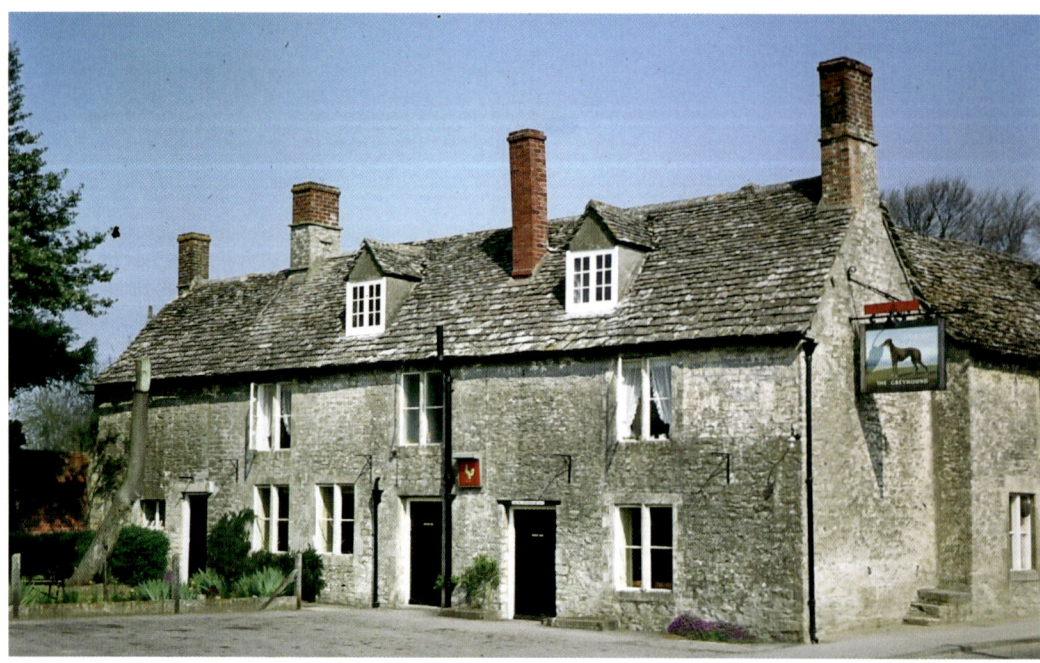

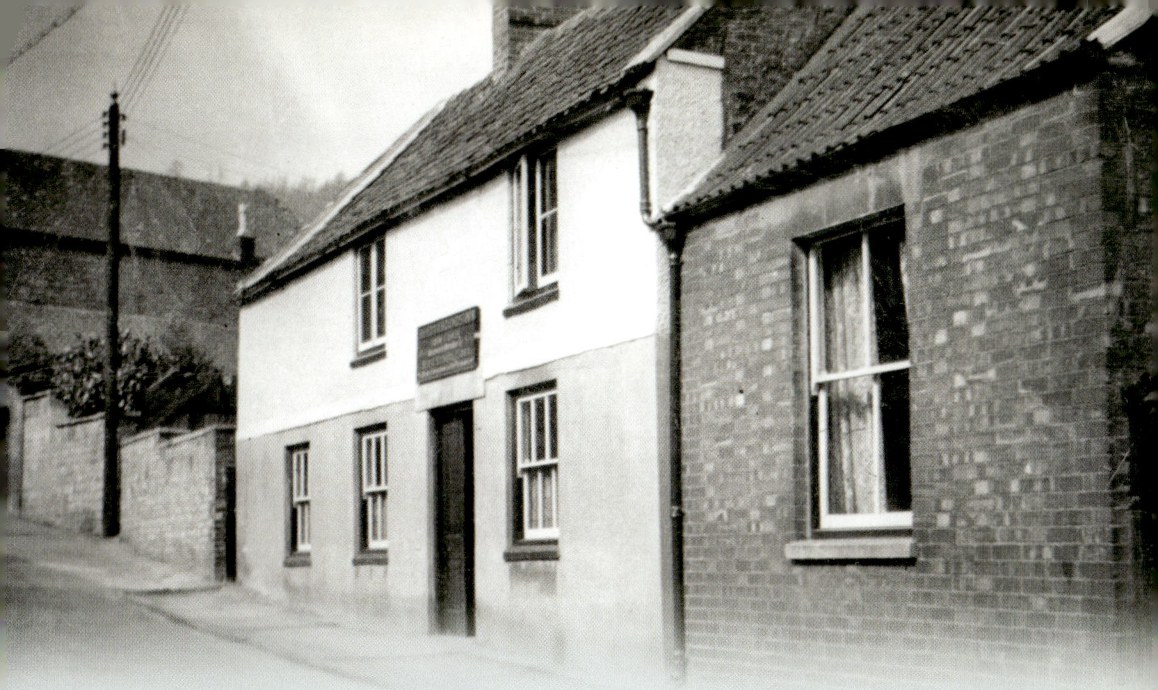

CHAPTER 3

Dursley

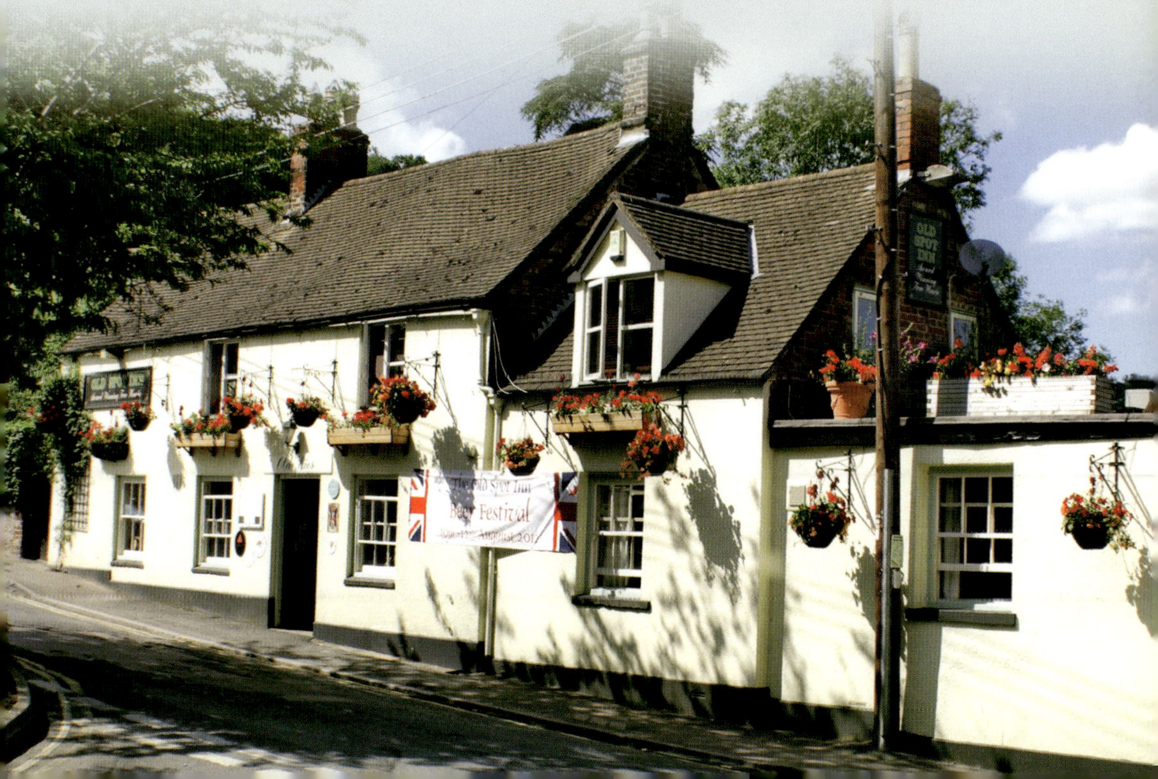

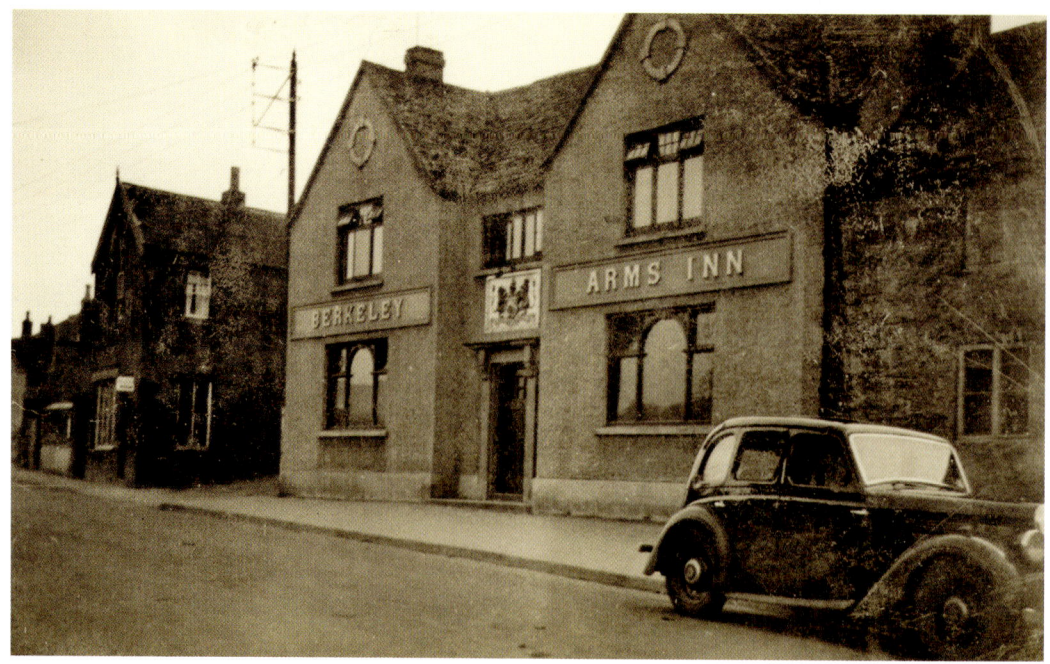

Berkeley Arms, Cam
The Berkeley Arms has a very successful darts team and is a sports orientated pub. Above the door is the French motto '*Dieu Avec Nous*' – 'may God be with us'. Before the London 2012 Olympics landlord Graham Ponting displayed the flags of thirty-two participating countries outside the pub. With Team GB gaining 65 medals – 29 Gold, 17 Silver and 19 Bronze – the Berkeley family motto turned out to be an accurate premonition.

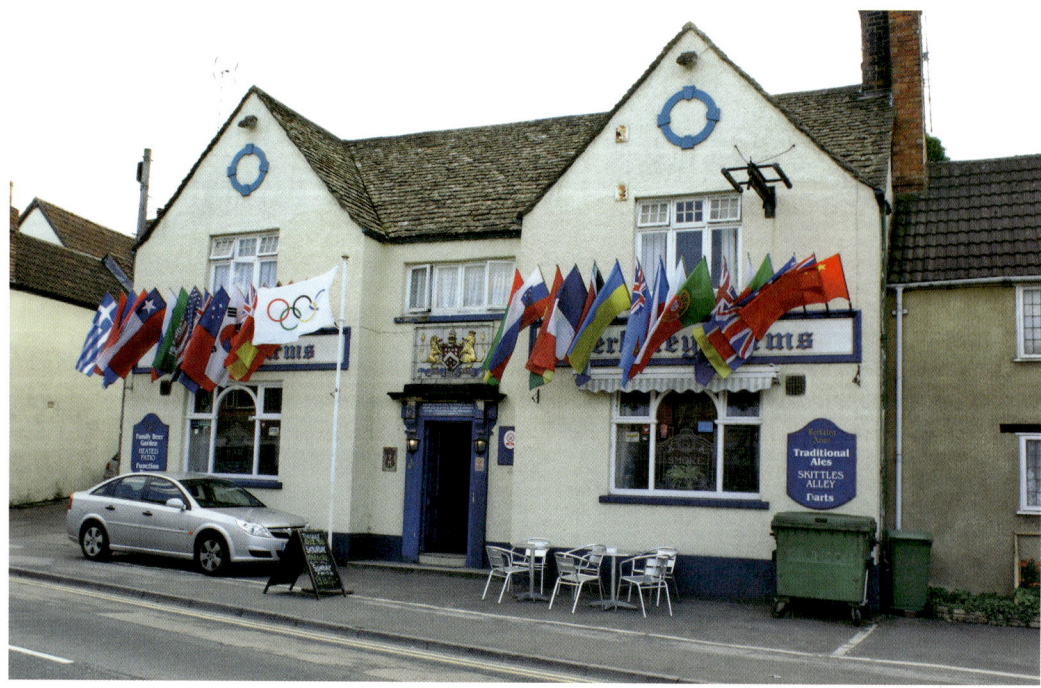

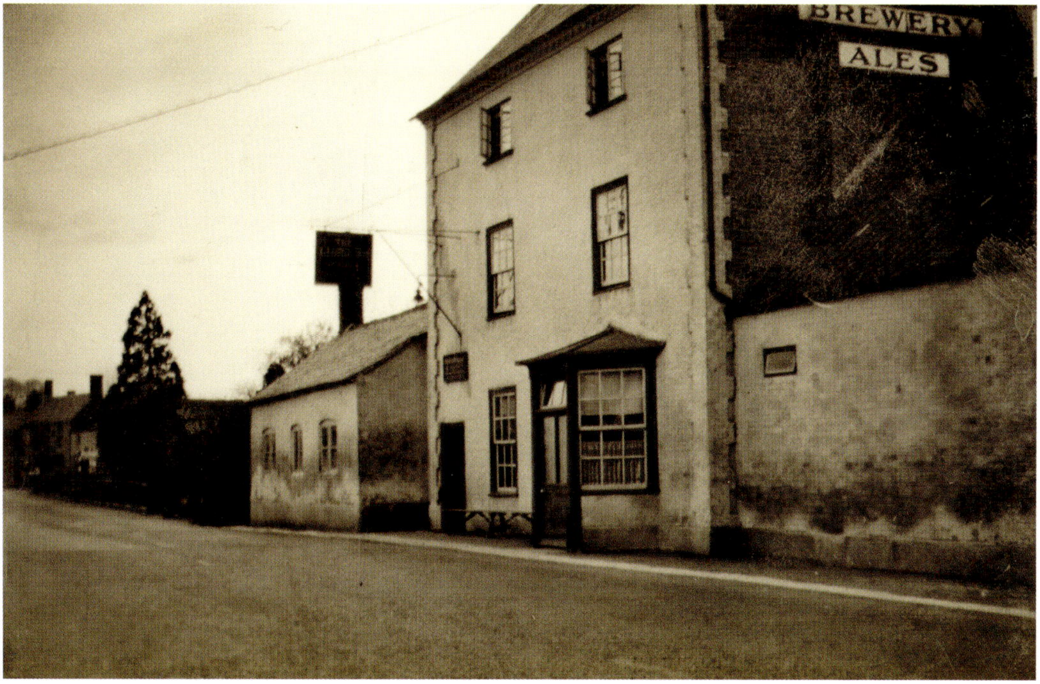

George Hotel, Cambridge

The George Inn was purchased by the Stroud Brewery from the Berkeley Estate in January 1945. However, Stroud Ales had been served at the George for many years before that under a leasing agreement. The landlord in the early 1960s, Cyril Tom Cooper, was a very talented pianist who ran the Dixie Cooper dance band. He died in October 1926.

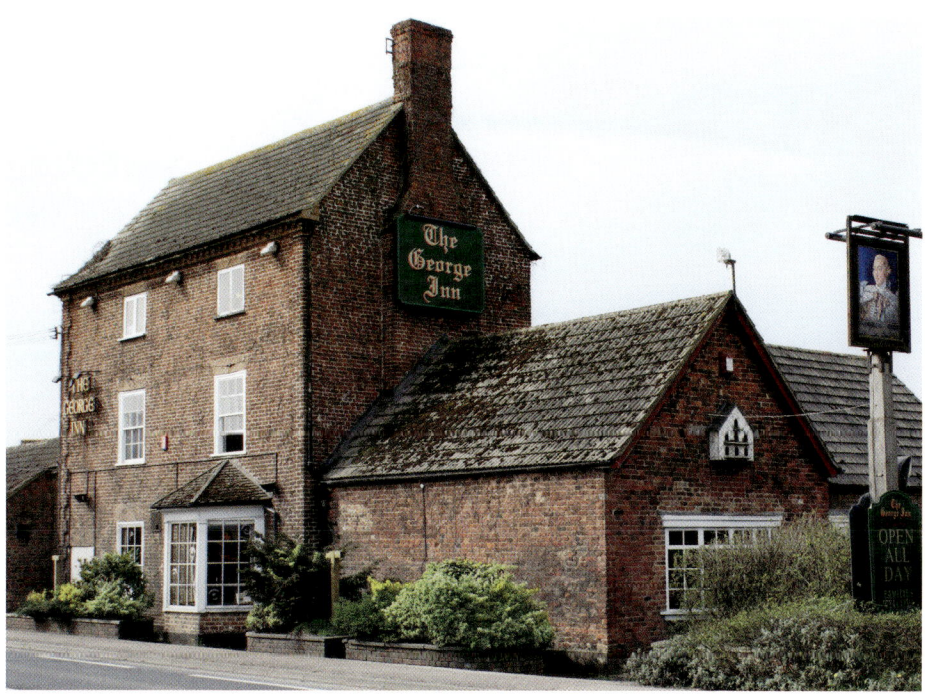

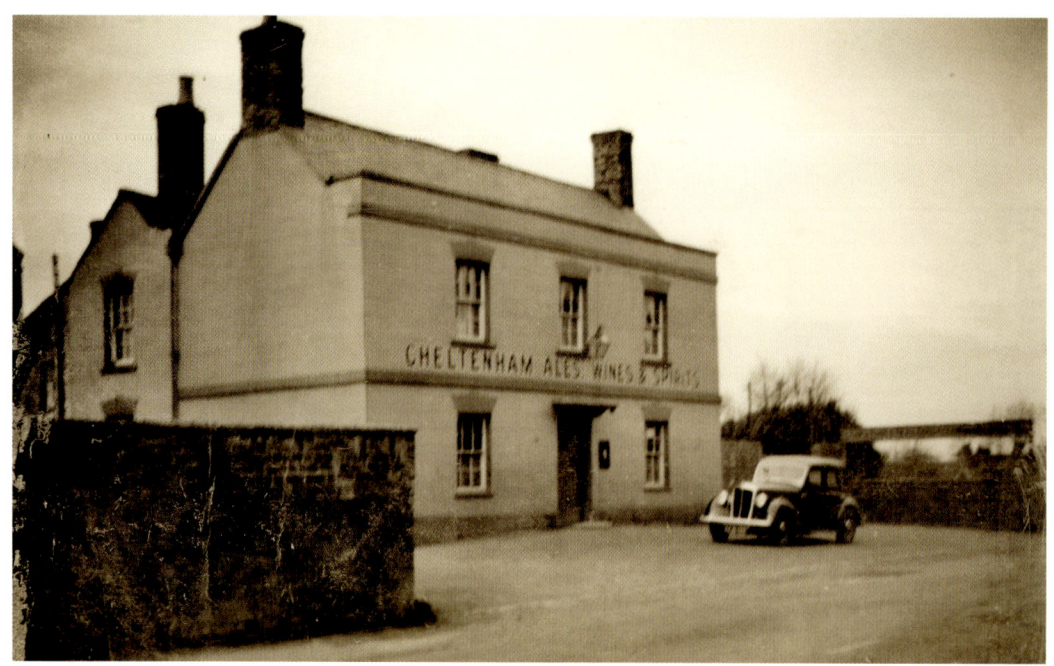

White Lion, Cambridge

The White Lion, on the main Gloucester to Bristol road, was once a busy inn with stabling for twelve to fourteen horses. The pub was still catering for passing travellers at the turn of the twenty-first century as there was a camping and caravanning site to the rear. The land was also used for car boot sales. Stroud District Council objected to the caravan site and the boot sales due to concerns of access to and from the busy A38. The White Lion closed at the beginning of 2012 and its future is uncertain.

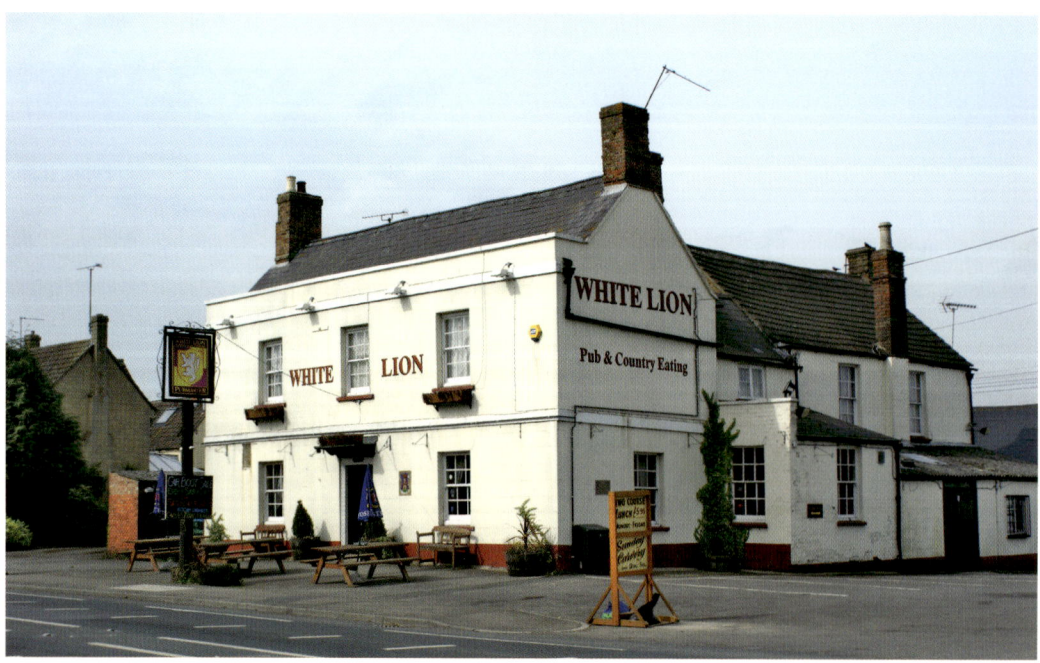

Fox and Hounds, Coaley

During the Second World War the Fox and Hounds doubled up as the local fire station and was manned for 24 hours a day. The fireman had their own vehicle and a hand operated pump. Their finest hour was probably when they extinguished a blaze at a local farm. The brigade were based in the old stables of the Fox and Hounds, which they shared with the local football team, Coaley Rovers.

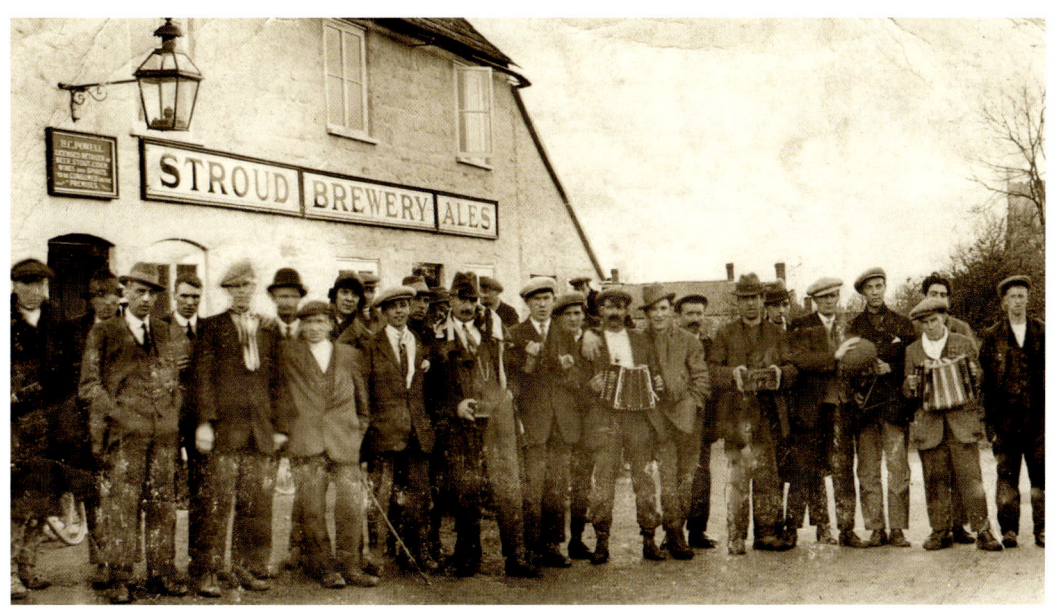

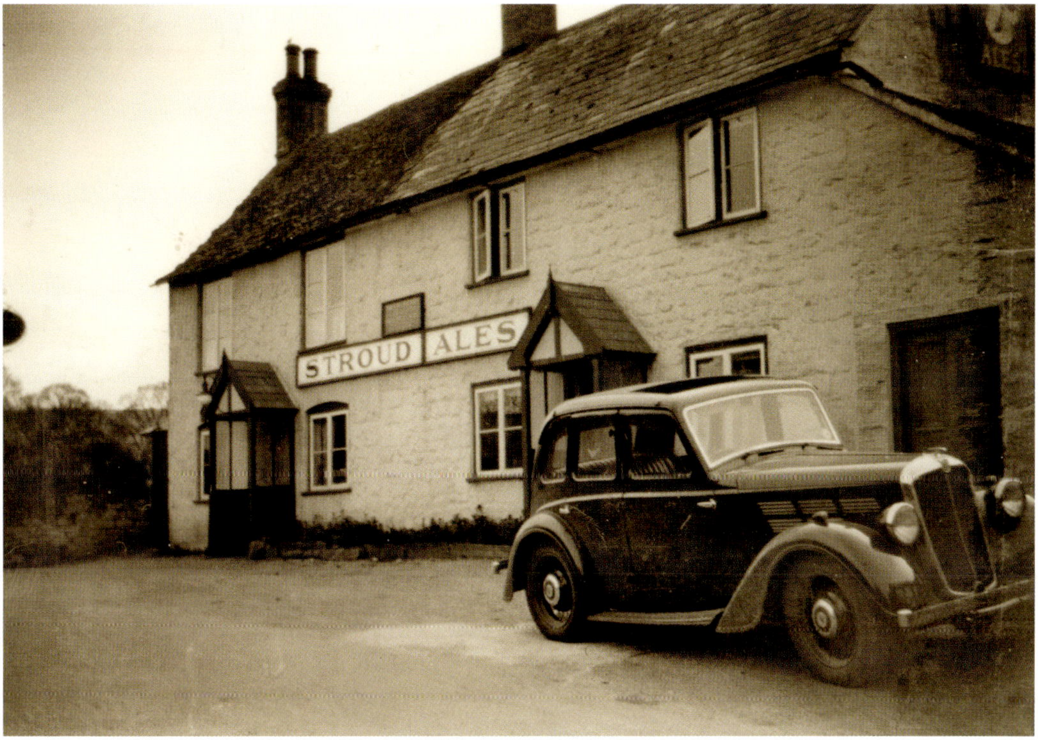

Carpenters Arms, Uley Road, Dursley

When Thomas Elvy bought the Dursley Steam Brewery and their pubs, including the Carpenters Arms, for £28,000 in June 1899, he went on a spending spree. An increase in rateable values at the pub from £14 10s 0d to £24 0s 0d between 1891 and 1903 suggests that the Carpenters Arms had a major facelift. In just seven years Thomas Elvy lost £33,000 due to expenditure on licensed properties with household and personal expenses exceeding income. He was declared bankrupt in 1906.

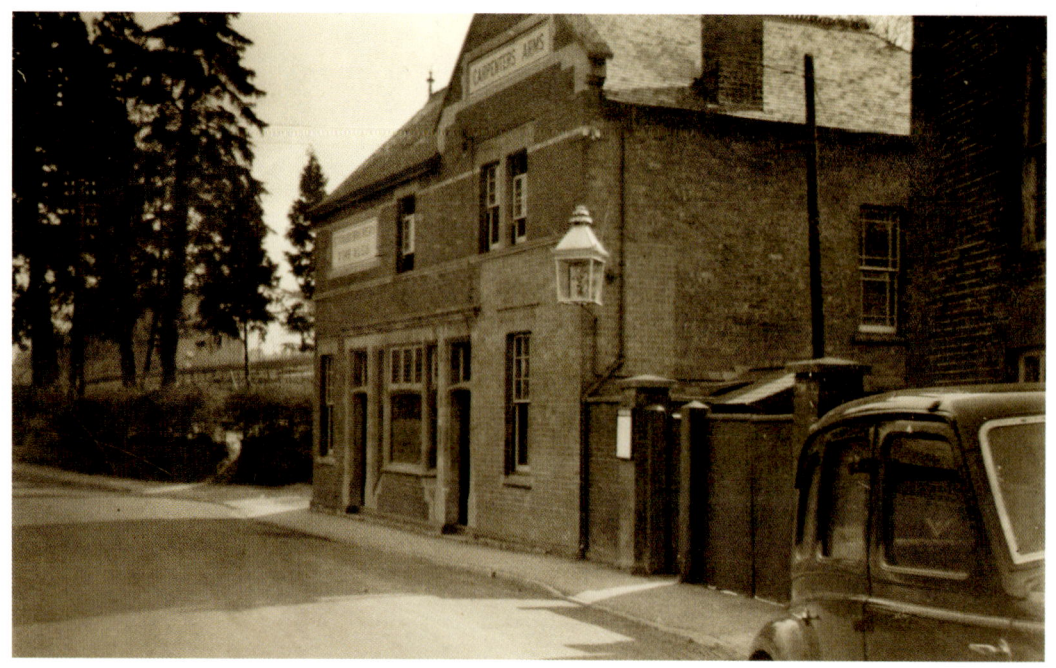

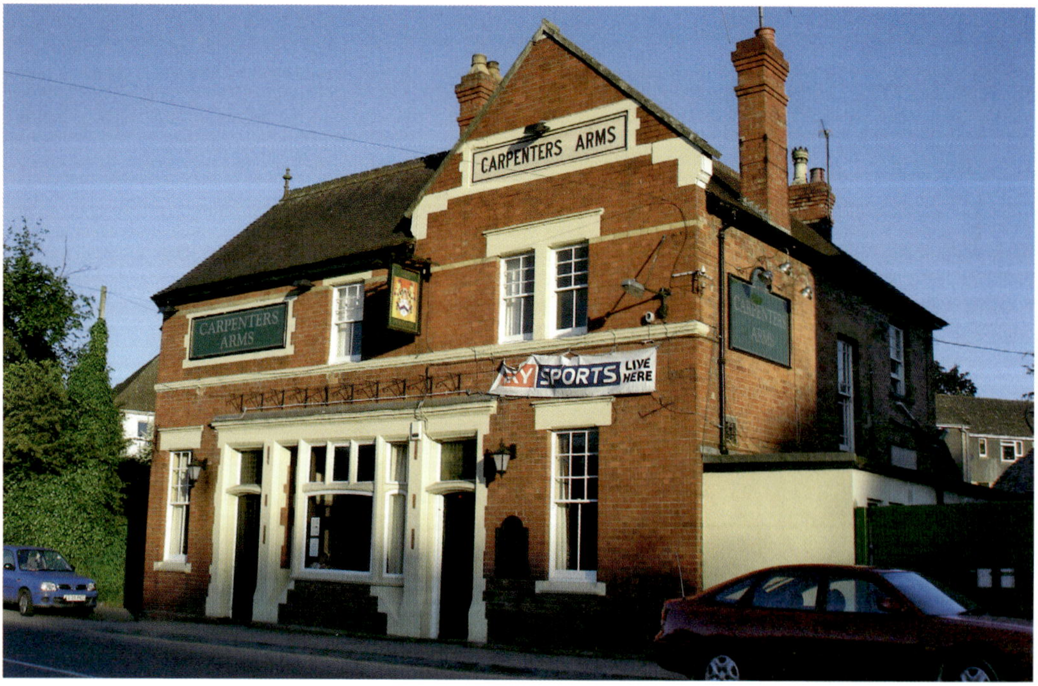

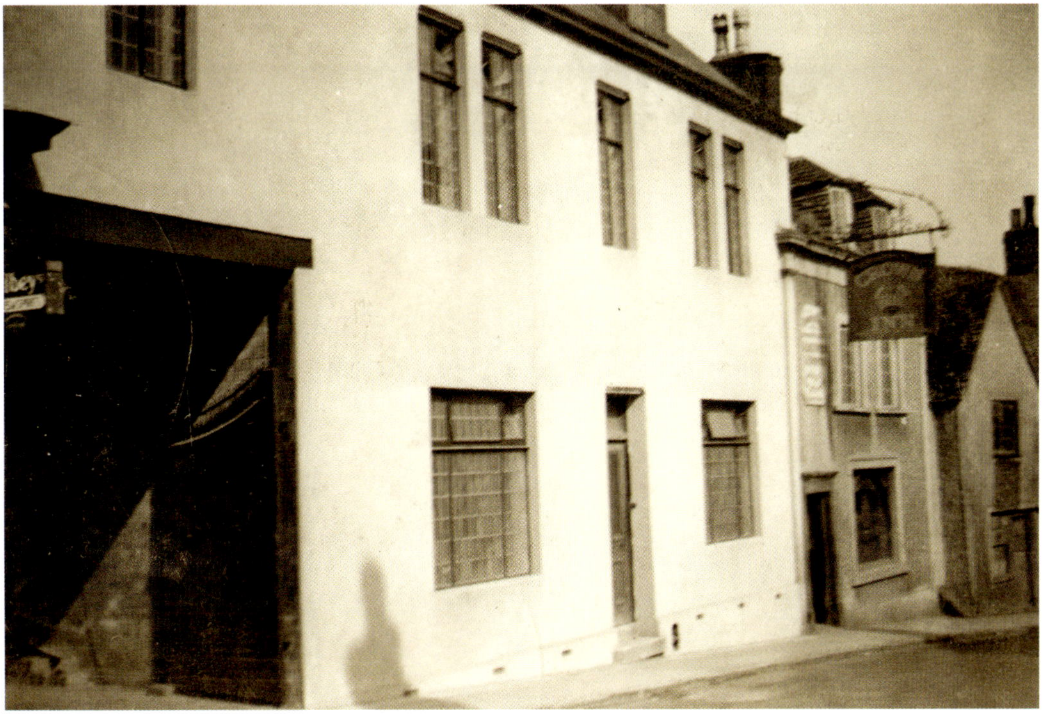

Crown Inn, Long Street, Dursley

The building that was originally the Crown Inn was converted to the Lodge Balti restaurant in August 1998 and is now the Dursley Tandoori. The Crown was later extended into adjoining premises (39 Long Street) where a West Country Ales 'Best in the West' ceramic plaque serves as a reminder of its previous history. The premises last traded as a pub in 1997 when it was known as the Inn Place featuring Cassocks Bar.

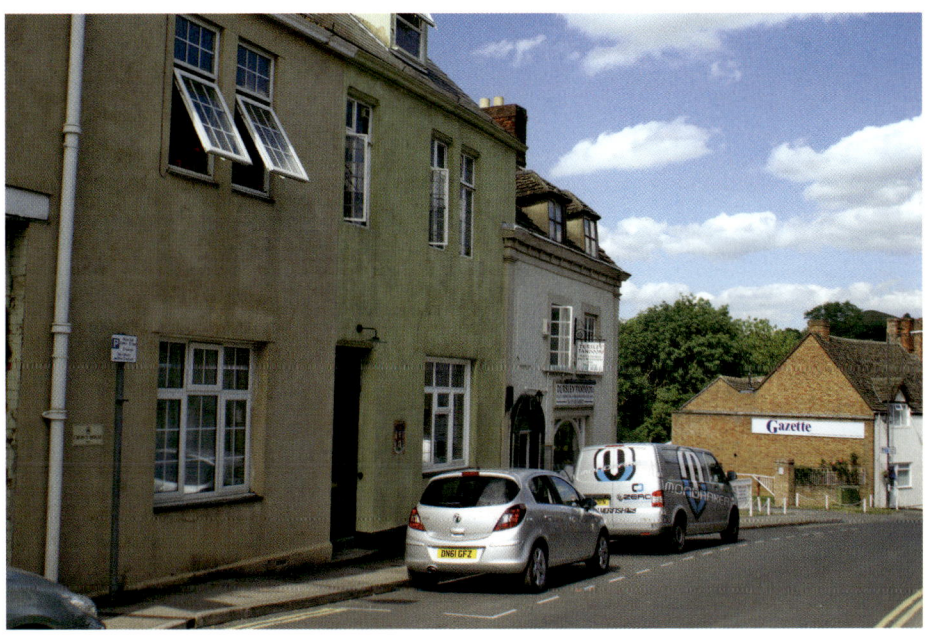

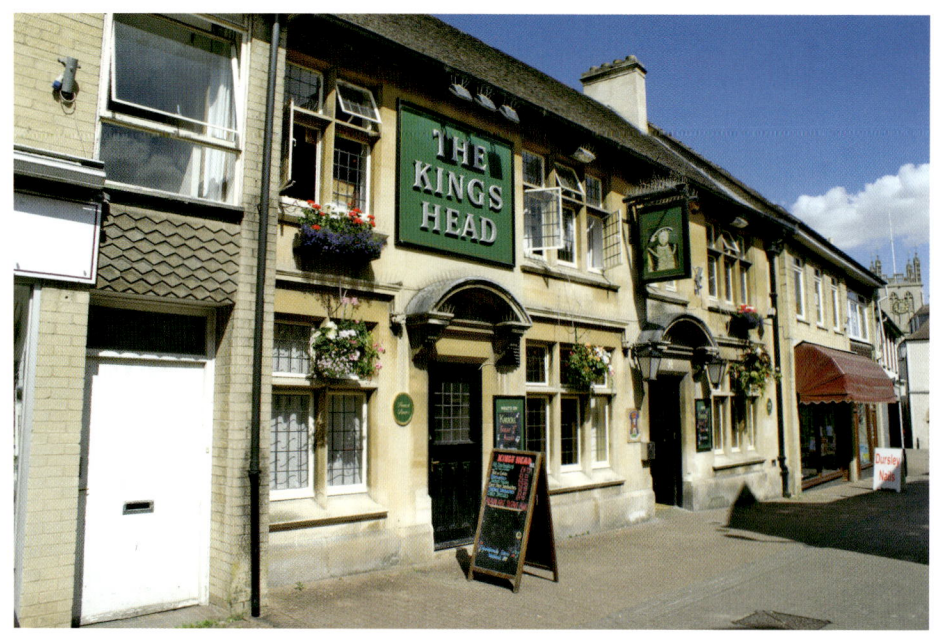

Kings Head, Parsonage Street, Dursley

For a short period in the late 1990s the Kings Head gained an enviable reputation for its live music, hosting some of the best established rock and pop acts on the pub circuit. Eighties pop megastar Paul Young played at the Kings Head twice. Seventies rock bands the Groundhogs and Wishbone Ash also played there. The live music stopped in April 2000 following a dispute with the tenant landlords and the brewery over the lease and entertainment licence.

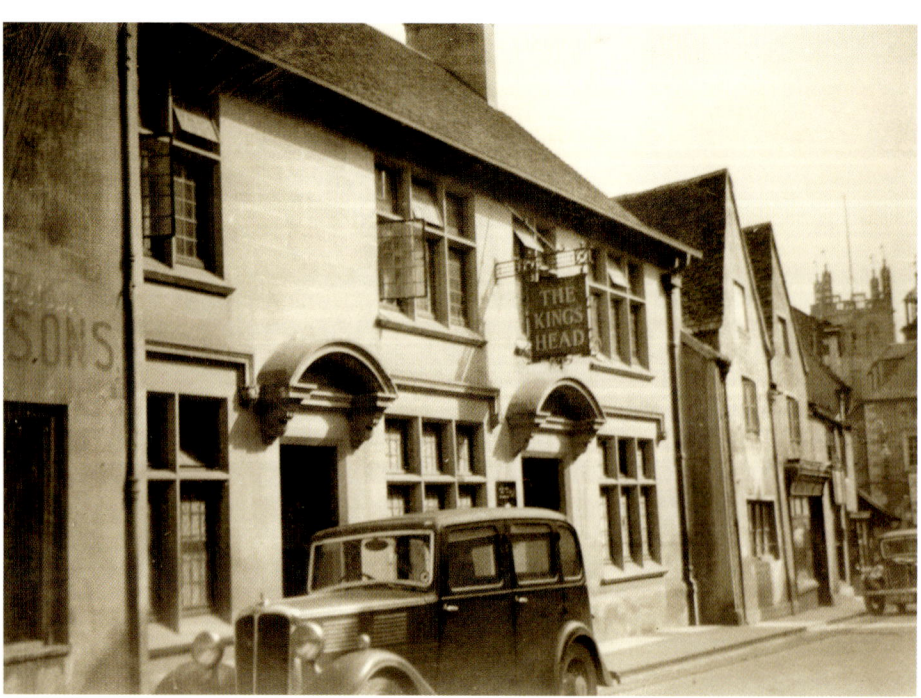

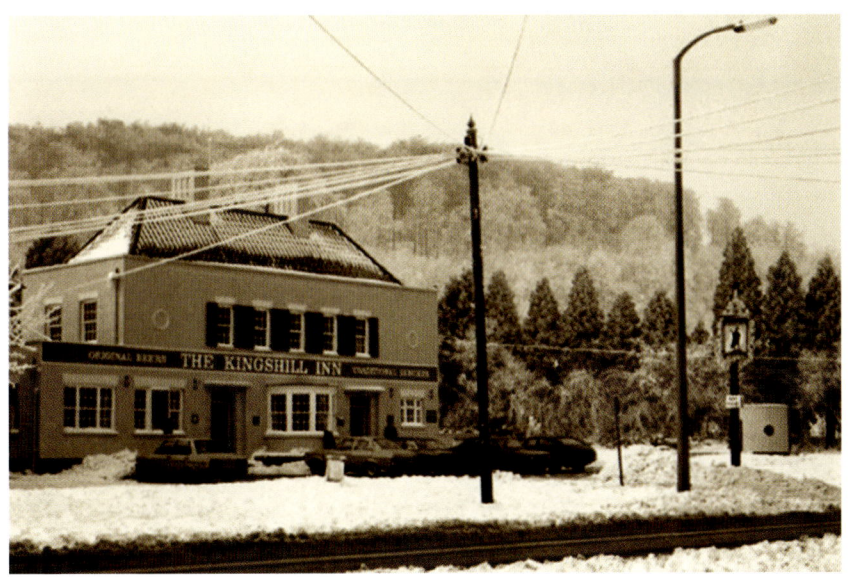

Kingshill Inn, Kingshill Road, Dursley

The *S. B. Courier*, the quarterly house journal for the Stroud Brewery Company Ltd, gave details of the Kingshill Inn in September 1949: 'This attractive inn was the last to be erected by the Company. It was opened for business on the day following the declaration of war in 1939. It has every modern convenience with spacious and comfortable public rooms, and Mr. and Mrs. L.W. Collins do their best to cater for the needs of their patrons.' Wadworth & Co. of Devizes acquired the pub from Whitbread in 1990.

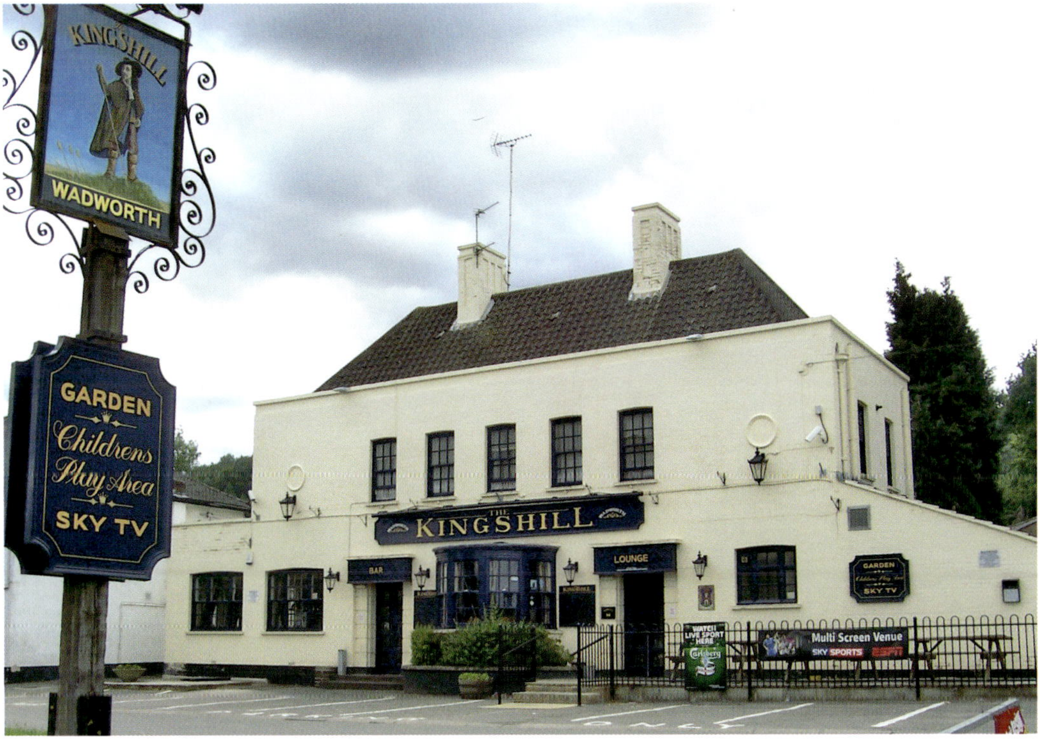

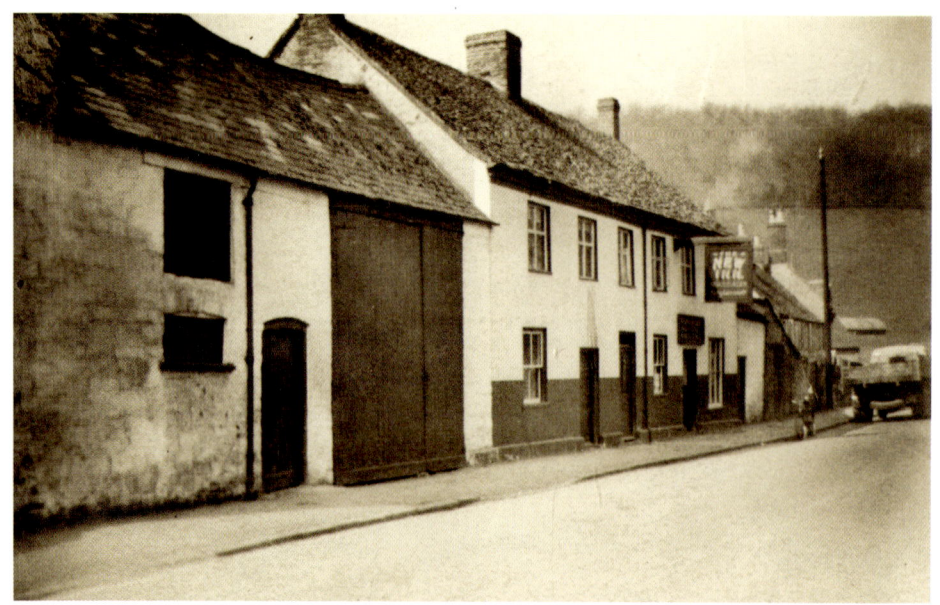

New Inn, Woodmancote, Dursley

A rather quirky, and certainly peculiar, tradition usually takes place during the first weekend in June when a team of six throwers compete for the annual Ball Throwing Contest which starts at the New Inn at Woodmancote and finishes, over the hill, at the New Inn at Waterley Bottom. The idea of the game is to throw a small ball all the way from one pub to the other, with the winners being the team who manage it in the least number of throws. In 2001 a team from the Old Spot managed it in thirty-three throws.

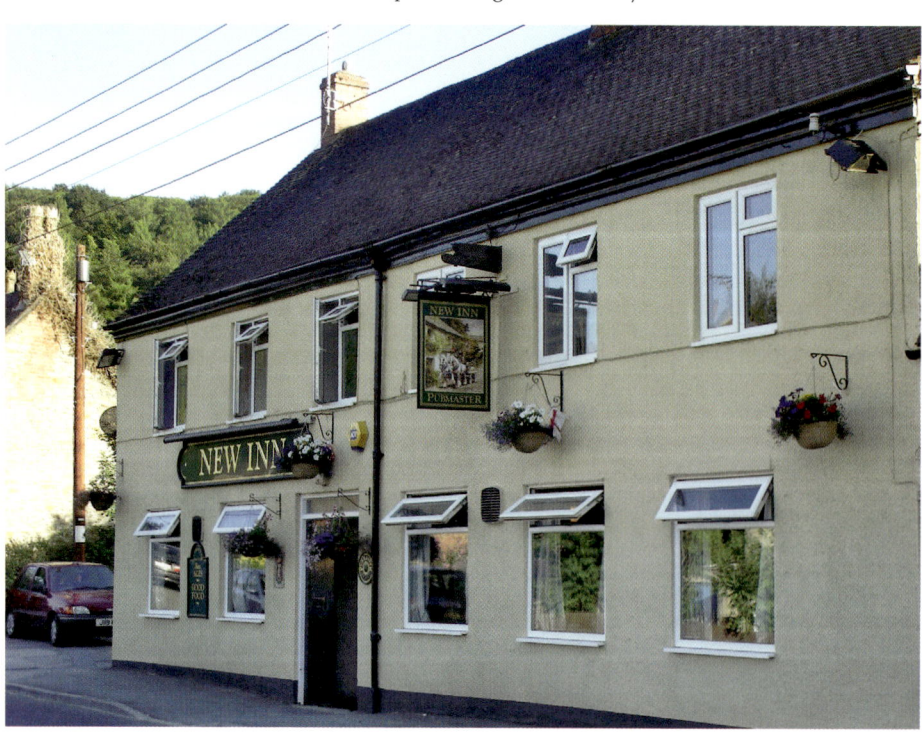

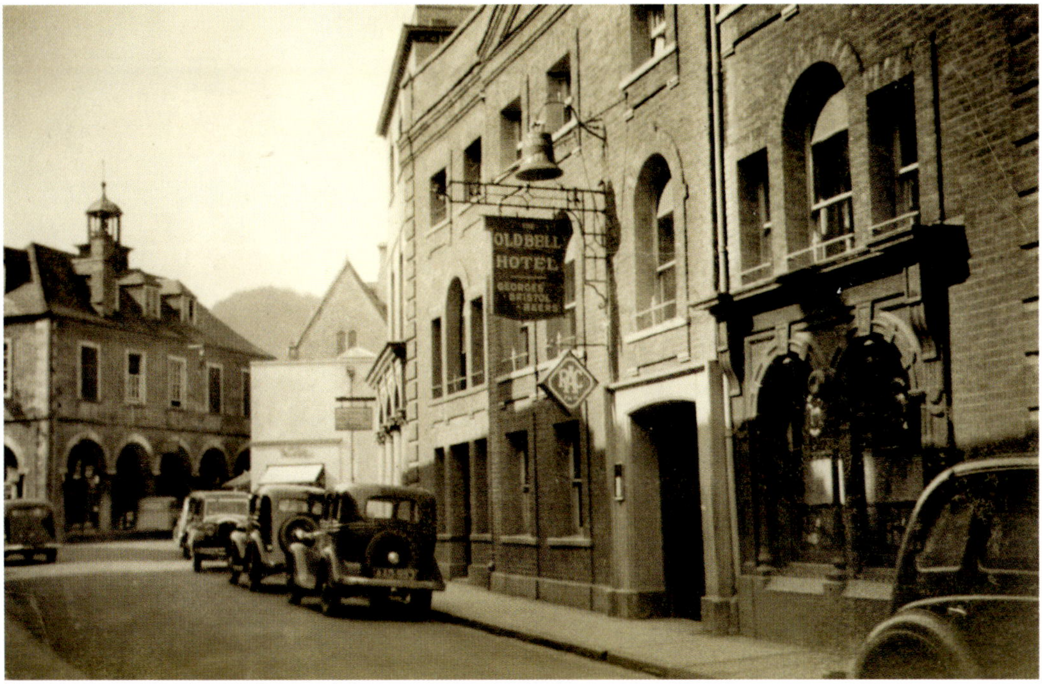

Old Bell, Long Street, Dursley
The Old Bell, a fourteenth-century former coaching inn, is reputed to have a secret tunnel leading to the church of St James the Great on the opposite side of Long Street. It has been said that one of the rooms of the Old Bell Hotel was once used as a local assize court, where the fate of criminals were decided by magistrates. Perhaps not surprisingly the pub is reputedly haunted. An investigation by a Cheltenham-based psychic research group early in 1997 apparently 'discovered' five apparitions.

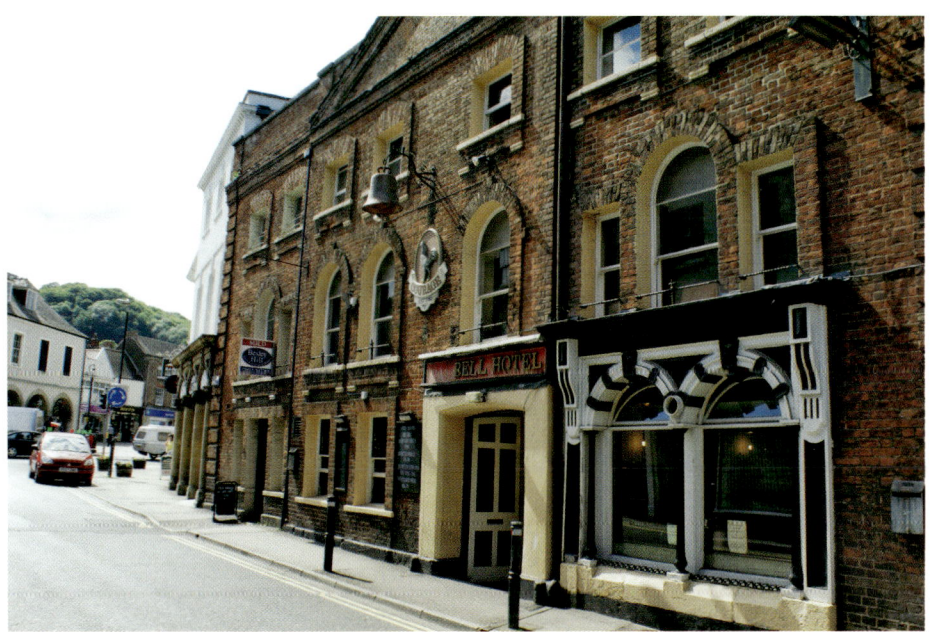

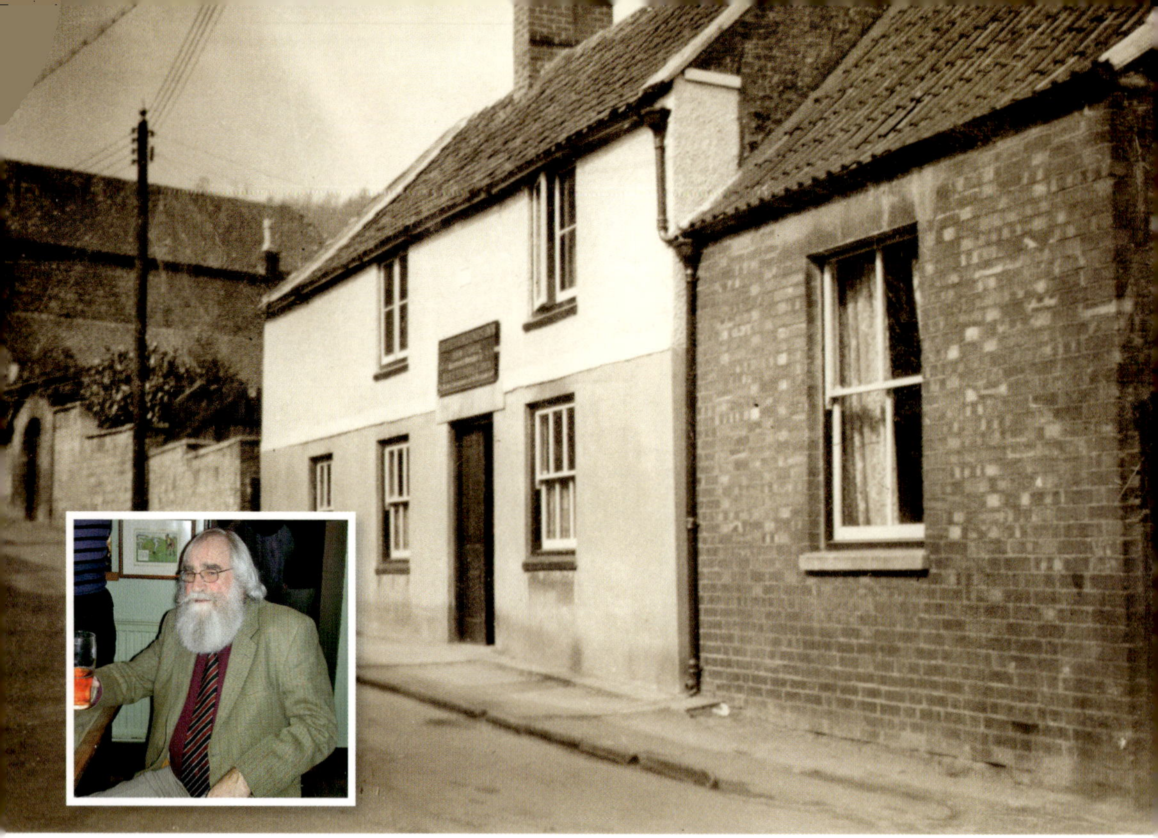

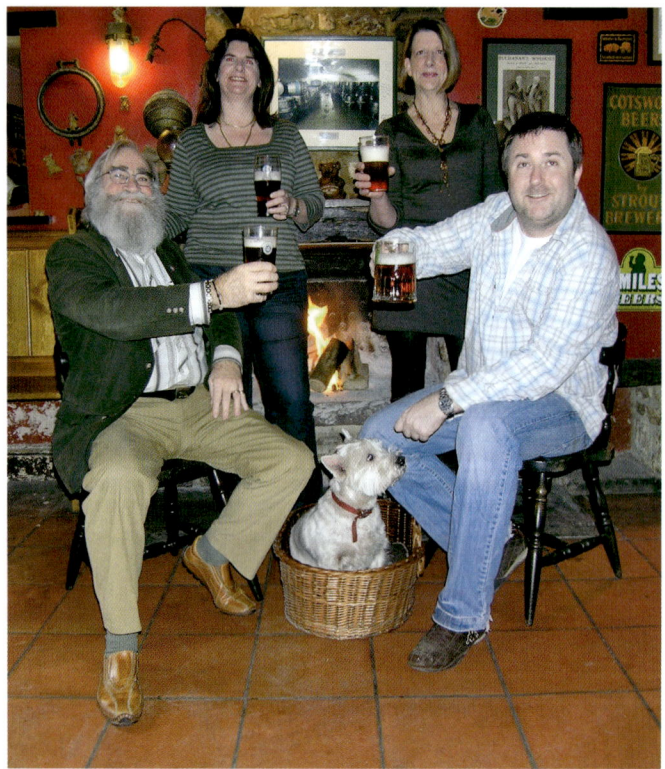

Old Spot, Hill Road, Dursley

In 1993 Ric and Ellie Sainty bought the Fox and Hounds from Whitbread and set about transforming the basic boozer into a superb real ale pub that was ultimately crowned the CAMRA National Pub of the Year in 2007. This amazing achievement can also be attributed to Steve and Belinda who have managed the pub in fine style since 2001. A presentation was made to the pub in February 2008. Sadly Ric passed away shortly afterwards whilst on holiday in France on 16 July. The spirit of Ric lives on at the Old Spot which, in September 2011, was crowned Best Cask Ale Pub in Britain.

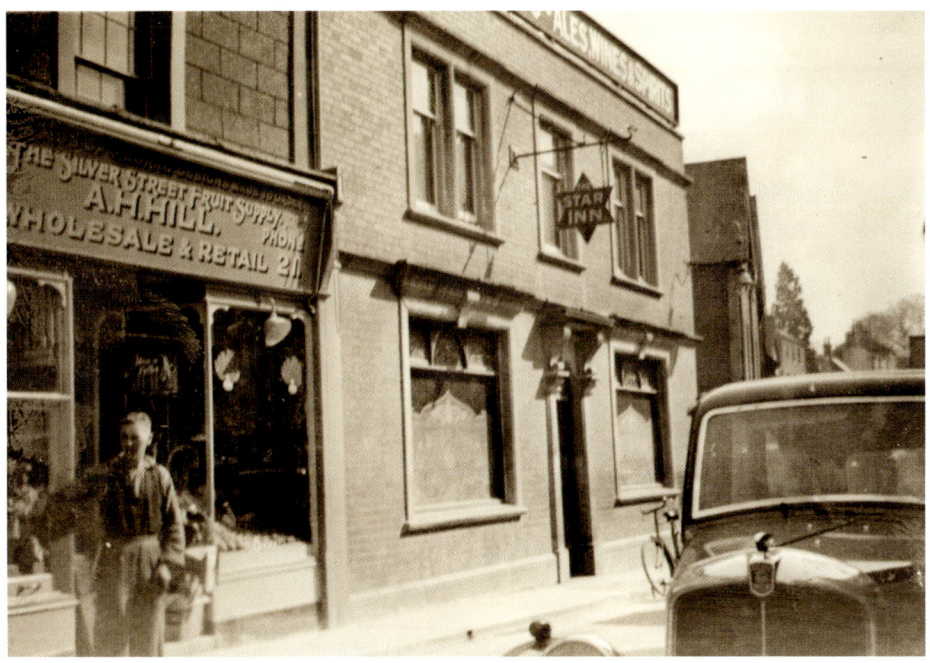

Star Inn, Silver Street, Dursley

The Star Inn was built by the Stroud Brewery at the end of the nineteenth century, replacing an earlier inn of the same name. Ironically, the Star was one of the closest pubs to the Dursley Brewery in Boulton Lane, certainly within smell and sound of the brewery, but it never sold the local Dursley ales. The Star Inn closed in the summer of 1984, when it was an ordinary Whitbread house selling the likes of Tankard and Trophy keg bitters. The building is currently in use as a ladies' hairdresser.

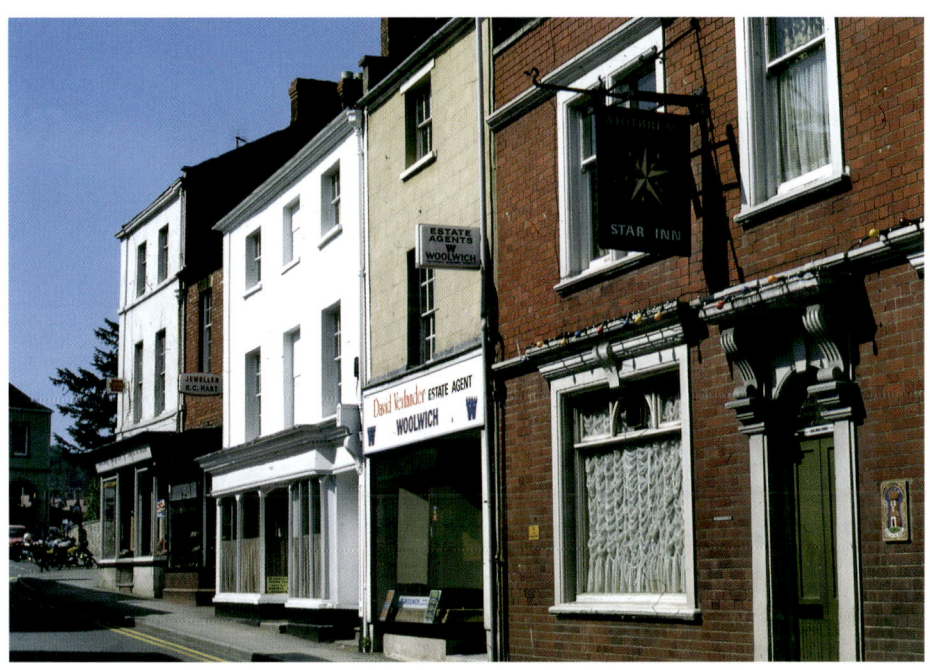

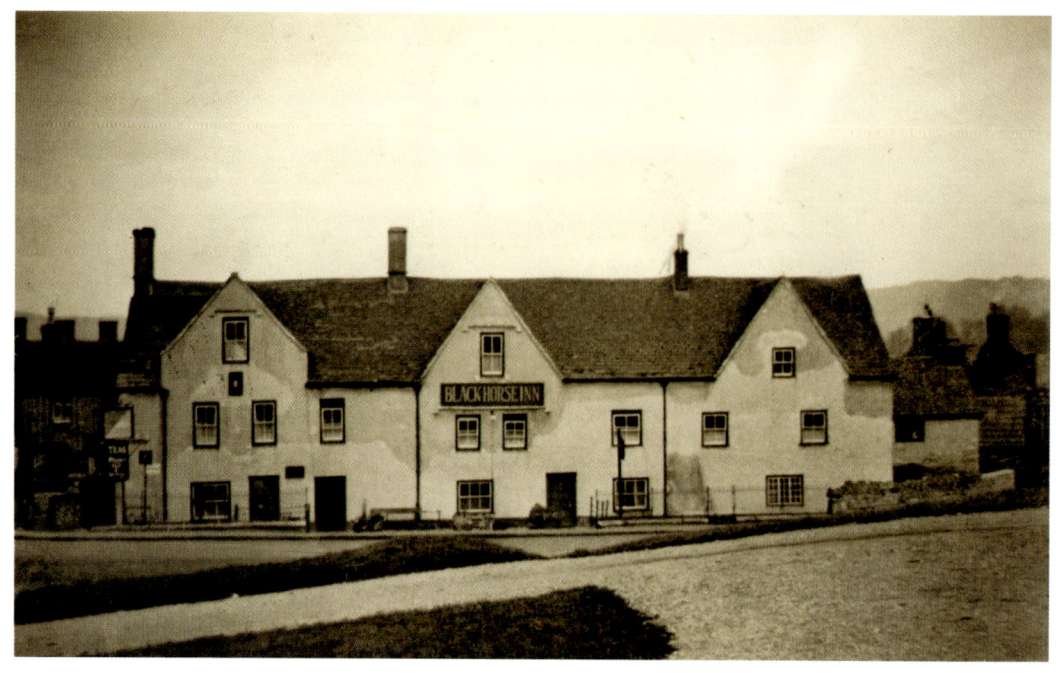

Black Horse, Barrs Lane, North Nibley

The present owners Chris and Sue Lewis bought the Black Horse in January 2011 after they stayed at the bed & breakfast and fell in love with the pub. The Black Horse sells three cask ales including beer from the Wickwar Brewing Co. A century ago the Black Horse was owned by Arnold, Perrett & Co. of Wickwar which ceased brewing in 1924. When the Wickwar Brewing Co. was established in 1990 by Ray Penny and Brian Rides brewing recommenced after a gap of sixty-six years.

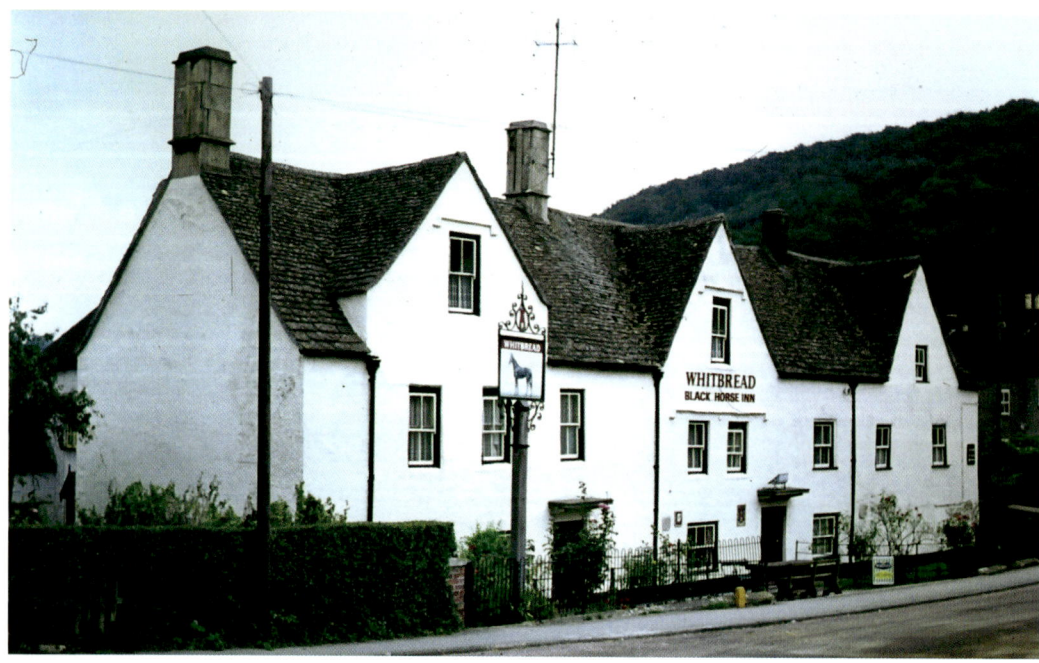

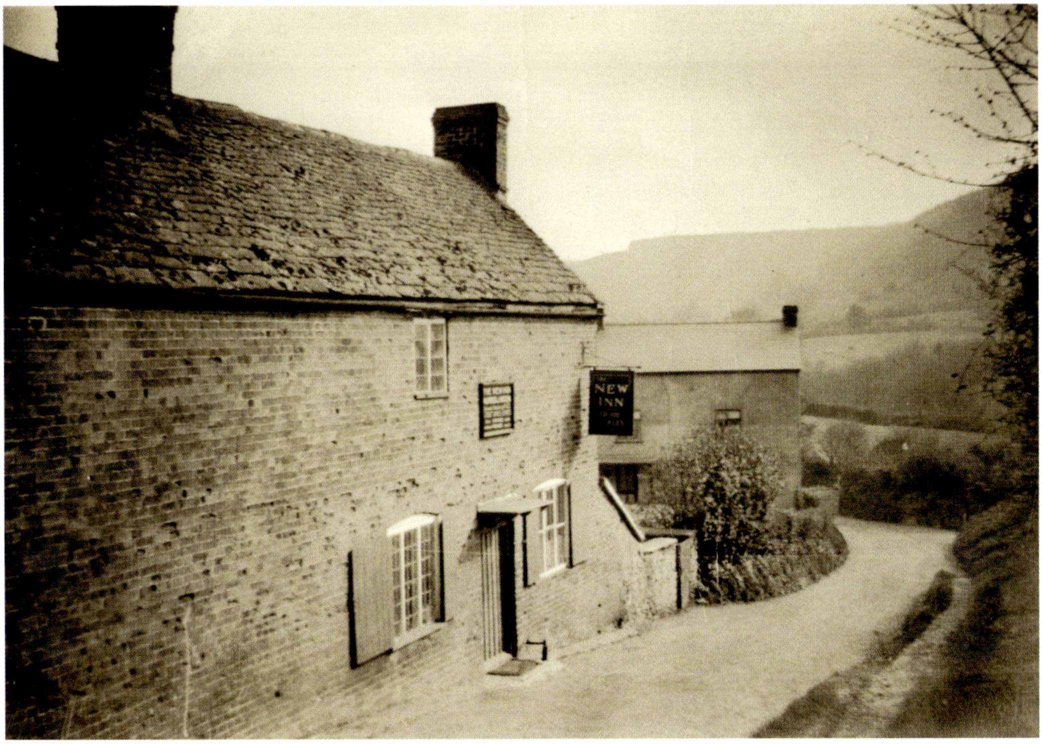

New Inn, Waterley Bottom, North Nibley

Tucked away down a warren of small country lanes, the New Inn can be a challenge to find for the first-time visitor. In 1912 the New Inn was owned by the Coombe Valley Brewery near Wotton-under-Edge. In the 1970s it was bought by Ric and Ruby Sainty who transformed the New Inn into a legendary real ale pub. Drinkers came from far and wide to sample Greene King Abbot Ale! In November 1998 a planning application to convert the building to residential use was submitted but refused.

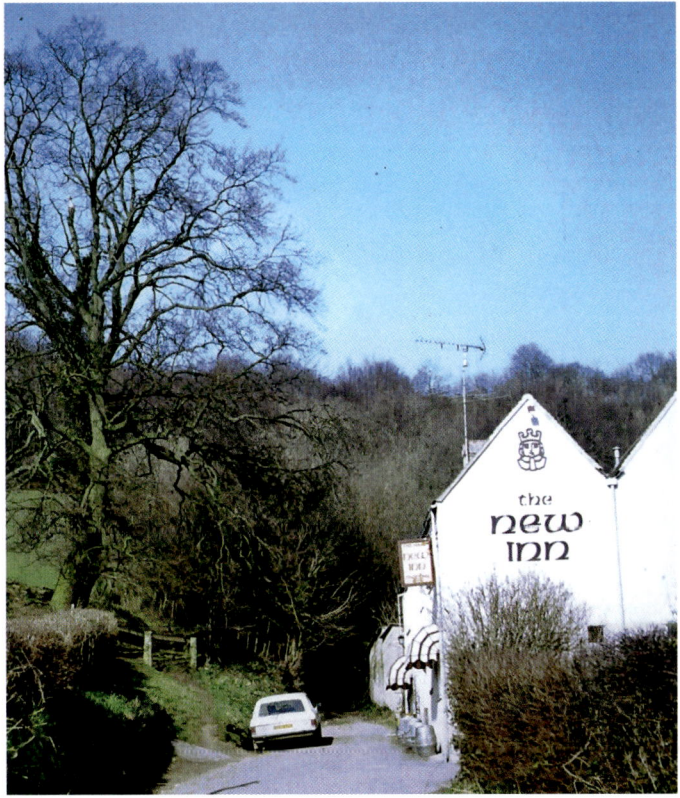

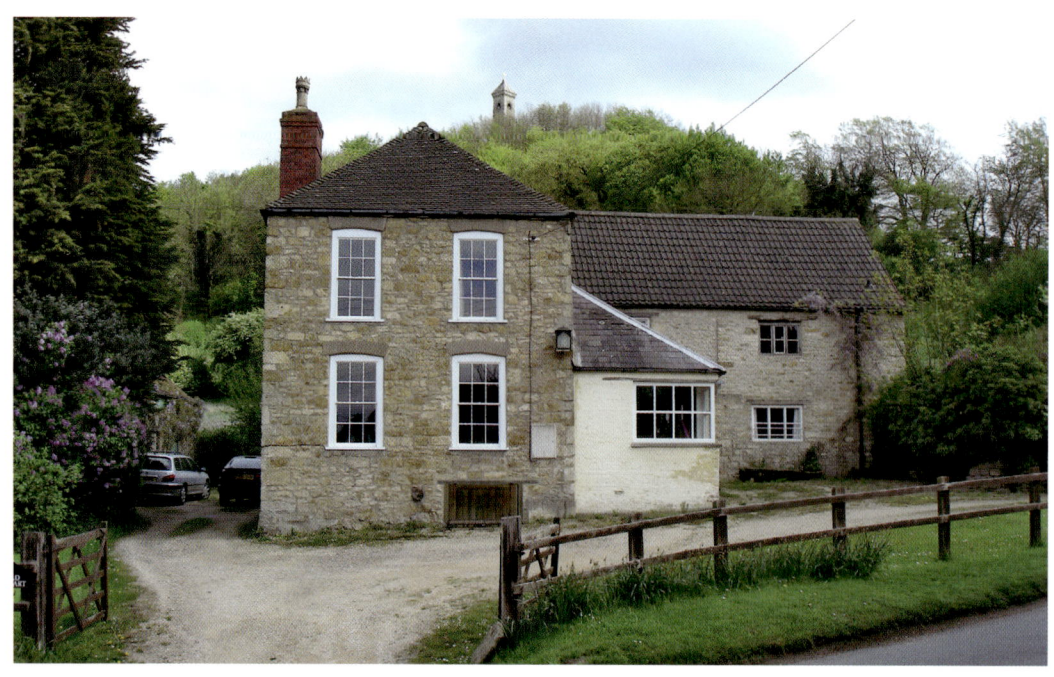

White Hart, Wotton Road, North Nibley

The White Hart was located directly opposite the Black Horse in the centre of the village. It was owned by Lord Fitzhardinge of the Berkeley Estate and leased to the Stroud Brewery Company. The White Hart closed in the late 1950s. In addition to the White Hart, Black Horse and New Inn there were once two other pubs in the parish – the Golden Heart at Pitt Court and the Kings Head in Nibley Green.

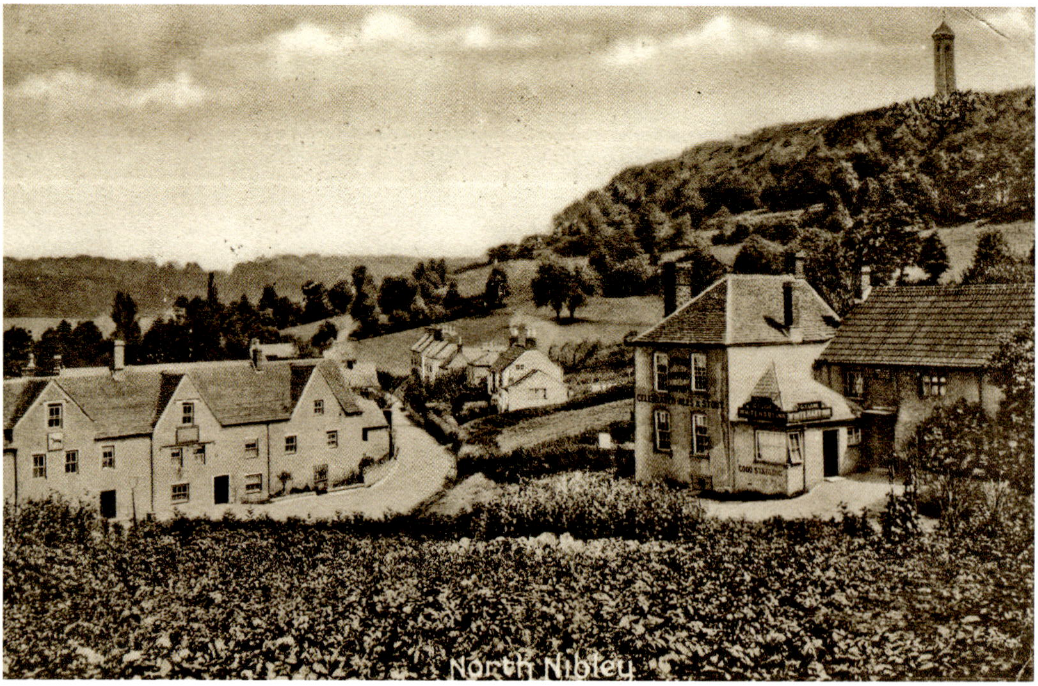

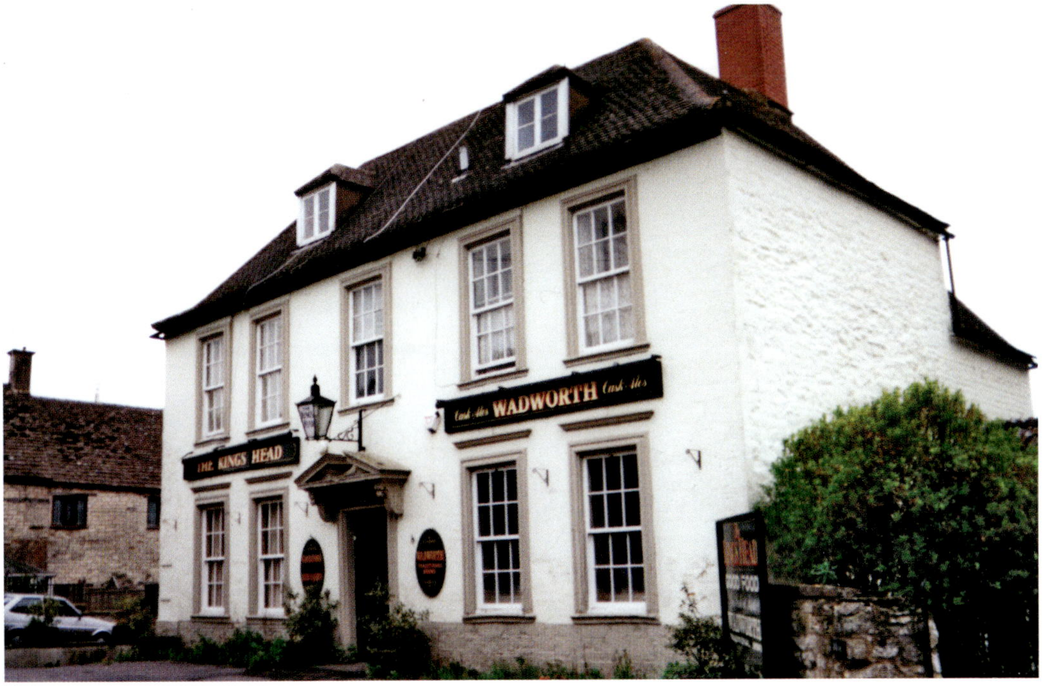

Kings Head, Uley

The eighteenth-century Kings Head was owned by Wadworth Brewery of Devizes, Wiltshire. An application was submitted to Stroud District Council in December 2000 for change of use from public house to residential. The Kings Head served its last pints on Saturday 9 April 2001. With a delightful twist of irony, the beers sold on the last day came from the Uley Brewery, located just a few yards away from the pub.

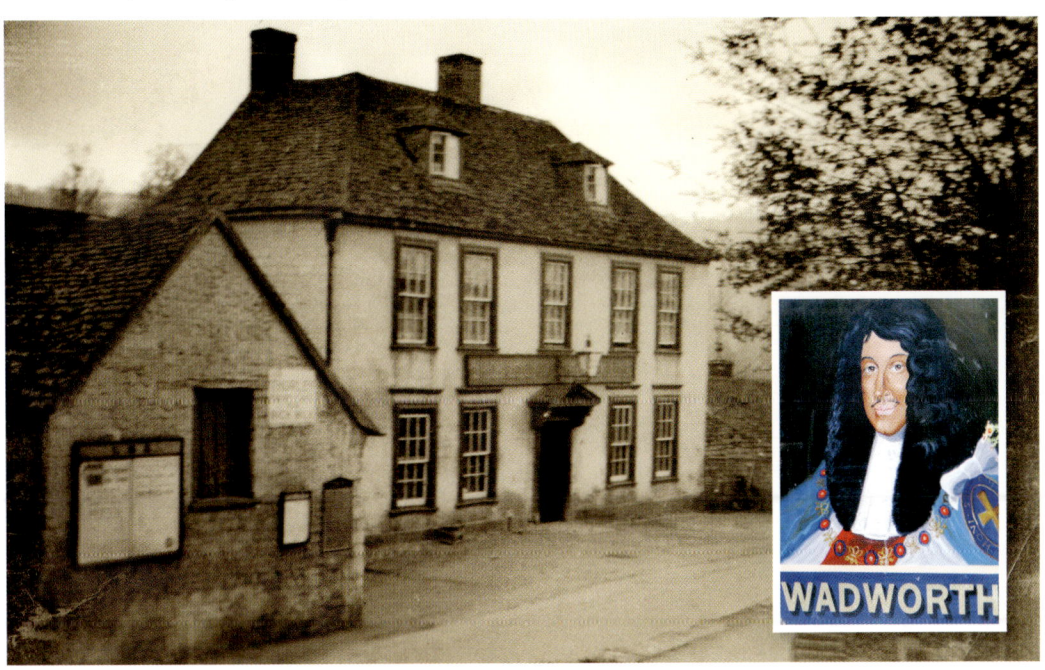

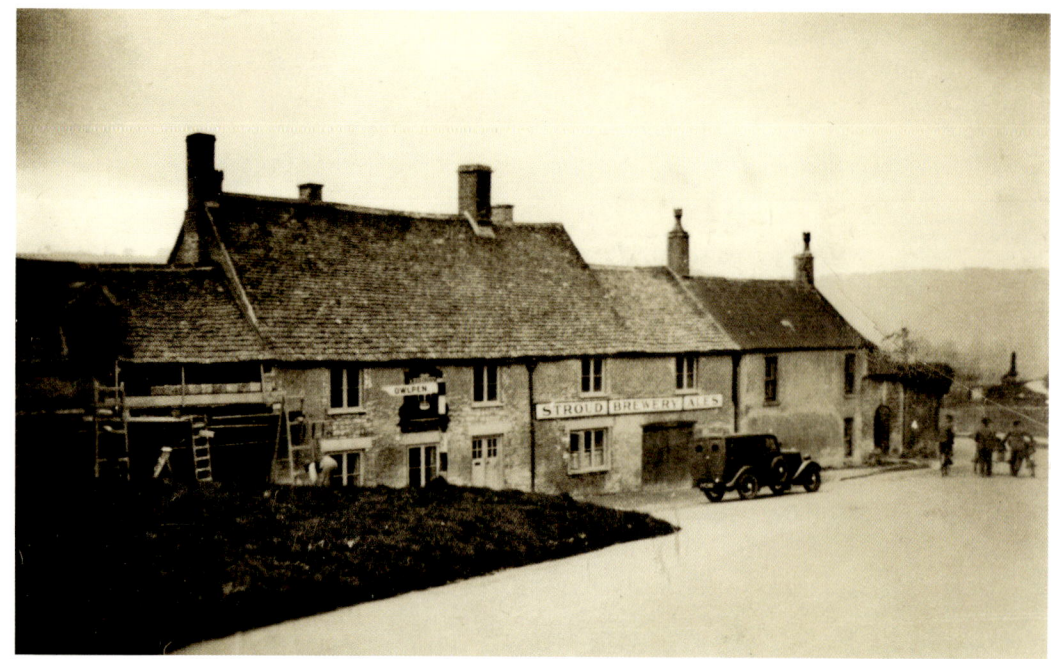

Old Crown, Uley
The Old Crown is sometimes referred to as the Top Crown to distinguish it from the long closed Lower Crown Inn which was a short distance further down the hill. The Old Crown was named the Pub of the Year by the Dursley sub-branch of the Campaign for Real Ale in December 2000. The Old Crown suddenly closed just before Christmas 2005. Thankfully, it reopened on 4 August 2006 and continues to be a genuine free house, serving the local Uley Brewery ales.

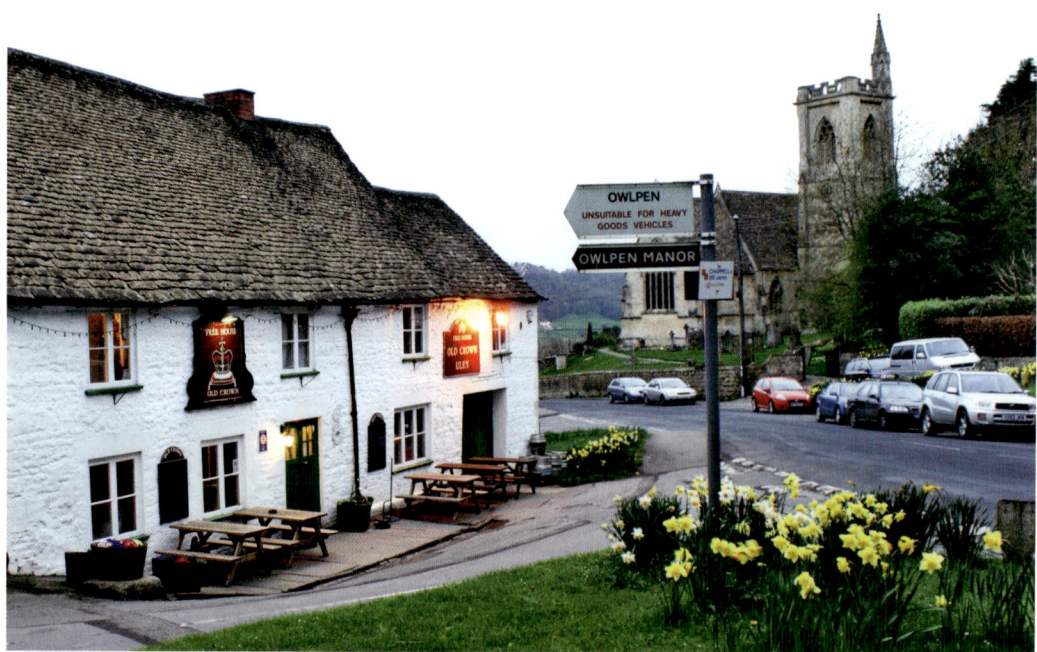

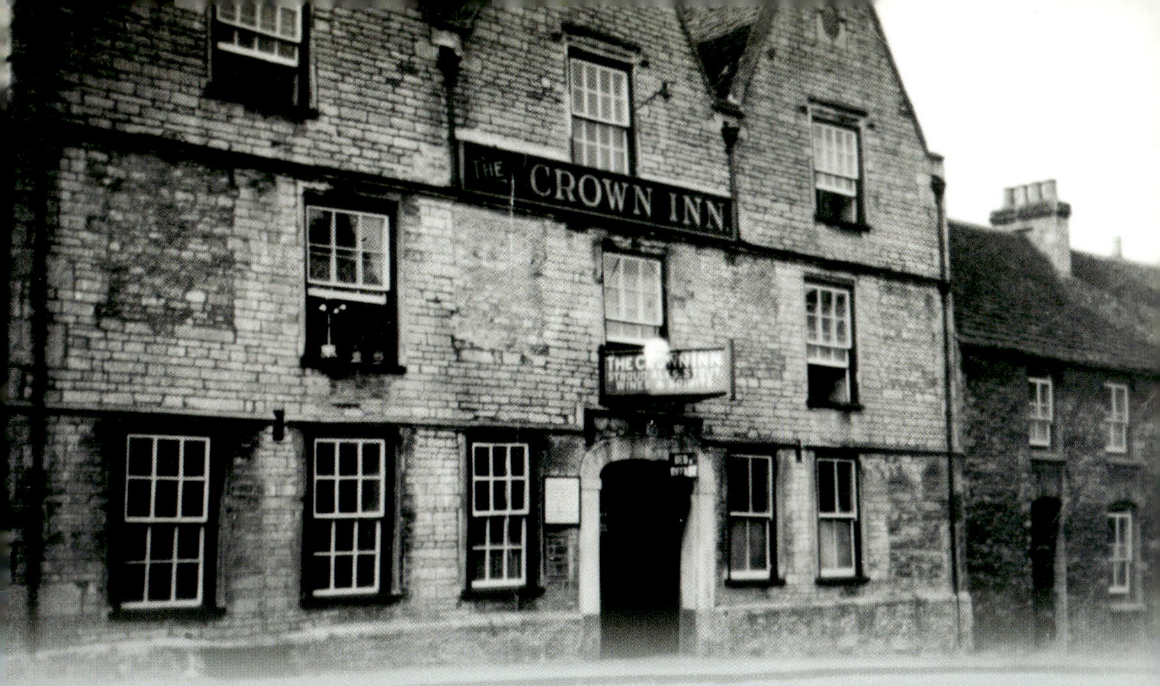

CHAPTER 4

Tetbury

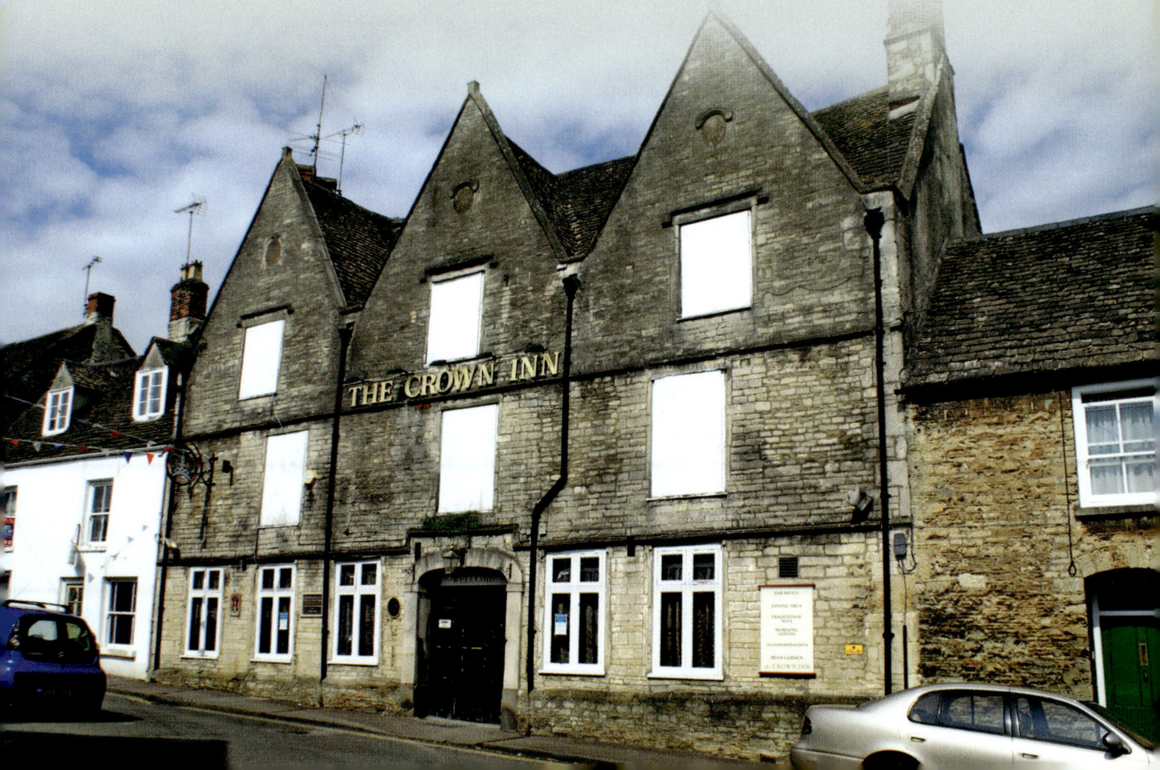

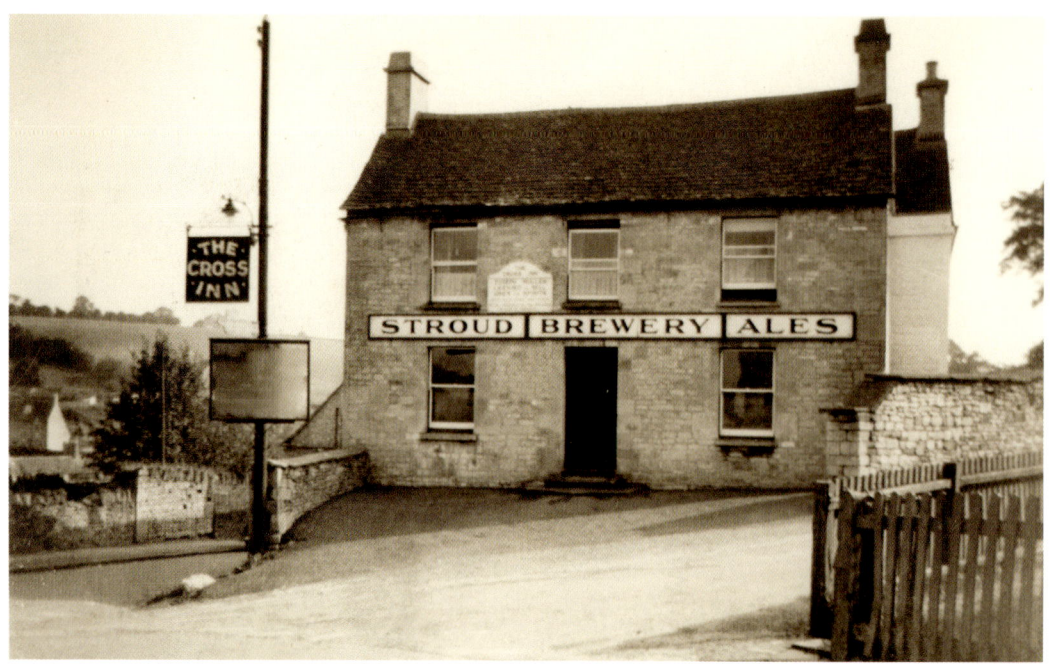

Cross Inn, Avening

In the austere years immediately after Second World War rationing was a part of life, with bread and other foodstuffs in short supply. A little-known fact is that comfy cushions were also in great demand. The *Stroud Brewery Courier* reported in June 1949: 'All customers over eighty years of age are to be provided with cushions in the public bar at the Cross Inn.' In true wartime spirit there are now allotments in the pub grounds and even the village shop has been at the pub since May 2010.

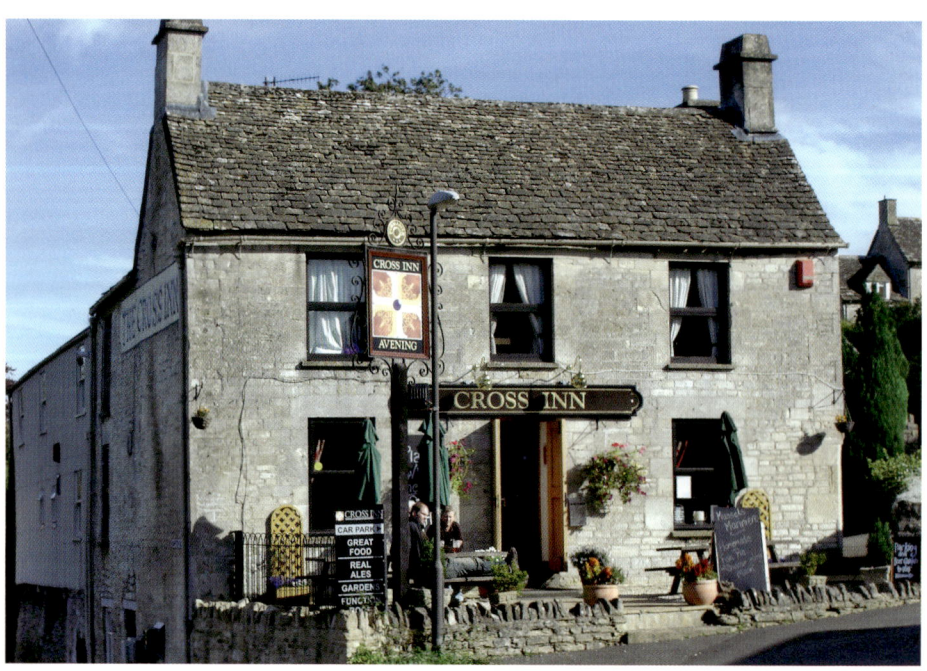

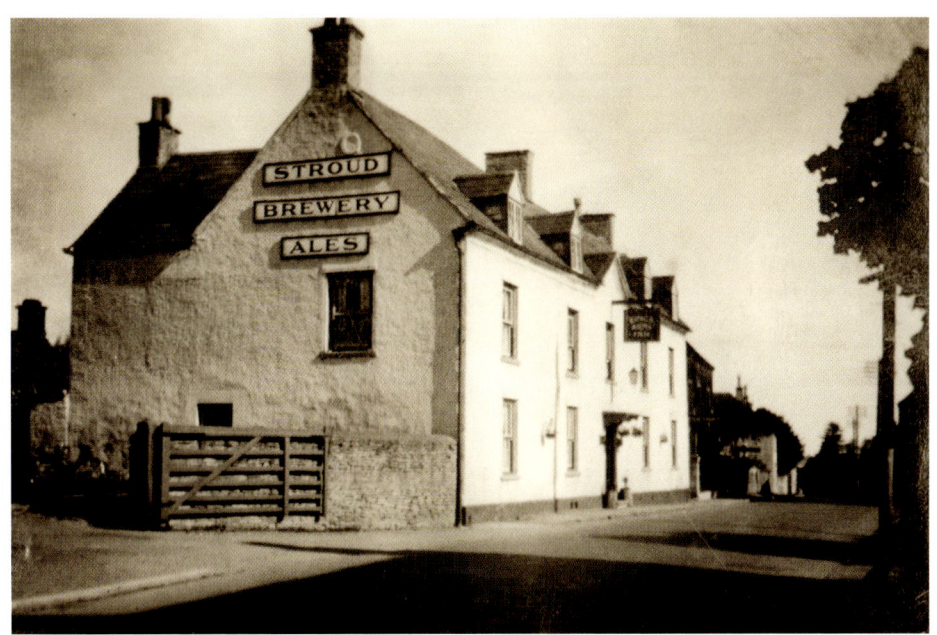

Kings Arms, Didmarton

The Kings Arms was built in 1652 as a coaching inn. In 1745 it was leased out from the Beaufort Estate for a period of one thousand years at 6*d* per annum. The Kings Arms was sold at auction at the Beaufort Arms at Petty France to Mr Cooke of the Tetbury Brewery for £750 in 1843. In 1992 an old custom was reintroduced – an annual rook pie supper. The landlady said: 'We dress up in black bin liners and sing an anthem as the rook pie is brought out of the kitchen.'

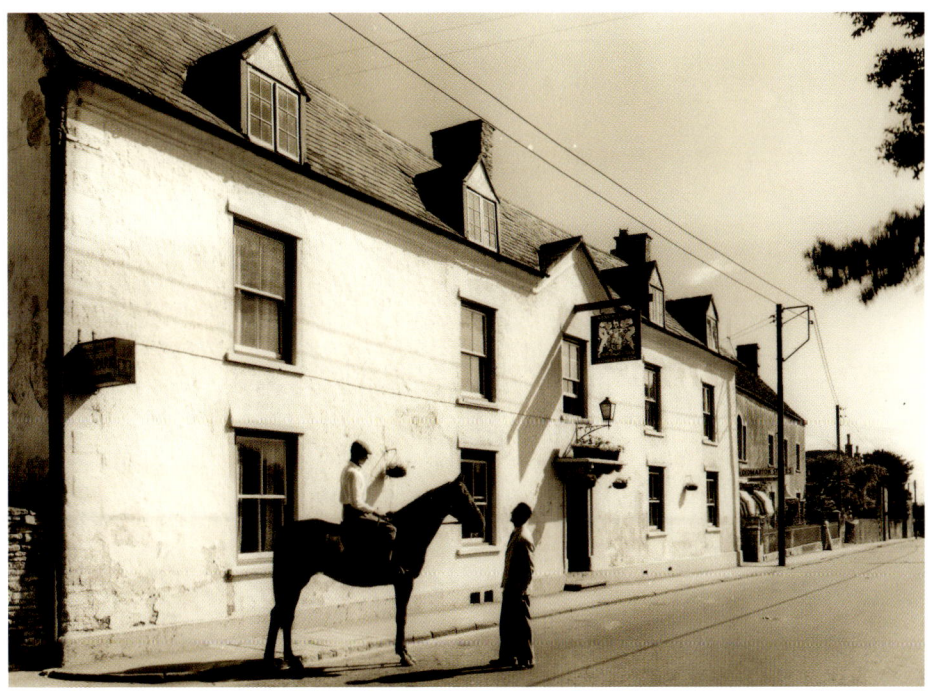

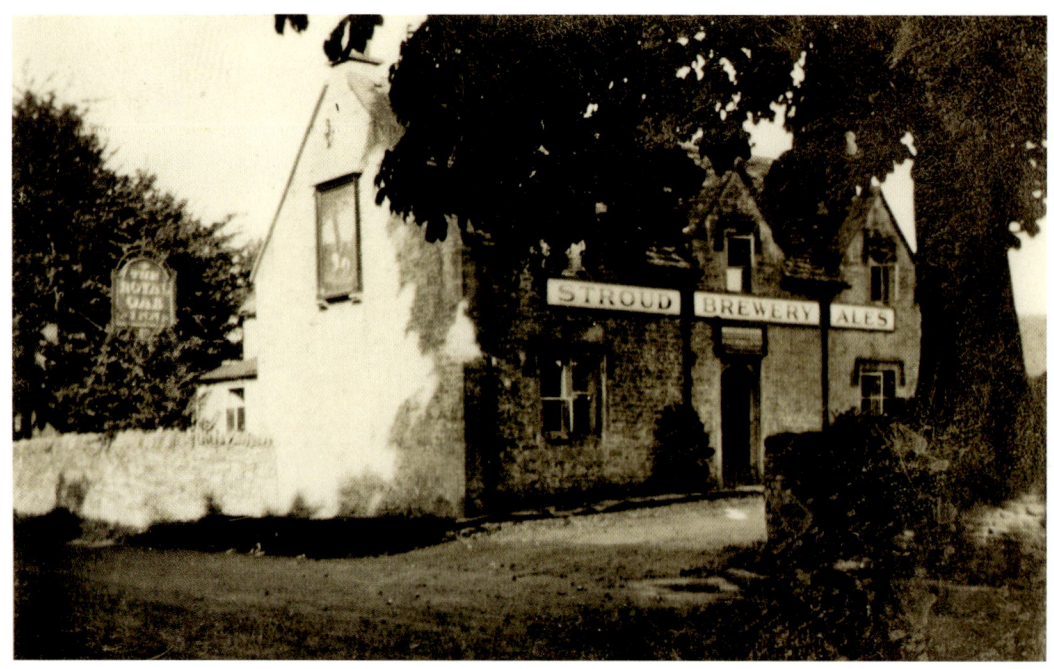

Royal Oak, Leighterton

The Cotswold stone building is at least 300 years old. It was sold to the Stroud Brewery in 1903 by the Huntley family of Boxwell Court. It is now described as a 'first class Country Pub and Restaurant' and is a popular free house serving good food and selling excellent traditional beer including those from Bath Ales and Cotswold Spring.

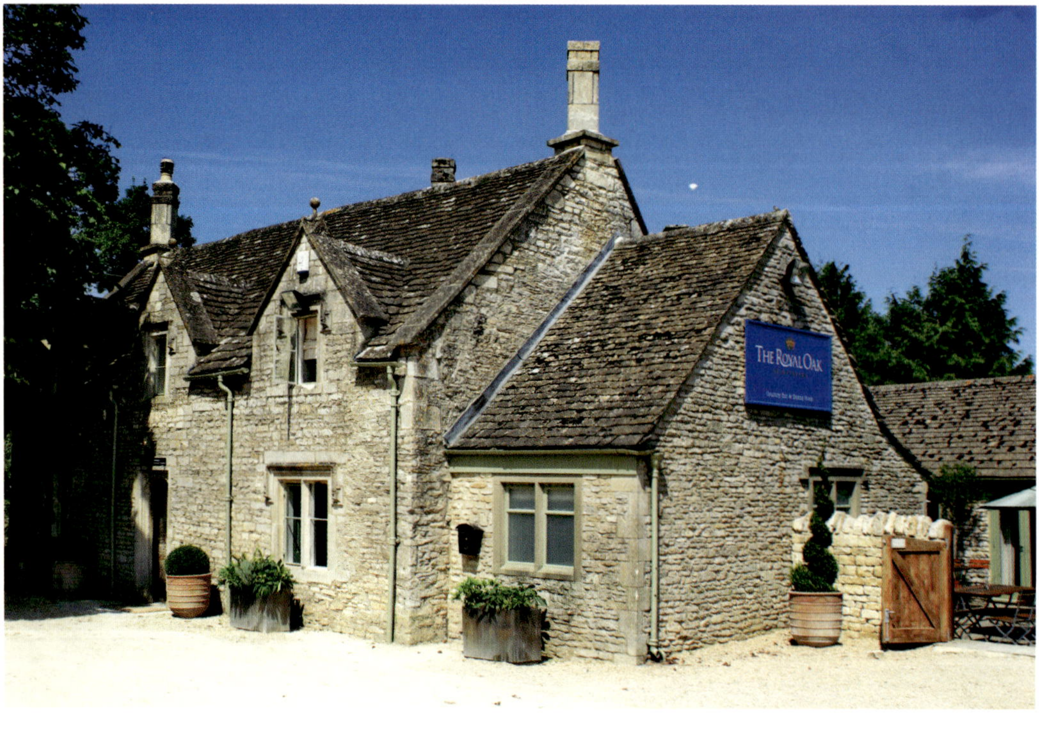

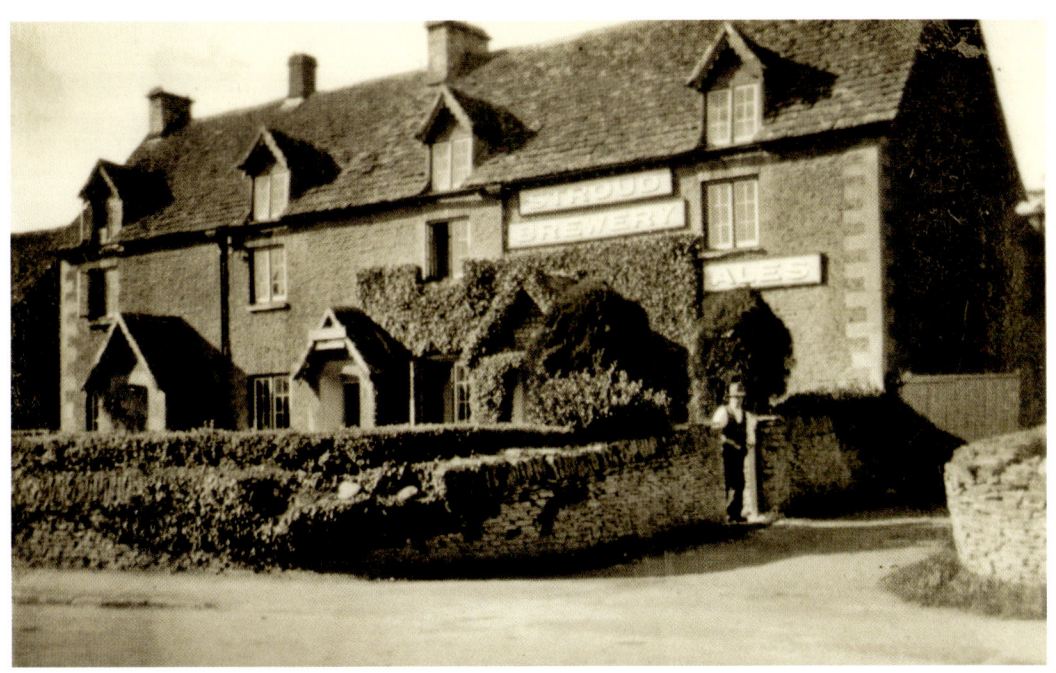

Cat & Custard Pot, Shipton Moyne

It is said that a director of the Stroud Brewery Company was reading the novel *Handley Cross* by R. S. Surtees, apparently a humorous account of fox hunting in mid-nineteenth-century England, when he came across the phrase 'Cat and Custard Pot'. It is difficult to ascertain what is supposed to be humorous – I've read funnier telephone directories!

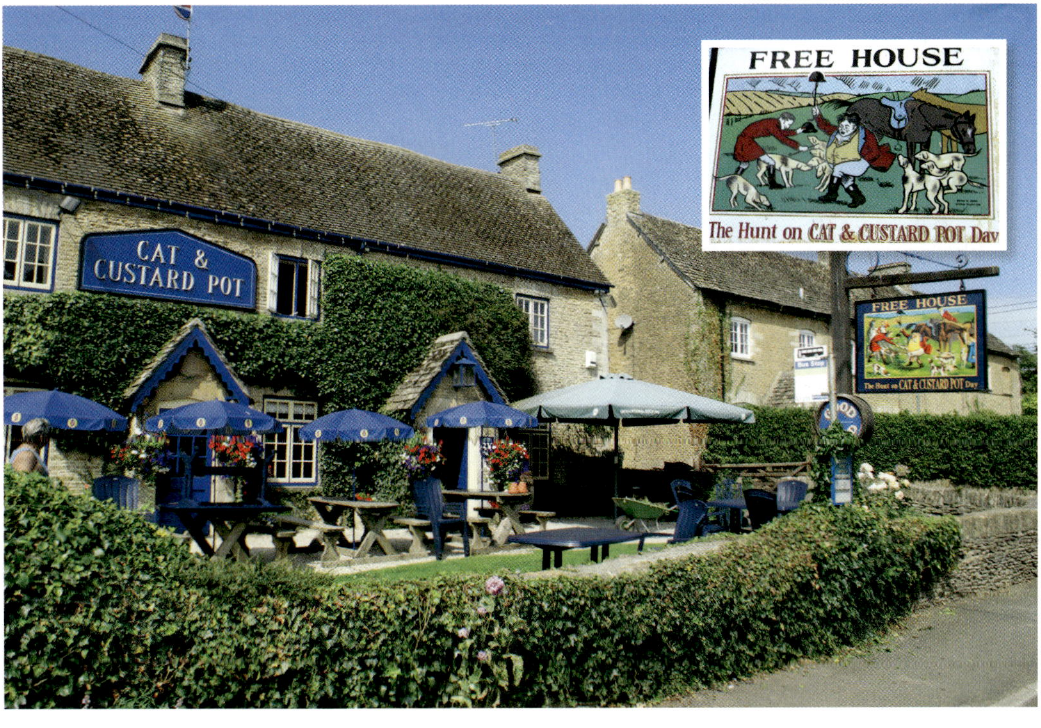

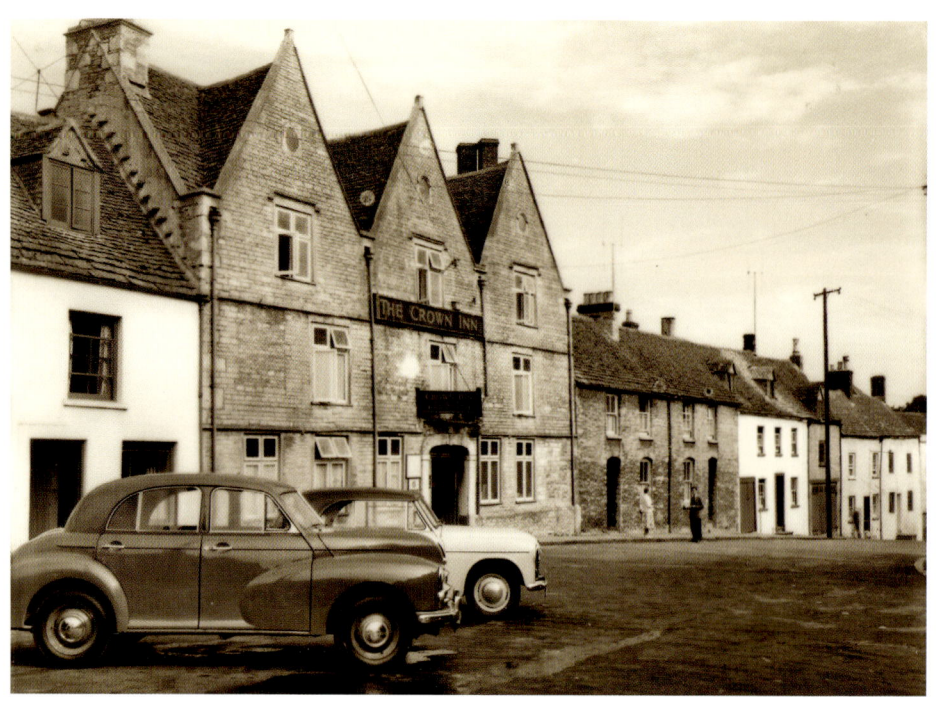

Crown Hotel, Gumstool Hill, Tetbury
The tri-gabled Cotswold stone Crown Inn dates back to 1693. At the time of writing (August 2012) the pub was closed. The Crown Inn is the starting point of the historic Woolsack Races held at Whitsuntide every year when participants carry 60-lb or 30-lb wool sacks on their backs downhill from the Crown Inn to the Royal Oak – a distance of 225 metres. The return journey up the hill is considerably more demanding!

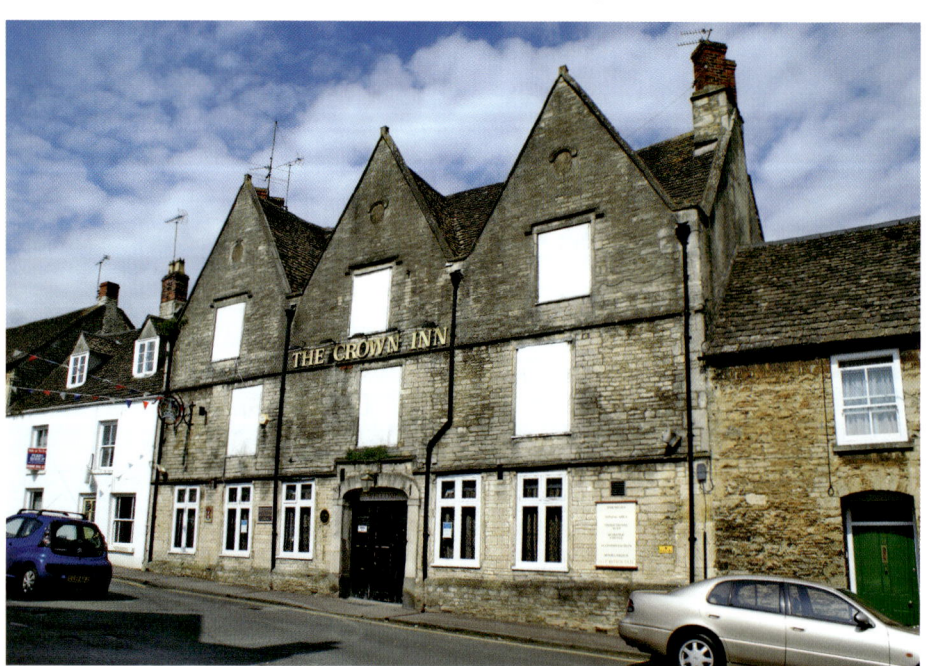

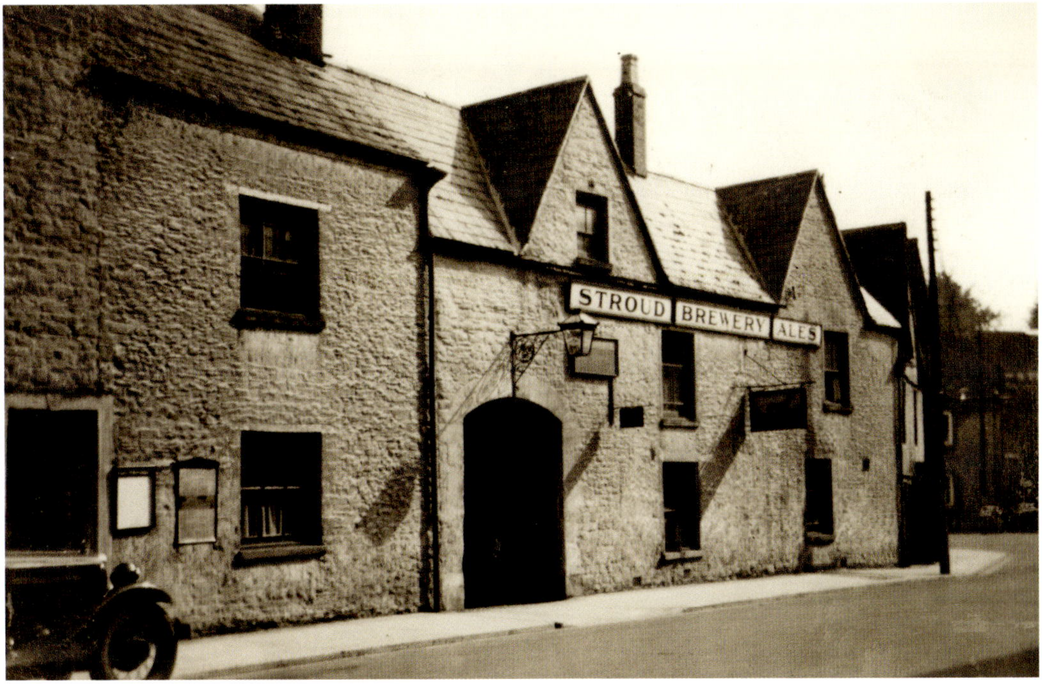

Greyhound Inn, Hampton Street, Tetbury

The Greyhound was directly opposite Cook's Tetbury Brewery and served as their tap house. The old Tetbury Brewery is now converted into luxury apartments. The Greyhound is the only 'local's pub' left in the town and in 2003 an advertisement for the pub said that it had the only dartboard in Tetbury.

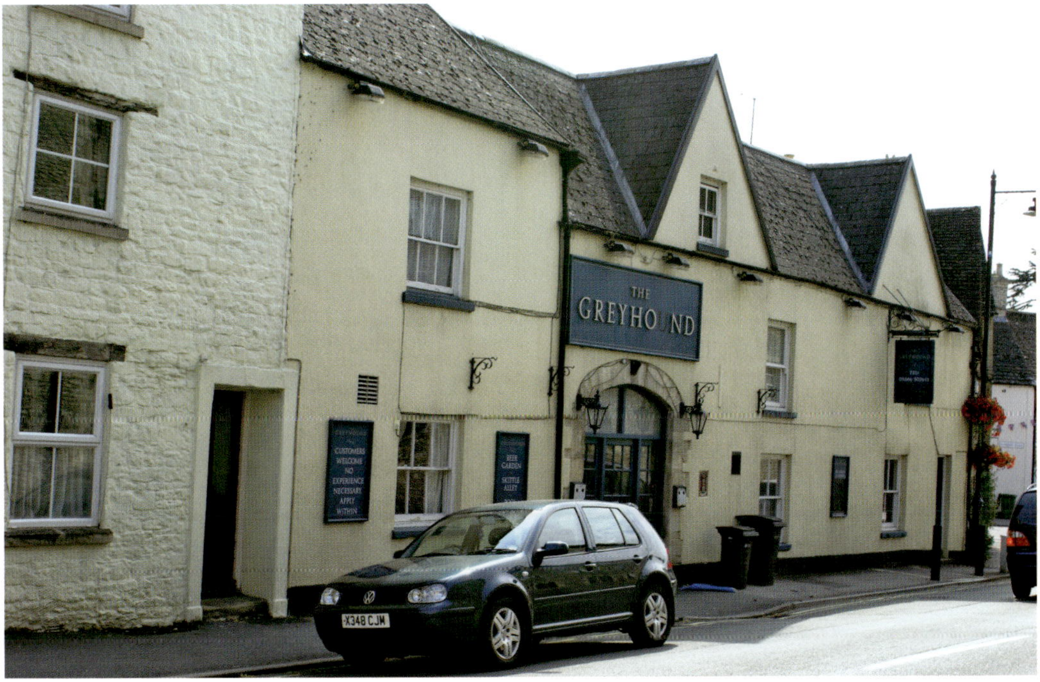

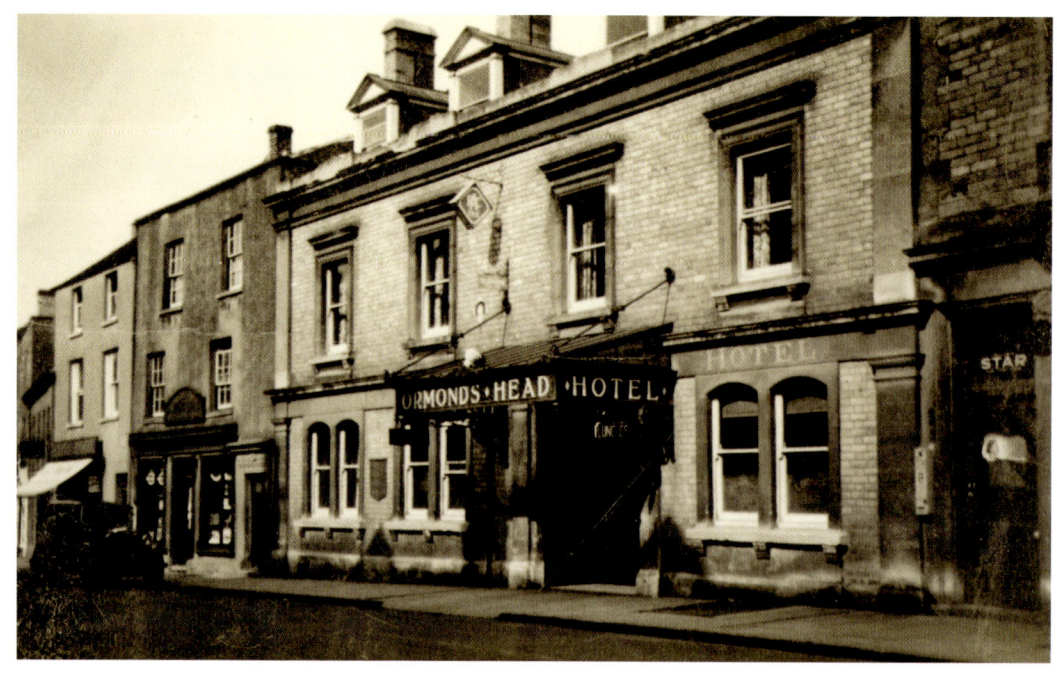

The Ormond, Long Street, Tetbury

During the seventeenth century the inn was known as the Lamb and then the King and Queen before becoming the Ormonds Head in honour of James Butler, the 7th Duke of Ormond. The original twin-gabled façade of the Ormonds Head was reconstructed in 1902. During the Second World War part of the building served as the orderly room for American troops stationed in the town. From 1987 to 1997 the premises was known as the Gentle Gardener but now trades as the Ormond, 'a comfortable blend of old and new creating an atmosphere which is relaxed, informal and individual'.

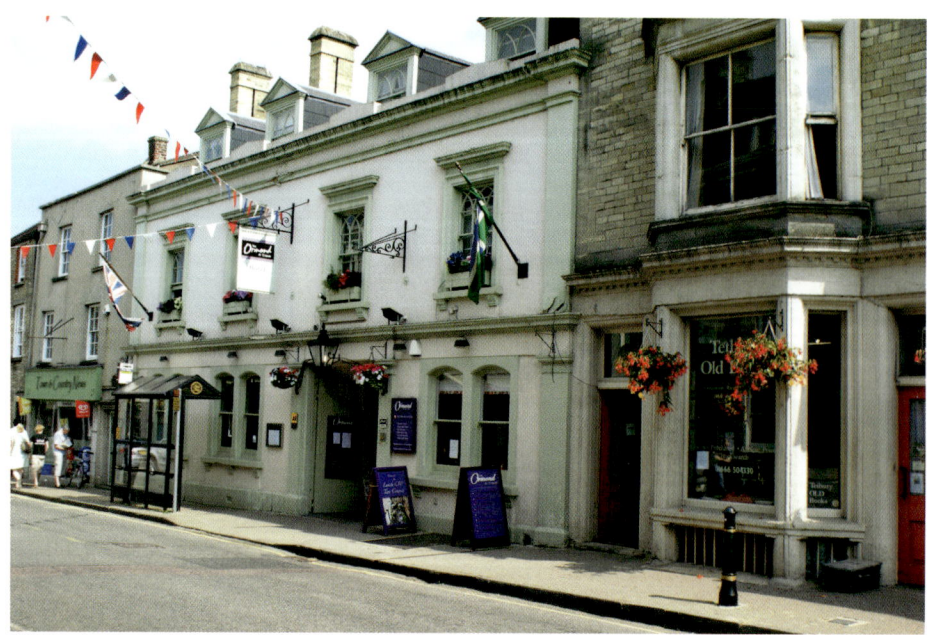

Prince of Wales, West Street, Tetbury

The Prince of Wales was an end of terrace 'basic one bar back street pub' in West Street. It closed down in the autumn of 1999 when landlord Fred Dyer, who had run the pub for thirty-two years, decided to retire. The vacant land (which was the pub car park) to the east of the Prince of Wales was acquired in the redevelopment of the site and a sympathetic conversion of the existing property and new build has created an extension of the terrace.

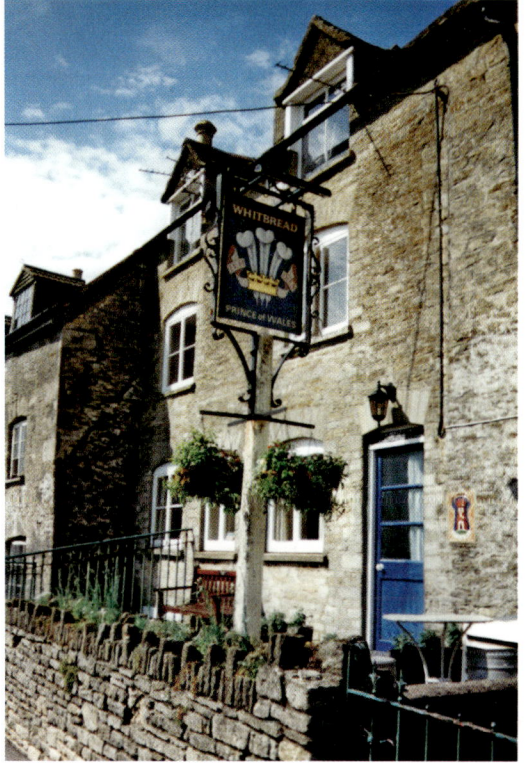

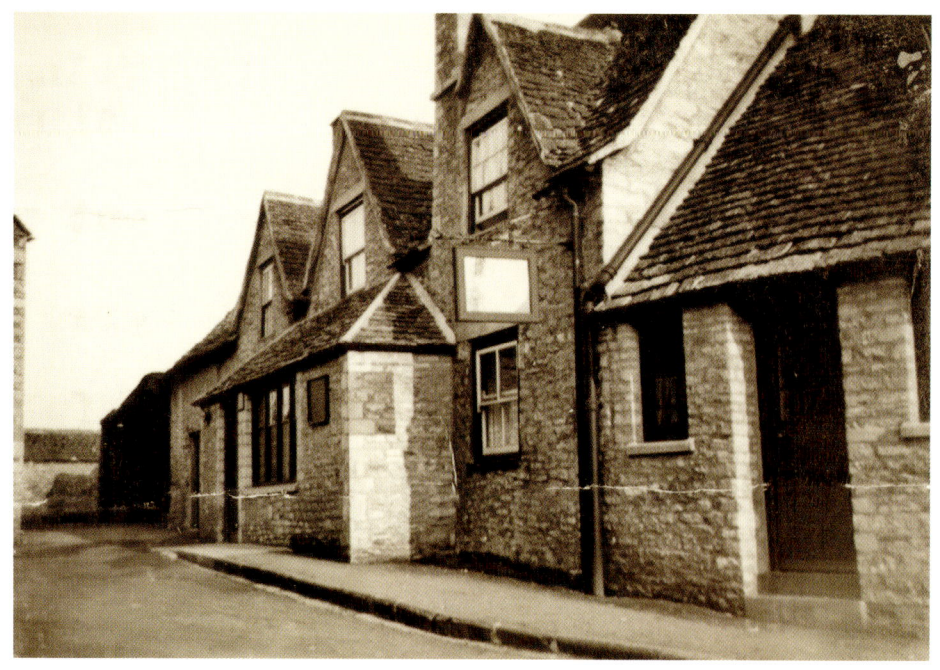

Royal Oak, Cirencester Road, Tetbury

The Cirencester Brewery purchased the Royal Oak on 11 February 1920, although it had been leased to the brewery before then. A plaque commemorates the visit of His Royal Highness the Prince of Wales to the Royal Oak on 23 December 1996; he probably called in for a swift pint and a game of darts with the locals on this way home to Highgrove! At the time of writing (August 2012) the Royal Oak is closed and for sale for £350,000 plus VAT with 'potential for alternate use subject to gaining the necessary permissions'.

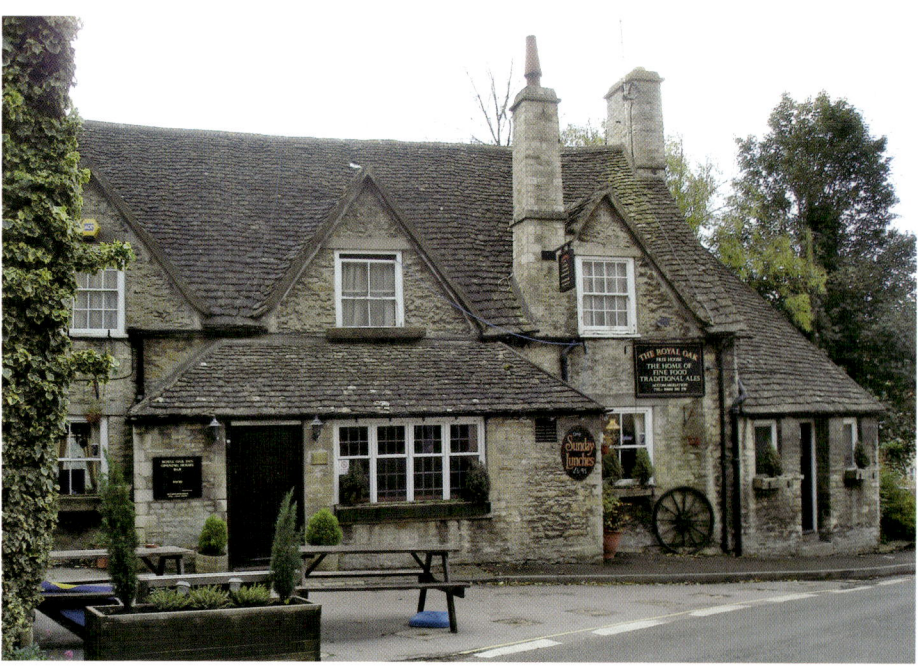

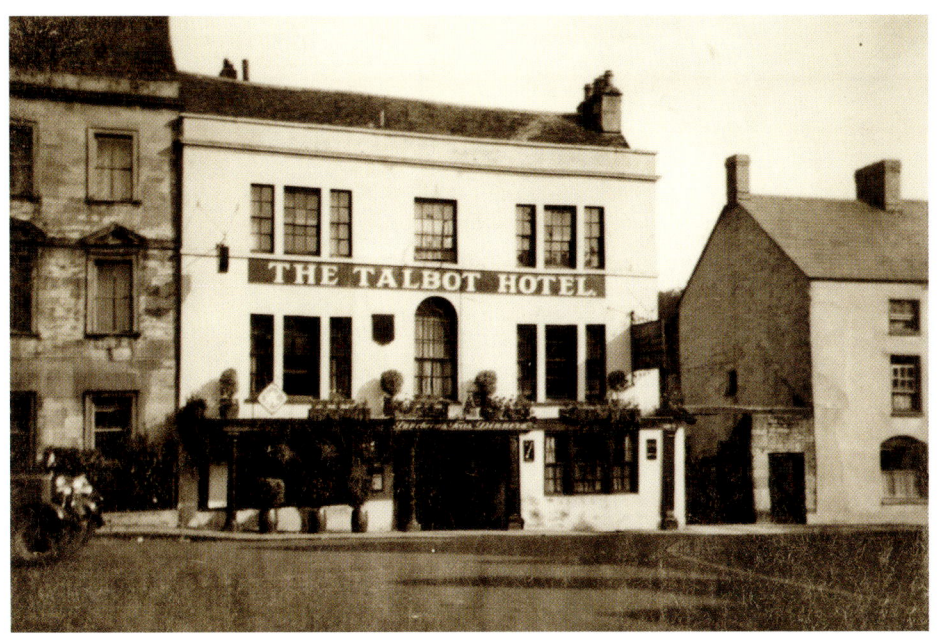

Talbot Hotel, Market Place, Tetbury

The Talbot was one of the most prestigious hotels in Tetbury. It did, however, have a skittle alley. Cecil Sims, a farmer and regular at the Talbot, was interviewed in the 1950s by Brian Johnston (of *Test Match Special* fame) for the BBC Home Service. Cecil was the chairman of the local skittle league and told 'Johnners' that there were six skittle alleys in Tetbury and the skittlers (forty men's teams and thirty-five women's teams) had collected over £1,000 for local charities. The Talbot is now converted into eight self-contained flats called Talbot Apartments.

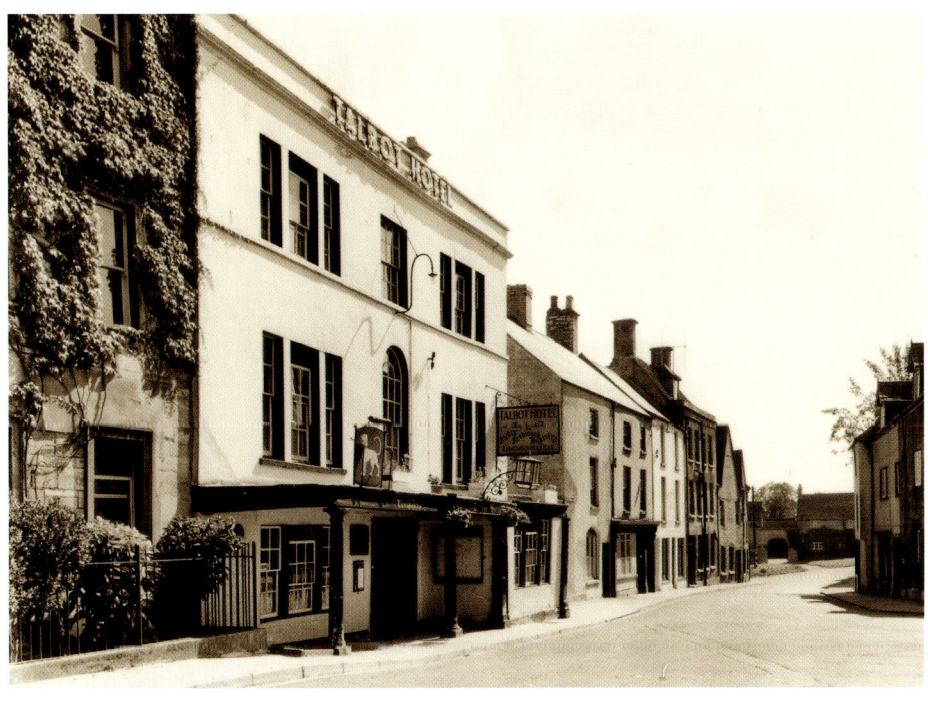

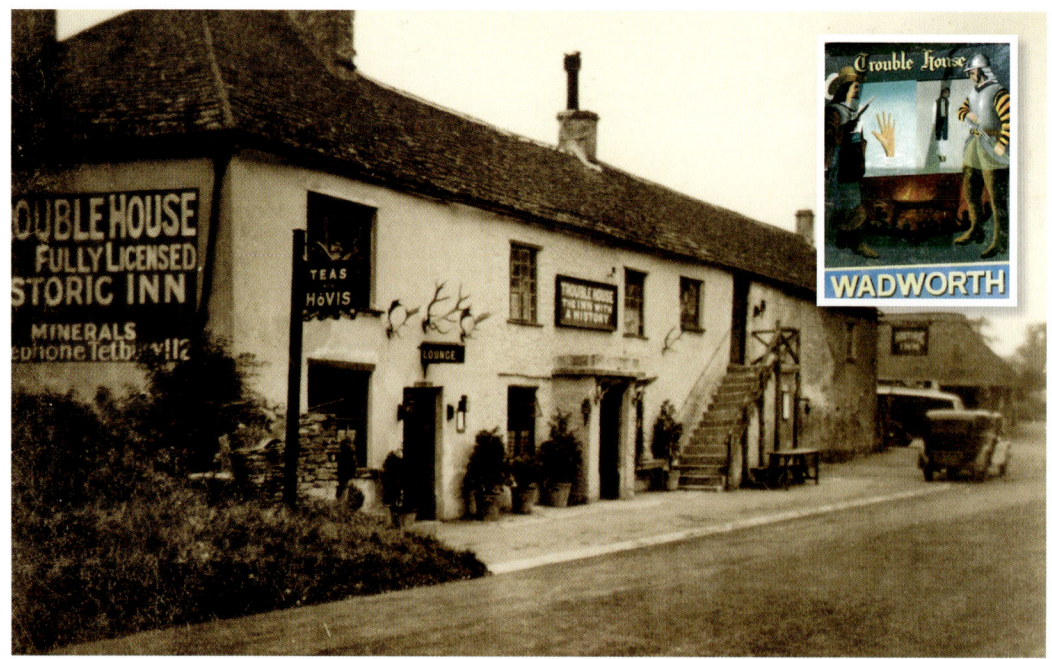

Trouble House, Cherington, Tetbury

The seventeenth-century Trouble House has a fascinating history that involve tales of tragic suicides, agricultural Luddite uprisings and several ghostly sightings – the most malevolent being the Lady in Blue. From 1959 to 1964 the Trouble House Inn even had its very own railway halt on the Kemble–Tetbury branch line. The platform, made of wood, was wet and slimy in the winter months. After drinking a few pints of Wadworth's beers the slippery surface must have provided much hilarity (and wet bottoms) as a result of unfortunate mishaps.

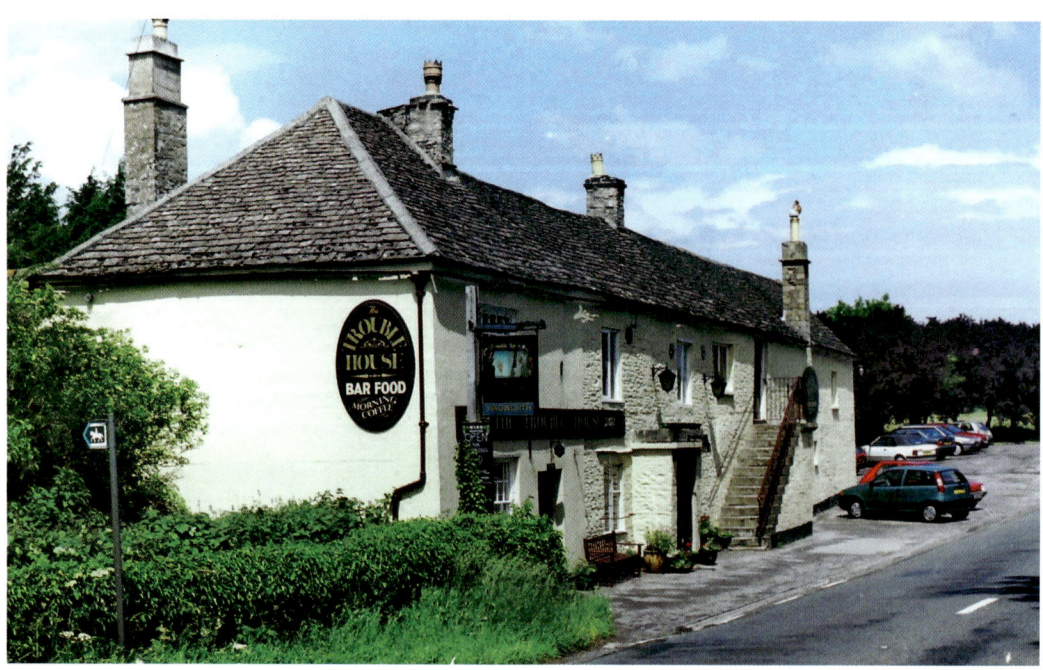

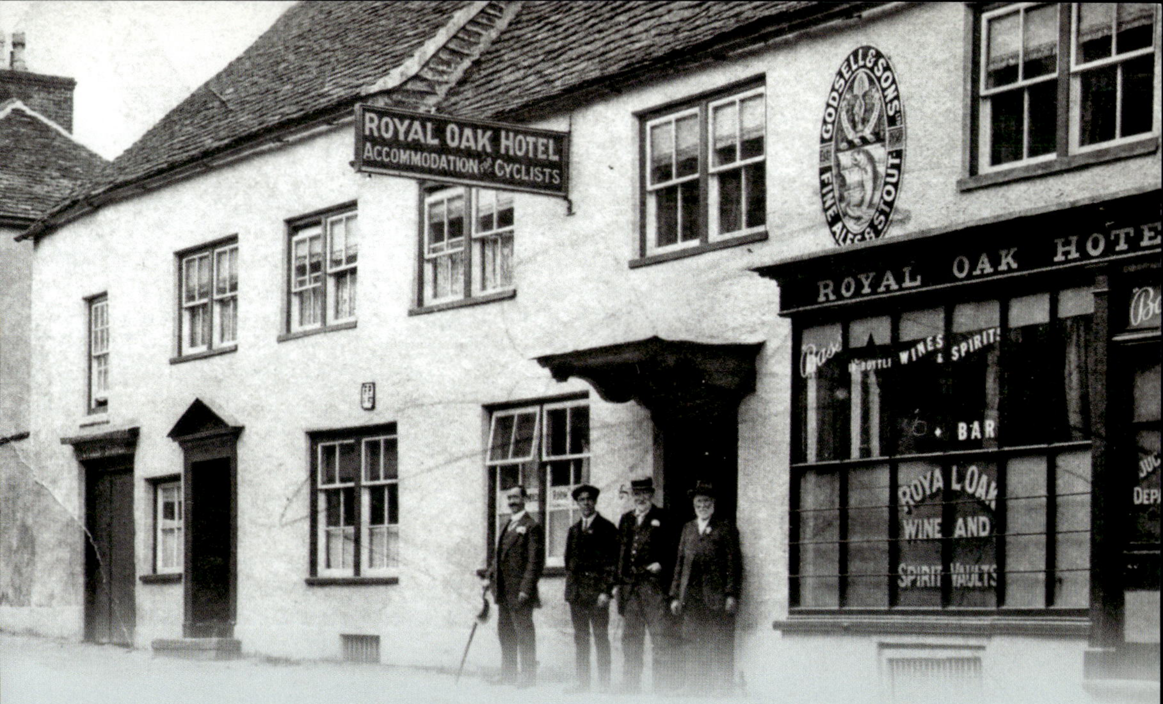

CHAPTER 5

Wotton under Edge

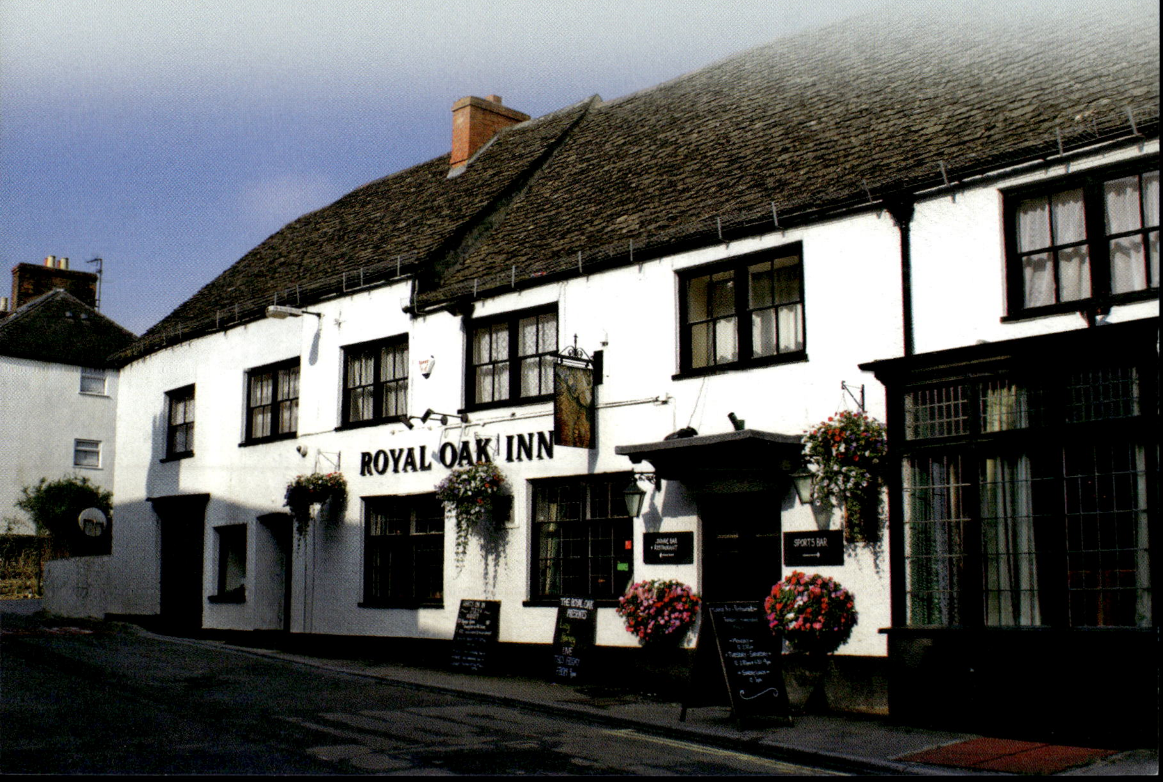

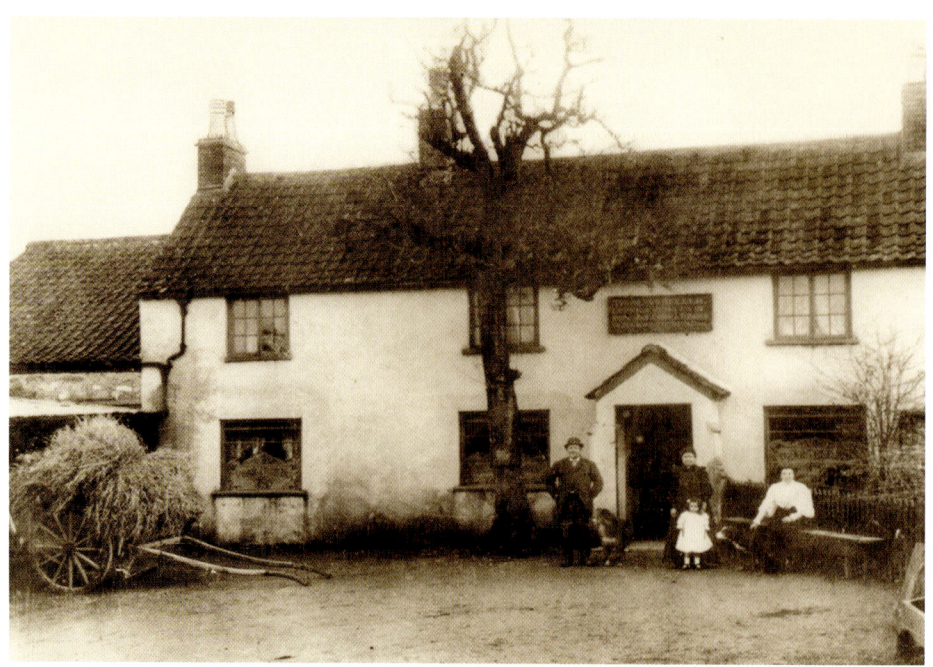

Pear Tree, Charfield

The Pear Tree dates back to at least the early 1800s and was originally cottages. The Pear Tree was once tied to George Playne's Forwood Brewery in Minchinhampton, a family business that was acquired by the Stroud Brewery in 1897. The landlady of the Pear Tree Inn in 1999, Anne Marie Marsh, had a passion for theatre and Shakespeare. The pub was covered in theatre memorabilia. 'Real Ale, Real Food, Real Pub' is how the Pear Tree website succinctly describes the pub today.

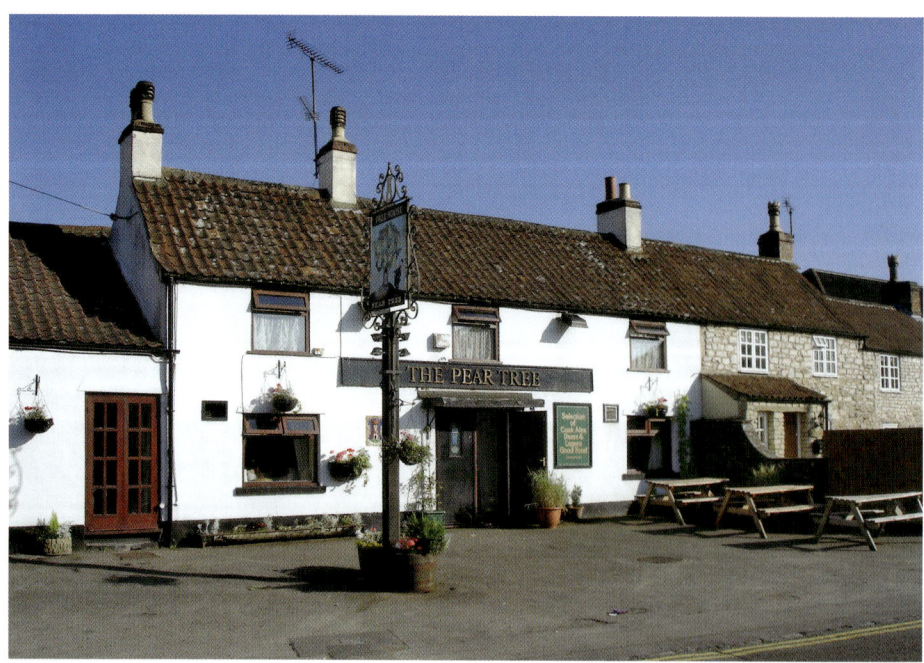

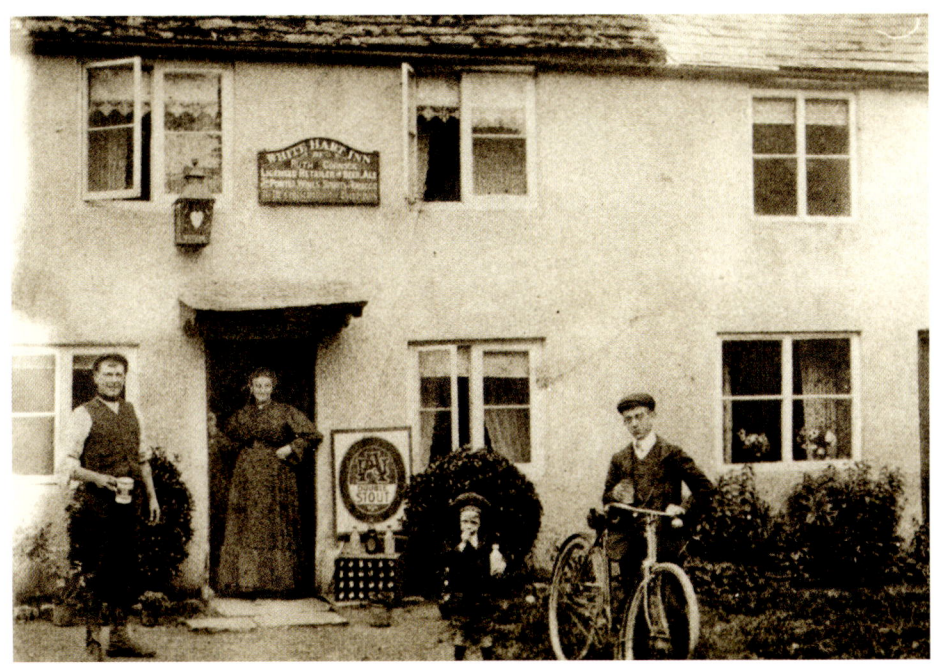

White Hart, Coombe
The White Hart was owned by Arnold, Perrett & Co. of Wickwar in 1891 and 1903, but by 1912 the pub was owned by the Coombe Valley Brewery Co. Ltd. The brewery was located nearby in a picturesque location. Coombe Valley Brewery was registered in 1905 to acquire the business previously carried on by A. J. P. and J. H. S. Annesley. It seems that over expenditure, possibly caused by the acquisition of property such as the White Hart, caused their downfall. In 1918 the licence of the Coombe Valley Brewery was lapsed and the White Hart at Coombe closed *c.* 1920.

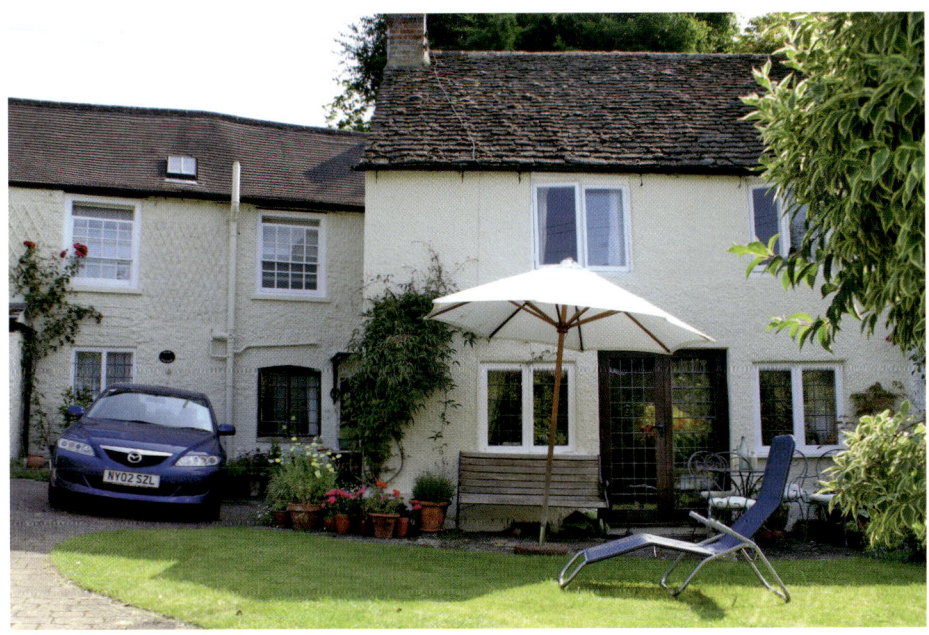

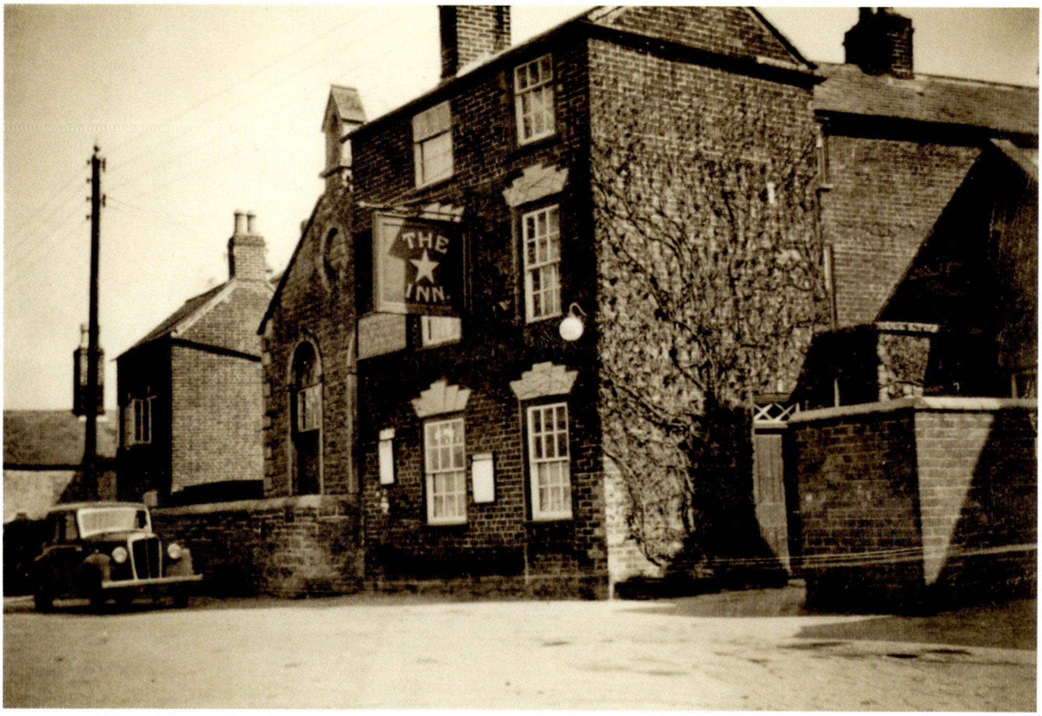

Star Inn, Kingswood

When Wadworth of Devizes acquired the Star Inn at Kingswood from Whitbread in 1991 the name was changed to Dinneywicks. The name refers to the name of a field at the back of the village. The owner of the field levied a toll because it straddled a highway. Another local story is that the nearby Dinneywicks Hill was a burial ground for horses in the English Civil War.

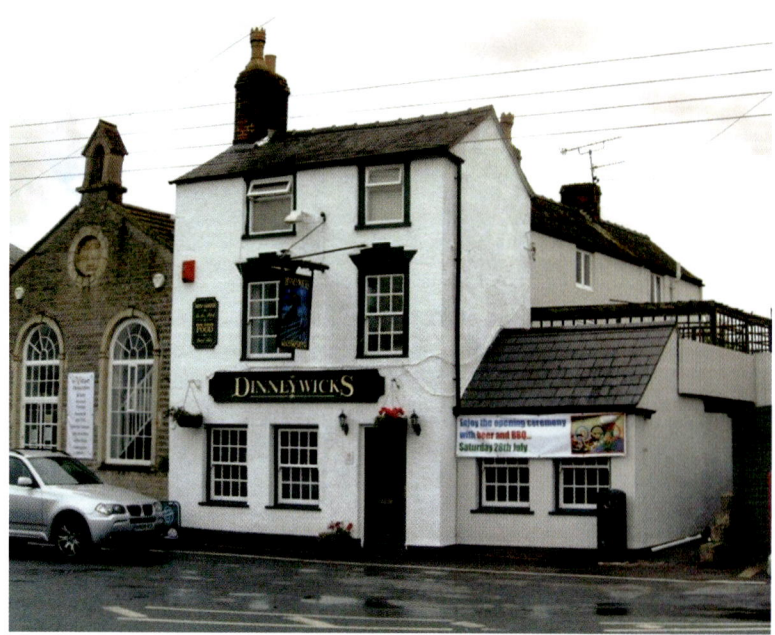

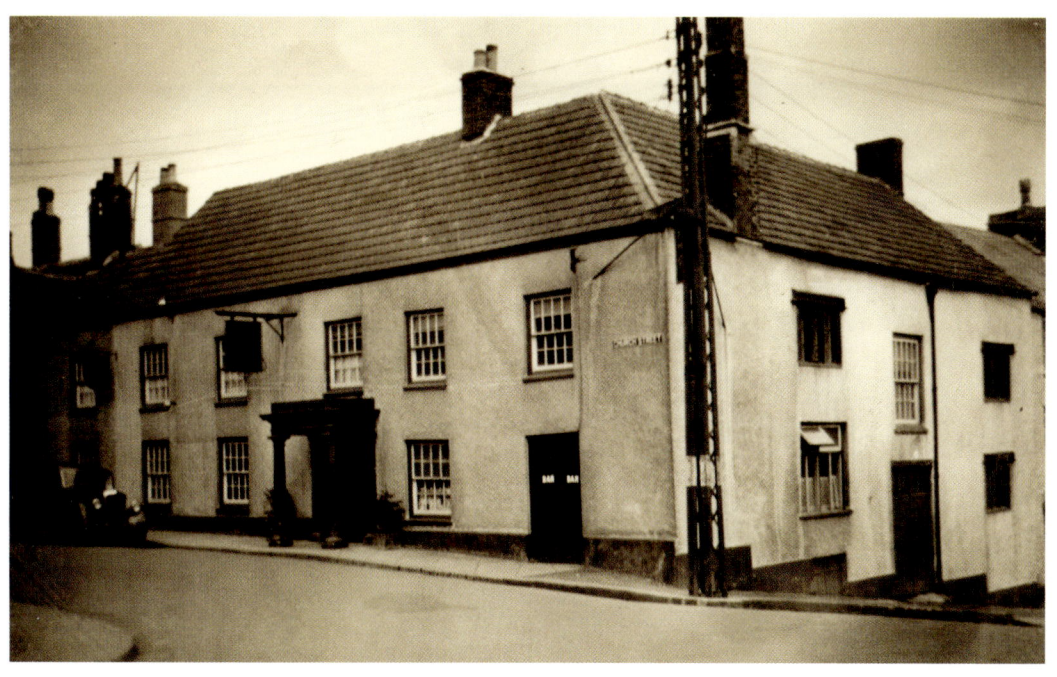

Falcon Hotel, Church Street, Wotton under Edge

The Falcon Hotel was the only pub in Gloucestershire owned by the Pickwick Brewery in Corsham, Wiltshire. The Pickwick Brewery was being run by Frederick & Henry Hulbert and Henry Padbury Manning in 1862. In December of that year there was a twenty-one-year lease agreement for the Falcon to be 'tied' to the Pickwick Brewery. By 1891 ownership of the brewery (and the Falcon Hotel) had been transferred to Thomas Pearson-Stevens. The business was acquired by Wilkins Brothers & Hudson Ltd of Bradford on Avon in 1896 with twenty tied houses.

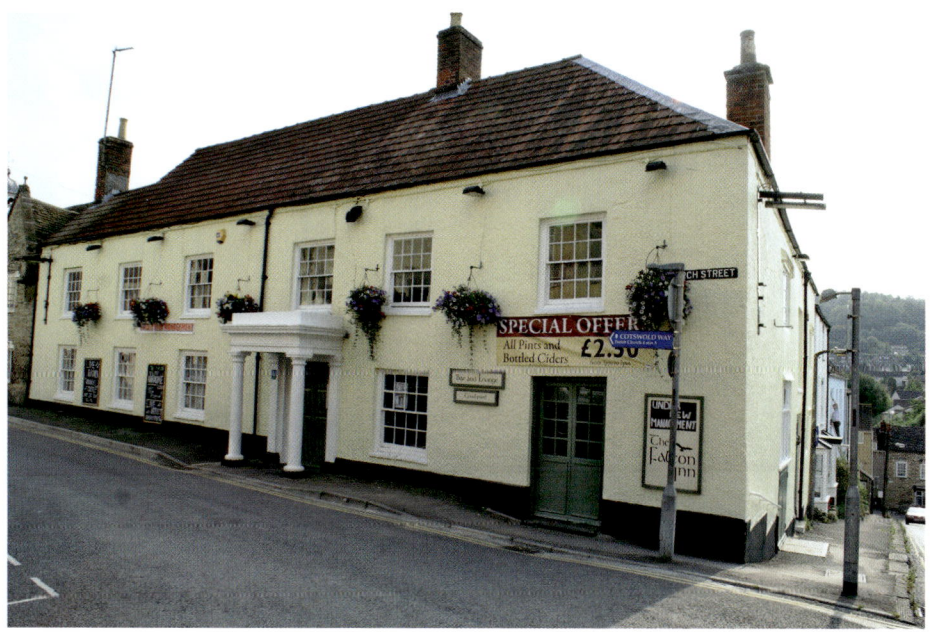

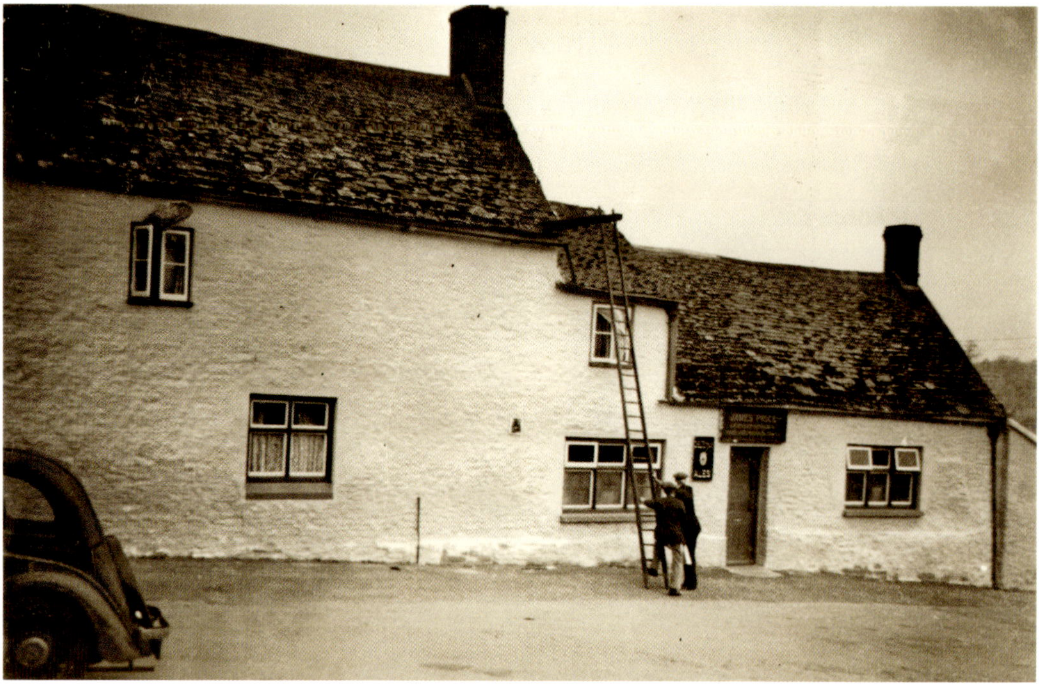

Full Moon, Synwell, Wotton under Edge
Behind the Full Moon there is a house called the Old Full Moon which was the original pub. This closed when West Country Breweries built the new Full Moon Inn in 1966 and the licence was transferred. On August Bank Holiday in 2004 Tinker and Tailor, two large bay horses kept by landlords Joe and Teresa Carly, greeted visitors to the Full Moon and offered cart rides around the area. Money raised went towards the Macmillan Nurses charity.

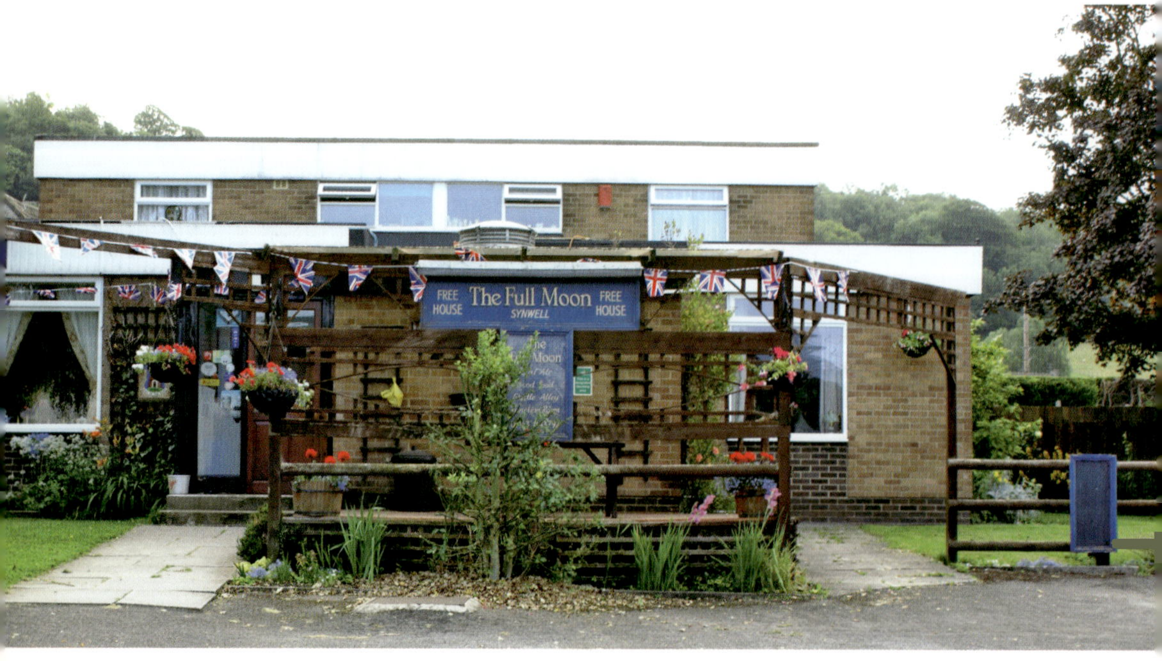

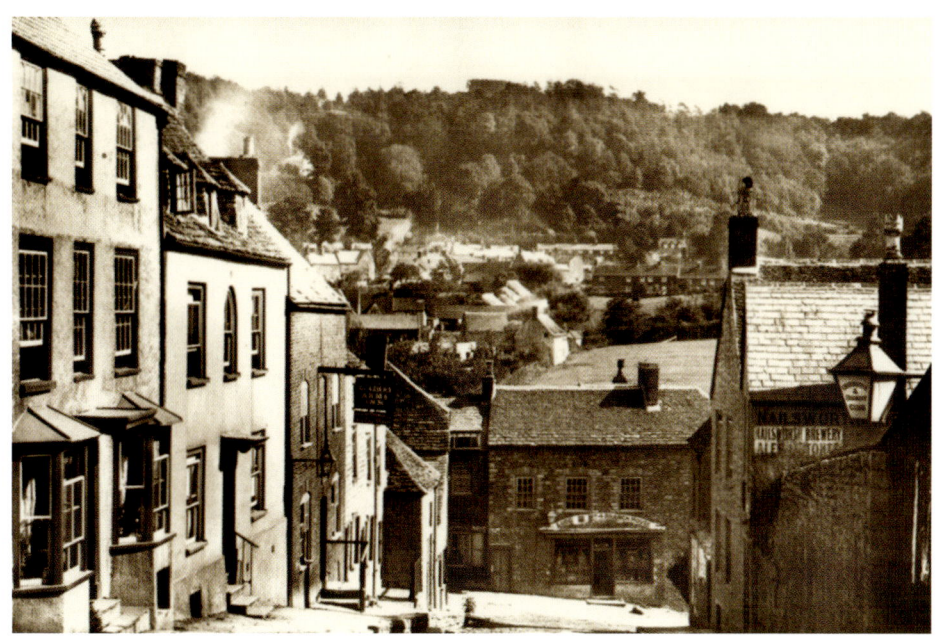

Glaziers Arms, The Steep, Wotton under Edge
The Glaziers Arms, which closed in 1908, was a Cook's Tetbury Brewery pub on the northern side of the Steep. The building is now known as Bremhill House. Directly opposite stood the Nailsworth Brewery Stores. This building was previously owned by John Keynton, owner of the Ludgate Brewery in 1891. It seems that the Nailsworth Brewery acquired the Ludgate Brewery. Was the brewery located in the same premises?

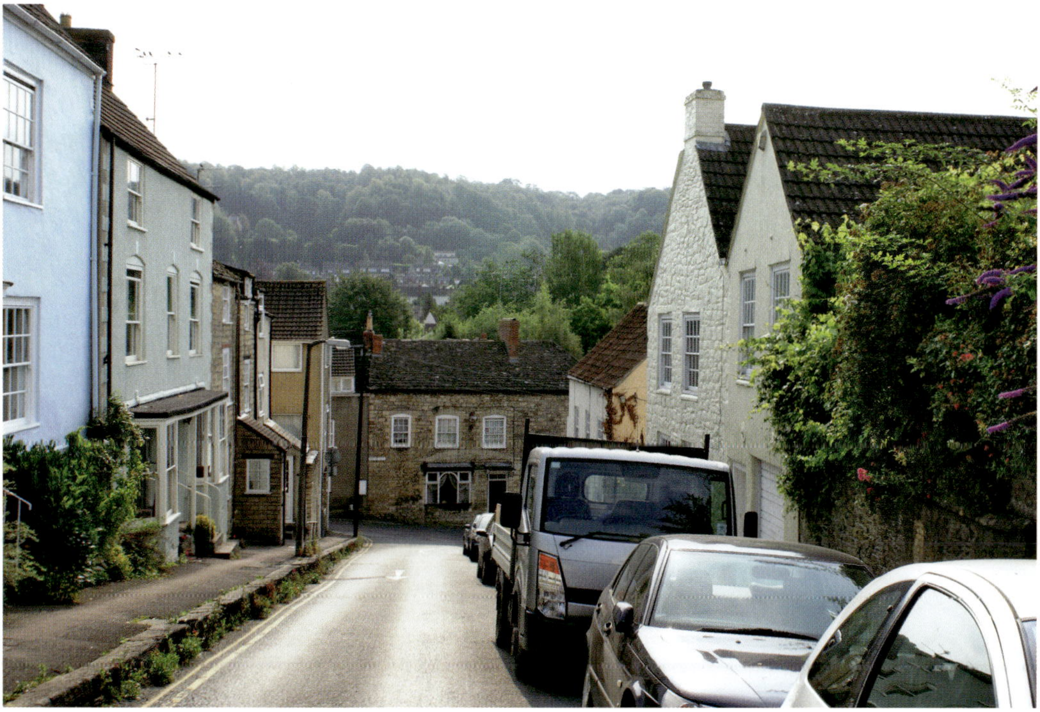

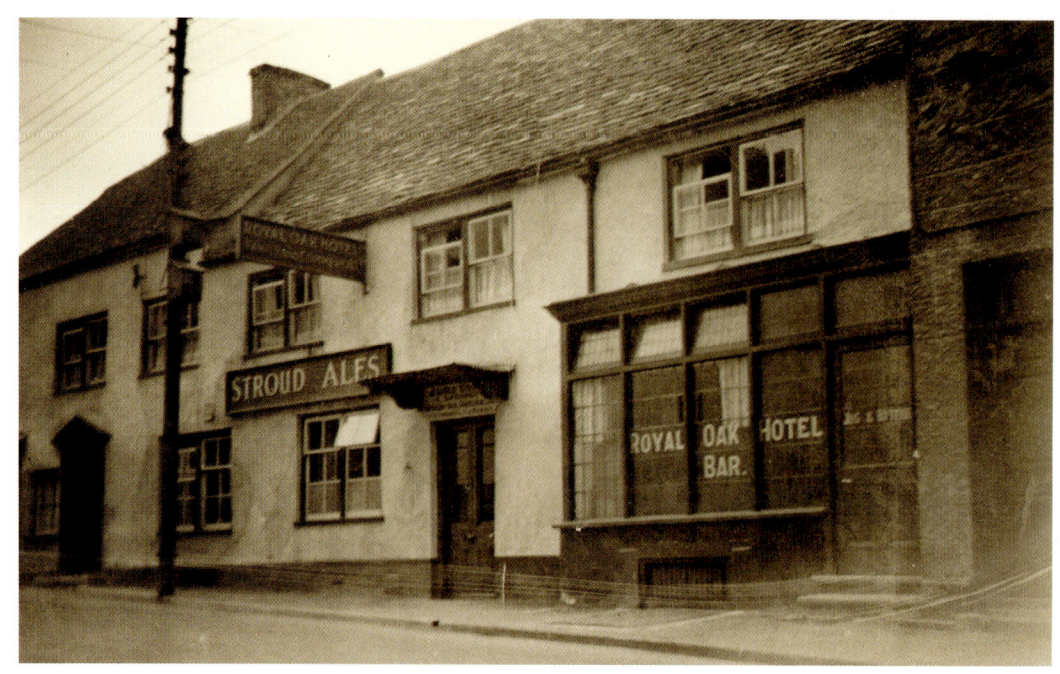

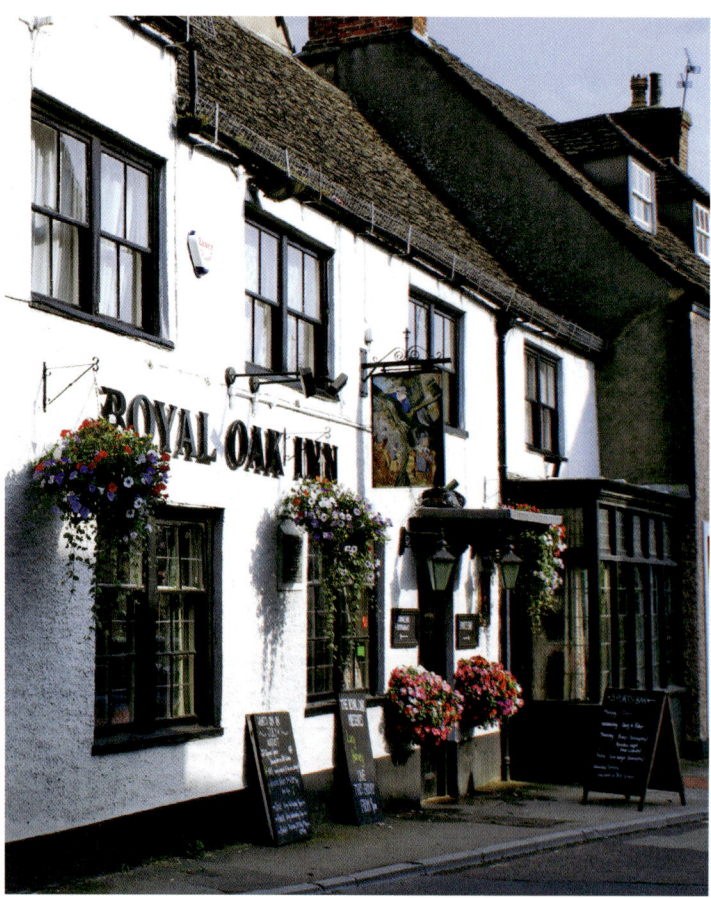

Royal Oak, Haw Street, Wotton under Edge

The Royal Oak was free of brewery tie in 1891 and 1903, in the private ownership of Joseph and Annie Marie Osborne. It seems likely that they sold the freehold of the Royal Oak to the Coombe Valley Brewery. When the Coombe Valley Brewery and its property was put up for auction on 6 July 1912, Godsell & Sons of Stroud were the successful bidders for the Royal Oak. In 1928, following acquisition, the ownership was transferred from Godsell's to the Stroud Brewery.

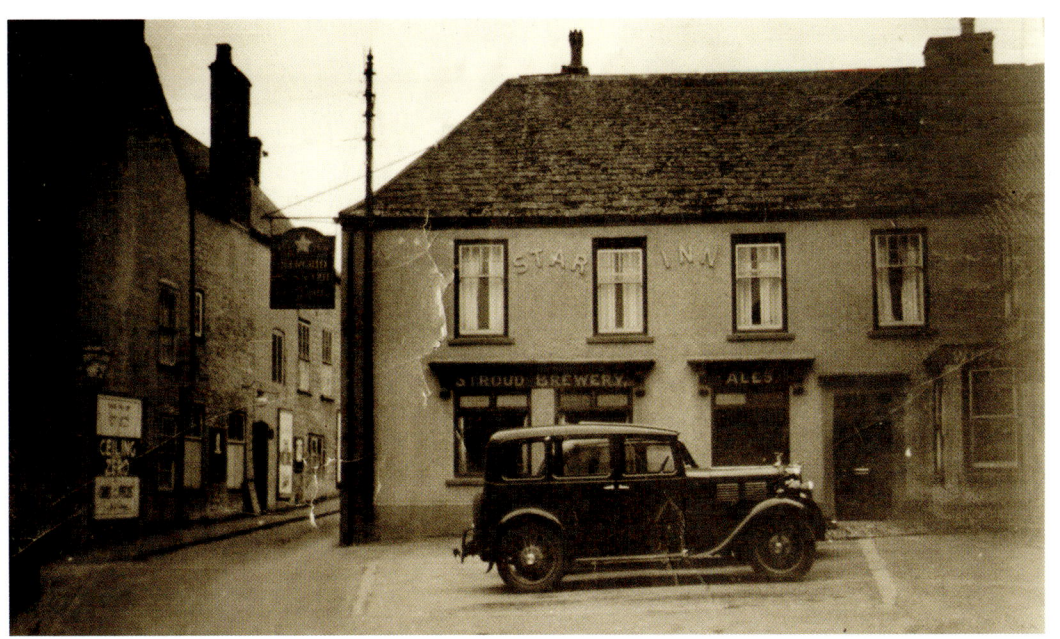

Star Inn, Market Street, Wotton under Edge

There is a wonderful legend associated with the Star Inn at Wotton under Edge and its link with the ill-fated RMS *Titanic*. John Cambridge was the son of Francis Cambridge, landlord of the Star Inn in the mid-eighteenth century. As a young adult John emigrated to Canada where he set up a timber business in Prince Edward Island for the ship building industry. John called his business White Star, named after his father's pub. Upon takeover, the name of John's business was used by the famous shipping company who later went on to commission the building of the *Titanic*.

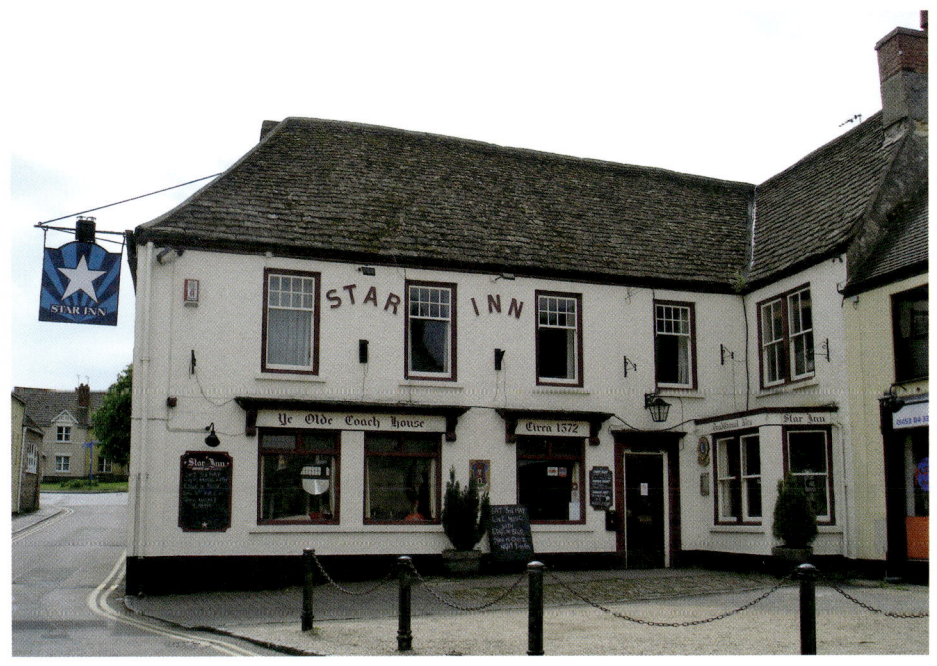

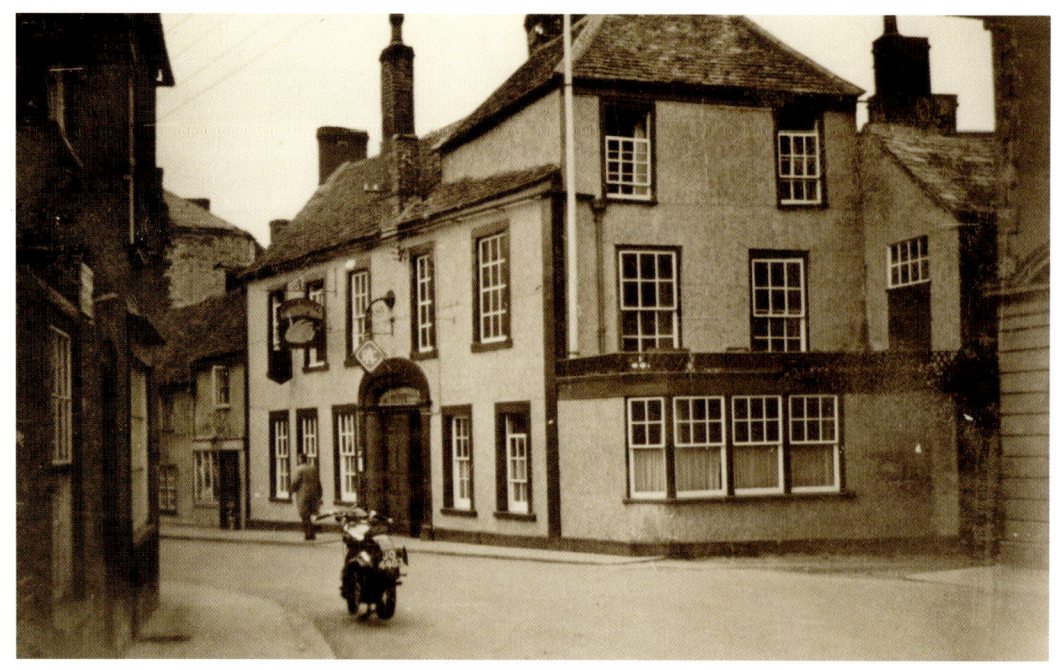

Swan Hotel, Market Street, Wotton under Edge

The Swan Hotel must have been one of Godsell & Sons most prestigious hotels. An advertisement in 1907 called the Swan 'one of the best and most comfortable in the district, with passengers met from every train calling at Charfield station on the Midland Railway'. Many celebrities have stayed at the hotel – David Niven, Vincent Price, Dick Emery, Wendy Craig, Rex Harrison and even Hilda Ogden (sorry, Jean Alexander)! Margaret Thatcher, Shiela Hancock and the Two Ronnies (not Kray and Biggs) have also dined there.

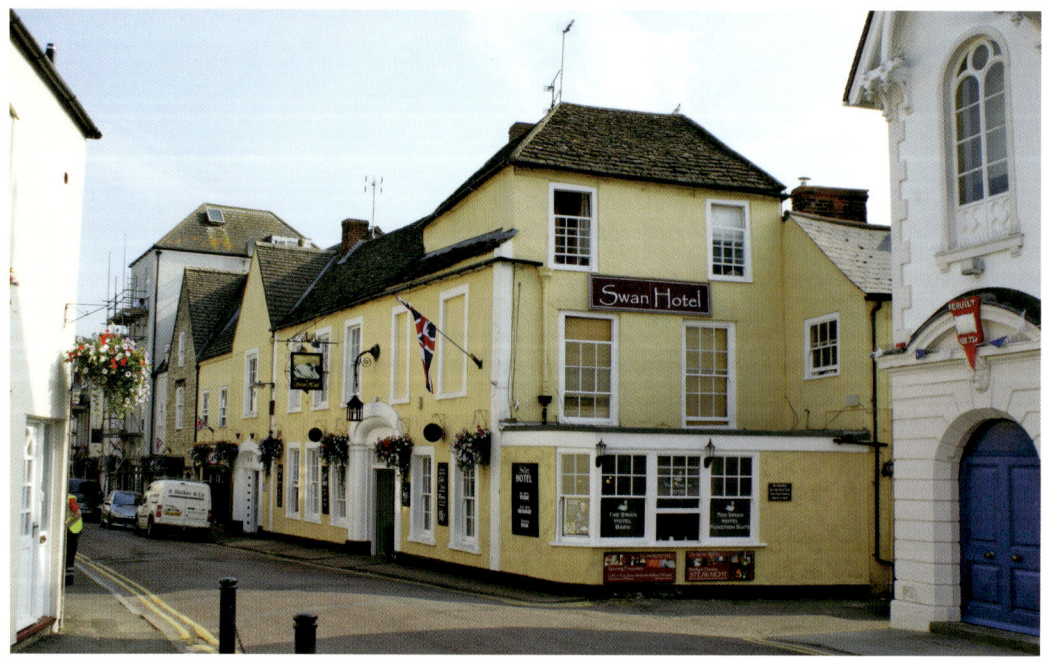

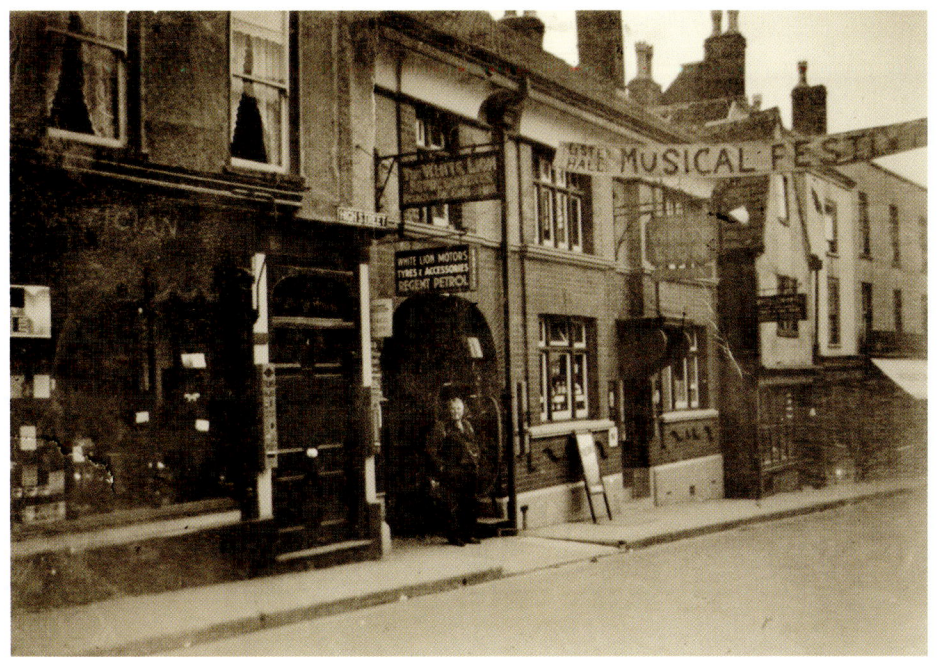

White Lion, Long Street, Wotton under Edge

The façade of the White Lion was substantially rebuilt at the beginning of the last century by brewers Arnold, Perrett & Co. The original pub was a plain rendered building but was replaced by a more ornate brick-built façade. 'Ted' Scadding, the landlord of the White Lion in the 1950s, was also the proprietor of a local coach company called, appropriately, White Lion Motorways. The blue and cream liveried Guy Arab coaches were stabled in the firm's garage in Bear Street, opposite the school. At the time of writing (August 2012) the White Lion is closed and boarded up, and faces an uncertain future.

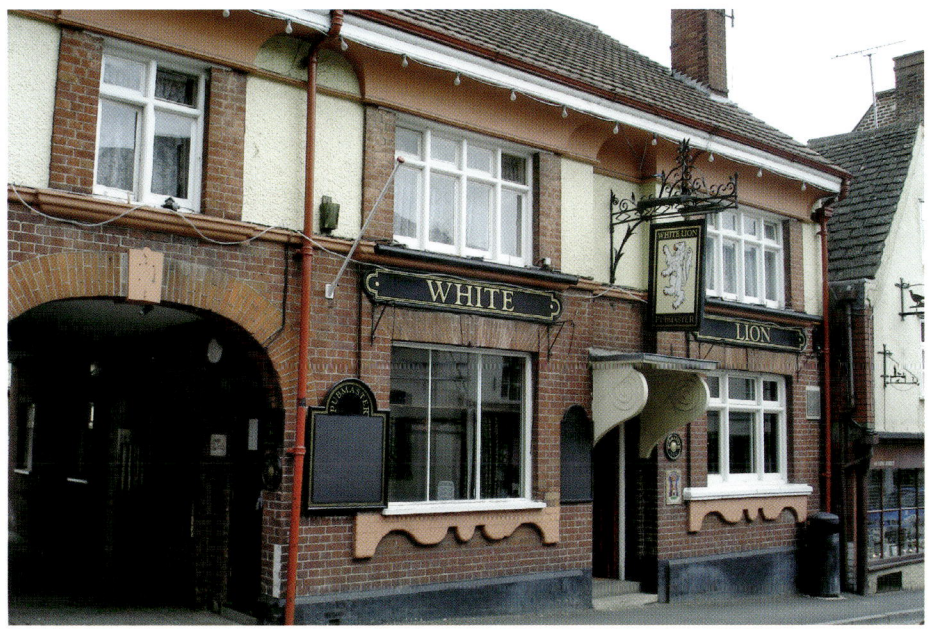

ALSO AVAILABLE FROM AMBERLEY PUBLISHING

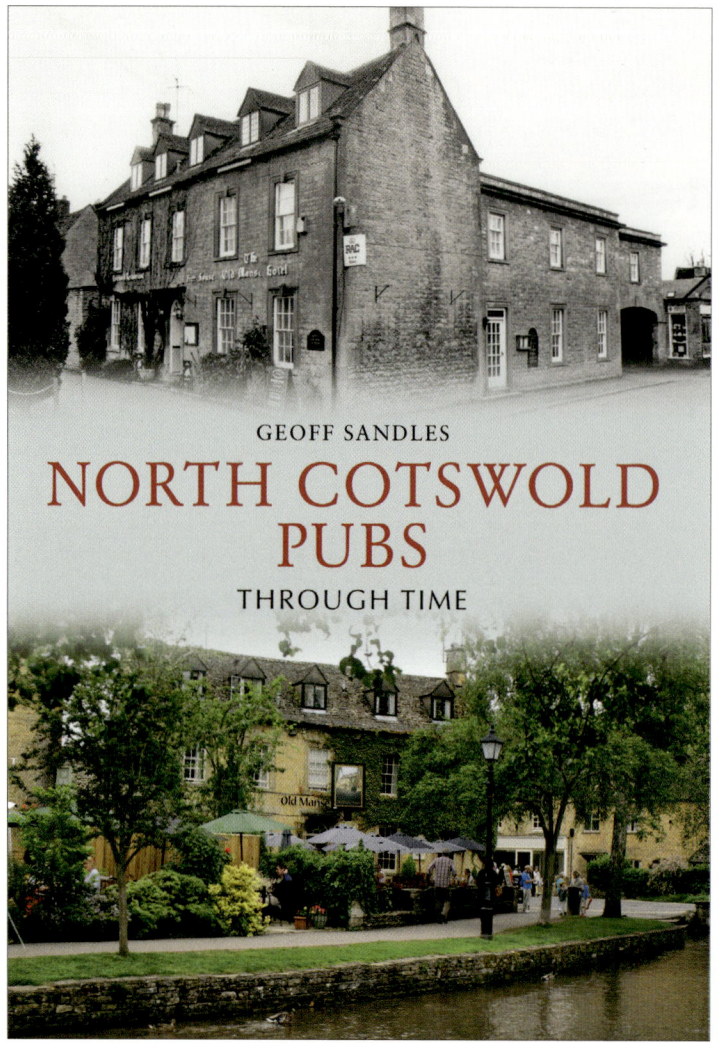

North Cotswold Pubs Through Time

Geoff Sandles

This fascinating selection of photographs traces some of the many ways in which North Cotswold pubs have changed and developed over the last century.

978 1 4456 0401 5
96 pages, full colour

Available from all good bookshops or order direct from our website www.amberleybooks.com